ENGLISH IN AMERICA

ENGLISH IN AMERICA

A Radical View of the Profession

RICHARD OHMANN
with a chapter by
WALLACE DOUGLAS

New York
Oxford University Press
1976

For permission to reprint essays from the works indicated, grateful acknowledgment is
made.

"The Size and Structure of an Academic Field: Some Perplexities" (Chapter One) is
from *College English*, February, 1967. Copyright © 1967 by the National Council of
Teachers of English. Reprinted by permission.

Chapters Eight and Nine are an expansion of "English Departments and the
Professional Ethos," which originally appeared in *New Literary History*, and is reprinted
by permission of the editor, Ralph Cohen.

Chapter Two is a revised version of "An Informal and Perhaps Unreliable Account of
the Modern Language Association of America." Copyright © 1969 by the Antioch
Review, Inc. First published in *The Antioch Review* Vol. XXIX, No. 3; reprinted by
permission of the editors.

Chapter Four is a revised version of "Teaching and Studying Literature at the End of
Ideology," which appeared in *The Politics of Literature*, edited by Louis Kampf and Paul
Lauter, and published by Pantheon Books, a Division of Random House, Inc.
Copyright © 1970, 1972 by Random House, Inc.

Robert Frost's poem "Design" from the poetry of Robert Frost edited by Edward Con-
nery Lathem. Copyright 1936 by Robert Frost. Copyright © 1964 by Lesley Frost Ballantine. Copyright © 1969 by Holt, Rinehart and Winston, Publishers.

Acknowledgments

Wesleyan University has generously supported my research and writing: parts of two sabbaticals went into this work.

The National Council of Teachers of English has also contributed. Editing its journal, *College English*, has taught me much. I thank the people of NCTE for interest and encouragement, especially Robert F. Hogan who, among many other kinds of assistance, urged me to set down some of these ideas for the first time.

I did much of my thinking and writing about the profession in collaboration with members of the Radical Caucus in English and the Modern Languages.

To Wallace Douglas, my gratitude for contributing a necessary chapter that I couldn't have written myself.

These people gave me special help—read parts of the manuscript, criticized it, suggested books to read: Neil Coughlan, Stewart Gillmor, Eugene Klaaren, Paul Lauter, Richard Vann, Martha Vicinus.

Louis Kampf did that and more. After seventeen years of talking and working with him I am not sure which ideas are his and which mine, but I know that I would not have written this book without his comradeship.

Contents

I

Introduction

CHAPTER ONE

Working in English
in America, ca. 1965

This book is about my profession, the teaching and study of language and literature in America. I hold that many things have gone wrong in it, these past decades, and that these things have roots outside the profession itself. My discontents—and those of many colleagues—seem to me to follow from the way the modern American university shapes our work and, more generally, from the way this technological society uses universities and knowledge. So the book is also about literacy and literary culture in America.

But I do not come at that subject traditionally, by discussing writers and their work, movements and trends, ideas and cultural debates. Rather, I look at the folkways of teachers, at English departments, at freshman composition textbooks, at the Modern Language Association of America, at the Advanced Placement system. The point is to understand some of the institutions *that are most responsible for the transmission of literacy and culture. Their forms often reveal more about culture than do public pronouncements on the humanities, art and society, audiences and interpretation. Kenneth R. Johnston, in an excellent article on our field, writes "School, not Later Life, is becoming the dominant fact of literary experience. . . ."* [1]

I also hope, but can't guarantee, that this book will indirectly describe other academic disciplines and their professors and, to a lesser degree, other professions. I mean to offer hypotheses about how this industrial society organizes the labor of people who work with their minds and whose work is anchored in bodies of knowledge and theory. To say that I am looking at knowledge and work under advanced capitalism would be far too grand but in the right direction. So I offer my book as a case study in the academic professions.

It is also—inescapably—a study of me. I do not want to overemphasize the confessional side of this book, because (naturally) I think my analysis is correct. *But if I have learned anything during its writing it is that ideas derive from the lives and needs of people and that attempts to deny this connection are at best futile and at worst deceptive. My argument is the argument of someone who is American, male, white, 44, and privileged; who has been marked by Shaker Heights, Ohio, by the Harvard Society of Fellows, by Wesleyan University, by professional successes and failures, by students and colleagues, by the Vietnam war, by the crises in American society these past fifteen years. I mean to speak of the connections between my life and my present argument when I see those connections as pertinent because, in part, the argument is a record of my changes of mind and feeling during the time of writing.*

I did not intend to write this book. I meant to write one on syntax and style, for which Oxford University Press wrote me a contract and made me an advance in 1963 and patiently waited until I offered them this book as a substitute. Then I wanted to write a book on speech acts and literature. These would have been professional books, advancing "our" knowledge and my career. But as I worked to that end, while teaching

1. "Aesthetic Personae in the Profession," *College English*, vol. 36 (April, 1975).

undergraduates, and then being an academic administrator, I began to feel uncomfortable about where careers were taking me and the people I worked with. I felt increasingly that a gap existed between what we said we were doing (and had set out to do) and what we were actually achieving. I found it harder to believe that Humanity was being served well by the academic humanities, as our official dogma held, or that the professional apparatus we had invented was a rational structure and not a Rube Goldberg machine. I began to give some strident talks, criticizing the profession and proposing reforms. Some of these were warmly enough received to convince me that I was not alone in my perceptions or in the malaise I felt.

The best way to get into my subject, I think, is to reprint one of those talks—one that is characteristic in tone, though perhaps more orderly and thoroughgoing than the rest. I delivered it to the College Section meeting at the 1966 convention of the National Council of Teachers of English, and then published it in February, 1967, in College English, *an NCTE journal I edit. I called it "The Size and Structure of an Academic Field: Some Perplexities." Here it is:*

To put it concisely, our field—the study of humane letters—is too populous to be organized as it is. Since it will get more populous before it gets less, we must do something about its organization or we will choke.

That is my theme, and, having articulated it, I might with decorum stop, for in a way the point is obvious enough. But the conventions of conventions forbid that form of self-effacement. And there is another, older convention that will keep me standing before you: a little noticed rule of rhetoric says that the most woeful discourse shall last the longest; neither Cassandra nor Jeremiah was famous for brevity.

I shall assume that we believe the study of literature to be the most central of our concerns—that, in fact, there would not *be* a field of English if literature did not exist. Our other concerns would then be distributed among linguists, communications experts, teachers of writing skills, and so on. Literature is what holds our interests together in a loose confederation, and I think it a safe guess that literature is what brought nearly all of us into the profession. Literature is our subject matter, and, this being so, an inquiry into the state of the profession must ask how we stand vis-à-vis literature: what are our responsibilities toward it, and how well are we executing them?

It will help to have a specimen before us, so that I can revert to it when the abstractions get too thick. I choose a familiar sonnet by Robert Frost, "Design":[2]

> I found a dimpled spider, fat and white,
> On a white heal-all, holding up a moth
> Like a white piece of rigid satin cloth—
> Assorted characters of death and blight
> Mixed ready to begin the morning right,
> Like the ingredients of a witches' broth—
> A snow-drop spider, a flower like a froth,
> And dead wings carried like a paper kite.
> What had that flower to do with being white,
> The wayside blue and innocent heal-all?
> What brought the kindred spider to that height,
> Then steered the white moth thither in the night?
> What but design of darkness to appall?—
> If design govern in a thing so small.

First, notice that this undoubtedly *is* a piece of literature. Even if I had not said so, you would have identified it immediately. The language is ordered in special ways; the rhetoric has a ceremonial quality that you would not expect from me, speaking *in propria persona;* and the speech act has an unusual ontology, in that it is divorced from present circumstances and from utilitarian concerns. It neither conveys information nor furthers an argument nor embodies a command nor passes a judgment. The questions it contains are not even real questions. One might be tempted to call it a meditation—but who is meditating, and when? The customary

2. From *Complete Poems of Robert Frost.* Copyright 1936 by Robert Frost. Copyright © 1964 by Lesley Frost Ballantine. Reprinted by permission of Holt, Rinehart and Winston, Inc.

relations of speaker and audience do not obtain, but are suspended in favor of an as-if rhetoric which is one of the things we go to literature for. This is a poem; other things are not; we do have a subject matter.

Second, in your role as professional students of literature, you probably do not have much doubt about your obligations (or your inclinations) toward the poem: to preserve it and to purify its text if necessary, to make it available by supplying whatever linguistic background is required, to understand it, to appreciate it, perhaps to judge it, certainly to teach it. The poem has intricacies of form; it is the business of criticism to display and honor them. Besides its internal order, it has a place in the order of literature: one of our professional obligations is to specify this position. The poem is a sonnet, and that makes a difference. It also contributes to and modifies the traditions of descriptive-didactic and of meditative poetry. It has the mythos of comedy somewhere in its background. The verse bears a close relationship to Wordsworth's and a more indirect one to Milton's; these need to be defined. Frost's play on whiteness is allied to Melville's; this and other associations should be brought out. Frost wrote other poems; this one may come clearer through reference to "Desert Places" or "An Old Man's Winter Night." And of course the poem has potentially interesting connections with the world outside of literature: with the rigors of Frost's life, with New England, with the place of nature in the American consciousness. Its skeptical play on the margin of theology is peculiarly modern, and a critic may want to consider the poem as a document in the intellectual history of the twentieth century. Now, this list comprises the barest scattering of possibilities, yet it is surely long enough to suggest that, in addition to a subject matter, we have an occupation. It is not far from a list like this to a program of study or research. The move is utterly natural, and in my opinion perfectly appropriate. We begin with the experience of a poem, convert the poem into an object of study and, with luck, are able thereby to preserve and deepen and communicate the experience. It is not with the move itself, but with the public and social *form* of the move toward research, that I want to take issue.

But consider, first, the aims and structure of a *scientific* disipline. Its goal is to establish the laws and principles that account for phenomena in its domain—to construct a body of theory that economically and revealingly describes a portion of reality—or perhaps *all* of reality as seen from a certain point of view. To this end scientists conduct research, which is calculated to uncover the relevant facts, to extricate them from "mere" data, so that theories may be confirmed or discarded or modified. Research has a tendency to become more and more minute, as theory becomes more sophisticated and the relevant facts become increasingly subtle. In order to carry out meaningful research, a man must have an extremely specialized competence. He will not be simply a biologist, but a geneticist or a biophysicist. The sub-fields proliferate—as do journals—but they do *not* declare their independence from one another. They are linked together by a body of theory, which is, in part, common to all the sub-fields, and to which all are attempting to contribute.

A colleague of mine has found a way to measure distant events a thousand times more accurately than could be done before. This is a minute technological achievement, but it is a necessary part of his efforts to see whether light bends as it passes near celestial bodies, and thus put the theory of relativity to experimental test. And if his experiment works well over a period of years, it will bear on the question whether gravity is a constant force (as most physicists now think) or whether it decreases gradually, perhaps in proportion to the age of the universe. Through a hierarchy of theories his research is linked to the most central questions about the nature of the universe, and thus to the research of other physicists. In short, the work of physicists is essentially *corporate*, no matter how fragmented their field into subdivisions and sub-subdivisions. (This is not to say, of course, that physicists do only valuable research; I imagine that the human impulse towards triviality and irrelevance is about as strong among physicists as among the rest of us. What I do suppose is that there are clearer *standards* of relevance in the sciences than in the social sciences or, especially, than in the humanities.)

Let me continue a while with this somewhat impudent discourse on scientific disciplines. I have said that a science moves irrevocably toward the minute and particular, but only in order to facilitate an *opposite* movement towards generality. The point of a theory is precisely its generality and economy. It is a device for reducing phenomena to their underlying similarities, for doing away with them as unique and special cases, for writing off a host of special circumstances and irregularities as simply not germane. A theory extends over an infinite range of events, past and future, that fall within its boundaries, and it plays no favorites among those events. Science needs data to be sure, but the instinct of any scientist carries him as quickly as possible from data to facts, and from special theories to general theories. Hence we congratulate Einstein on having shown Newtonian mechanics to be only a special case, and we prefer a grammar that builds on linguistic universals to one that refers only to the language in question.

A striking consequence of this abstractive tendency is that although the knowledge of a guild of scientists may double every fifteen years, or whatever the appalling figure is, countervailing forces of compression are steadily at work. The intellectual holdings of a field are constantly being put in better order, subjected to more inclusive theories. This means putting them in a form that requires less special *experience* for comprehension. One values an entomologist, I suppose, not because he is personally acquainted with thousands of bugs, but because he has an integrative understanding of bugdom.

Thus the movement toward abstraction is also a movement toward public knowledge, toward accessibility. This may seem a strange claim, in view of the utter remoteness, to most humanists, of scientific work. But a moment's reflection on the scientific curriculum will substantiate it. Students in elementary physics or biology cope with material that they would not have encountered until graduate school twenty years ago, and that was not even known fifty years ago. They can get farther into a subject in a short time, not because students are brighter now, and not just because of curricular reform. Rather, curricular reform is possible and necessary because of radical simplifications in the field. Research supplements and supports teaching not only in that an active, specialized researcher is

constantly in touch with central theoretical problems, but in that the
results of research lead toward elegance, generality, and simplicity—
that is, toward something that is communicable in the classroom.

Ideally, then, the extremes of specialization, the proliferation of
journals and professional organizations, and the great emphasis on
research all are manageable within the framework of scientific fields.
One must allow, of course, for human venality, for the curse of
opulence, and for the siren songs of the federal government, but on
the whole the scientific disciplines seem to have a workable, and
even admirable, structure.

I should like to suggest now, that our own academic field is built
on much the same model, that the model is inappropriate, and that
it will become untenable as time passes.

Before speaking of science I mentioned a number of ways to study
Frost's poem. Presumably, anyone who studies the poem and
publishes his findings does so with a view toward making a
"contribution to knowledge"—knowledge of or about the poem. To
publish this contribution is to put it in the public stock of known
things, and augment by just so much our total knowledge of
literature.

But this conception leads to trouble. A minor difficulty arises from
the word "knowledge" itself, used in this context. How much of what
we discover about the poem deserves the name of knowledge? Take
the lines.

> Assorted characters of death and blight,
> Mixed ready to begin the morning right . . .

The last phrase sounds exactly as it would if "morning" were
"mourning" and "right" were "rite." [3] *This* is firm knowledge. But is
the pun really a part of the poem? That is harder to say; the answer
depends on whether the speaker's tone fits with the secondary
reading, whether the notion of a ceremony of mourning accommo-
dates itself to the wry, half-mocking simile of the witches' broth,

3. Credit to my colleague John Hackett.

whether the human emotion required for mourning is compatible with the abstract and inhuman horror the speaker claims to find in the three "characters," and so on. It is wrong to think of one reading or the other as a piece of knowledge, not simply because we can establish neither with absolute certainty (*all* knowledge is uncertain to one extent or another) but because to think of settling all such questions is to come at literature in a debilitating and unfruitful way, to expect literature to be what it is not.

The other difficulty is more crucial. To whose knowledge does an interpretation of "Design" contribute? A good reading of the poem will enlighten those who come across it, and possibly those they teach, but short of mysticism it is hard to see how a reading can contribute to knowledge-in-general. Knowledge does not finally count unless one mind can encompass it, at least in its broad outlines. Such outlines are precisely what a body of theory supplies, in the sciences, and what we lack in literature. We have no coherent system of principles which relates every finding to every other one, however remotely—and, incidentally, which permits us to adjudicate among competing interpretations of poems. For this reason, the phrase "contribution to knowledge" is particularly misleading in our field. It implies a gathering together, a consolidaton, in men's minds, whereas in fact the consolidation can only take place in an archive or an information retrieval system. In literary research, after a point, more is less and less is more. I think we must look squarely at the unpleasant fact that our research will become more nearly inert as it increases in volume, whether its quality improves or not. If one has a taste for apocalypse, he may imagine a time when each literary scholar knows only his *own* research, and we perish, not through entropy but through solipsism.

Now of course this is a wicked exaggeration, to be tempered and modified in calmer moments. But one counter-argument I shall *not* accept is that our system of sub-fields ameliorates the situation. It is perhaps true that eighteenth-century scholars can still talk to each other and keep up with each other's work, but if so, it will not be true much longer. In 1963 I contracted to review the year's crop of books on modern British and American literature. By the time I was done I had reviewed over 75 books. Modesty does not prevent me from conjecturing that I am the only person in the world who has read all those books and, indeed, that I shall be the sole possessor of that distinction until my death. I do not plan to hasten the latter event by trying to duplicate this feat in 1967 or in any other year, excellent though many of the new books are. No one can "keep up" with the modern field any more; soon fiction of the twenties will be enough, or Robert Frost *tout seul.* Our sub-fields do not contain our research and direct it to the common good; they simply provide categories for it to spread into and suggest ways of forming new categories when the old ones no longer suffice.

A still more serious charge may be brought against these sub-fields: not only do they make for specialization, they actually pull *against* the formation of a literary theory that might draw our efforts together. For the conceptual system that underlies our division of research labor, our journals, and our graduate programs is that of history—not even sophisticated history, but chronology. We inherit this scheme from a time when the goal of liberary study was the reconstruction of the past.[4] Our goals seem more complicated now, and though they still have something to do with historical consciousness, they are on the whole badly represented by divisions such as Blake-to-Keats or Eighteenth Century, First Half. I know that a great deal of scholarship vaults over these chronological fences, but the fences are there, setting artificial boundaries to the professional lives of graduate students, diverting research into a non-literary structure, and cutting off possibilities of humane discourse among colleagues.

And here is the point of nearly everything I have said so far: our scheme of professional organization is destructive of community. Partly owing to the academic necessity for *some* scheme of divisions, partly owing to the origins of our field in philology and history, and partly owing to the successful model of the sciences, we have inherited an elaborate system that ill suits our needs. For our main

4. See James Holly Hanford, "The American Scholar and His Books," *PMLA*, LXXIV, ii (May, 1959), 32.

goal is not the accumulation of knowledge—and in any case we do not have the theory to master our knowledge. Our goal, I think, is the fostering of literary culture and literary consciousness. If so, a prior responsibility is to our own community, our corporate identity; and it is precisely that identity that seems most threatened by our present means of conducting and presenting research. What an unsatisfactory state we have achieved, from the point of view I am urging upon you, when most of what we write drops quickly into a permanent non-circulating file, unassimilated, and even unread except by a corps of specialist colleagues and by unusually diligent committees on promotion and tenure.

Let me return, now, to science, in order to establish another contrast. I spoke of the abstractive tendency in science, the impulse to say "all other things being equal. . . ." Of course all other things never *are* equal; there is no perfect vacuum, no frictionless plane, and so on. But a scientific theory achieves one of its ends when it succeeds in extricating the regularity from its penumbra of untidy detail. There is no need for the scientist as scientist to return to particulars once he has accounted for them.

Our situation is quite different. We need generalization and theory, to be sure—indeed, I hope I have indicated that in my opinion we need far more and far better theory than we have. But finally, our theories should be the servants, not even of facts, but of the experience that lies beneath facts. The most ardent literary theorist would be unhappy, I suppose, to have arrived at a point where he could close the books on literature and say, "Here is a set of formulas that account for all poems and their effects upon us." At the end of literary study resides the work itself, in its complexity and uniqueness. We value the uniqueness above everything else, and wish to preserve it, even—if a choice has to be made—at the expense of theory.

I may make this point more graphic by glancing again at Frost's poem. This sequence of words might be an object of linguistic study, rather than of literary study. In that case it would have a certain interest. It instances a transformation that permits an adjective to appear after a noun when it is paired with another adjective, though not when it stands alone ("a dimpled spider, *fat and white*"); it contains some examples of complex apposition; and so on. But it serves linguistics only *as* an instance; its singularity is unimportant, except as something to be brought under the rubric of a complete grammar of English. For linguistic purposes, the first few lines are quite on a par with:

I discerned a spider. The spider was sitting on a white flower and was holding up a moth, which somewhat resembled a white piece of cloth whose rigidity suggested satin. The spider itself was corpulent and pallid.

It is not just that science seeks to achieve a neutrality towards particular events; the activity of theorizing is essentially neutral.

   Now linguistic concepts have a bearing on the critical interpretation of Frost's poem, as I would be the first to insist. Consider again the octet of the sonnet:

> I found a dimpled spider, fat and white,
> On a white heal-all, holding up a moth
> Like a white piece of rigid satin cloth:
> Assorted characters of death and blight
> Mixed ready to begin the morning right,
> Like the ingredients of a witches' broth—
> A snow-drop spider, a flower like a froth,
> And dead wings carried like a paper kite.

The poem opens by presenting the three elements of its image in a particular conjunction in space and time, which is delineated by syntax. "Found," places the event in the past, and the participle "holding" indicates that action of holding was contemporaneous with that of finding. The spider and the moth are related, in deep structure, as subject and object—related, that is, through action. The spider and the flower connect in space as well, through the prepositional phrase "on a white heal-all," which occupies a slot labeled "location." One might notice also that in the deep structure "spider" appears six times, "heal-all" and "moth" only twice each: the spider distinctly presides over the image. Thus the three "characters" bear a complex relationship to each other, one that deploys space, time, action, and emphasis.

These facts of syntax and semantics would scarcely be worth noticing, however, but for what follows the first three lines. Beneath the line, "Assorted characters of death and blight" are the underlying structures, "the spider was a character . . . ," "the heal-all was a character . . . ," and "the moth was a character. . . ." The three structures are identical, and thus accommodate themselves to conjunction. The moth, flower, and spider come together under the single rubric, "assorted characters," which makes no distinction among them. The arrangement in space and time has disappeared, as has the difference in emphasis. The next two lines certify this equation of the three (all are "mixed ready to begin the morning right" and all are "like the ingredients of a witches' broth"), and thus prepare for the simple conjunction of the final two lines:

> A snow-drop spider, a flower like a froth,
> And dead wings carried like a paper kite.

Frost has radically altered his image. The configuration in space and time has given way to an order that is neither temporal nor spatial, one in which action plays a minor part, and the emphasis is evenly distributed. In short, what began as a physical arrangement has changed into a purely conceptual one: the spider, moth, and flower are ranged in the speaker's mind, rather than in nature.

I have already gone well beyond the linguistic facts, and to see the significance of those facts it is necessary to go still farther. The poem is about design. It builds to a question about the possibility of a malevolent ordering force in the world, then backs away from the question with the odd twist of the last line: "If design govern in a thing so small." The syntactic and semantic patterns I have been discussing go a good way toward explaining the rightness of this conclusion. In moving from the random scene of spider, moth and flower to a neat conceptualization of them as equivalent, the speaker has supplied a pattern where none existed: he has, in short, imposed a *design*. That design can be seen "in" nature, but it takes a certain kind of human being to see it there, and to ask ominous questions about it. The speaker knows that he has allowed his imagination some leeway; thus, even after he has frightened himself with his questions he can turn and challenge the very premise of his meditation: that one does not have a design without a designer. Or perhaps the poem has shown the designer to be the poet himself.

But in offering such a reading of the poem—and only a tiny fraction of a reading at that—I have left linguistic rules and theories far behind, and appealed again to the unique configuration of the poem, which is what finally interests us, however much help we may get from theory along the way. What I have meant to suggest is that we have no satisfying way to compress the results of literary inquiry, since that inquiry seeks always to preserve an infinitely complicated and irreducible reality. It does not follow that there should be an end to inquiry; inquiry is one way we have of celebrating the uniqueness we value in the literary work. But what I have been saying does raise a vexing question about the payoff of research: if research is to honor the uniqueness of poems, can we afford to have the results of research deposited mainly in archives, rather than in minds?

In another, closely allied, way, our field differs sharply from those it seems to be emulating. A scientific inquiry has a certain ethic—that of disinterestedness—but its *results* are morally neutral, and, as I have said, it maintains a moral neutrality toward the objects of its attention. A biologist may hold the life of planaria in reverence, and his research may even contribute to his attitude, but such a morality is only a fringe benefit of that research. On the other hand, behind every teacher of literature lurks a moralist, and for good reason. The experience of literature is quite inseparable from moral experience, even less than from esthetic. Frost's poem gives us a figure of a man subjecting his encounter with spider, moth, and flower to theological scrutiny of a kind typically human, and yet, through a self-ironic tone and through the reversal of the last line, holding onto a measured agnosticism—and at the same time hinting, without terror, at a world even more terrifying than one governed by malevolent design: namely, one with no design at all. This complex of attitudes, simultaneously held, compactly defines a moral position (one, incidentally, that recurs throughout Frost's poems). One of our main efforts as literary people is to bring ourselves (and our students) up to the point of entertaining such moralities, without necessarily accepting them. One of the functions of a literary culture is to extend our moral experience.

I repeat this truism because it is easy to forget, especially in the organization of our professional lives. Our activities of research and publication imitate those of the sciences, whose effort is toward the abstract and impersonal. The model is a bad one for us, since our inquiries point ultimately toward the concrete and personal. A critical book or article does not simply record a finding; it demands to be felt, argued, and assimilated into the moral lives of its audience, and it admits of no guild limitations on that audience. Our machinery of publication scarcely permits that kind of response, and, as the field grows, will forbid it entirely, and make our enterprise increasingly irrelevant to the business of being human.

We are not growing because the field needs growth, but because the population of the world is growing, and because we can afford to have 2500 colleges, hundreds of journals, five thousand books and articles on English and American literature each year, many thousands of graduate students in English, and so on. We did not ask for a population explosion in the literary wing of the academy, but we are having one—and of course we need one, so long as the rest of the population is also exploding, because we want to teach the teachable and thus exert the good influence literature is capable of exerting on culture. Yet this cultural aspiration has always been somewhat at odds with our professional aspirations, and as both the profession and its professional*ism* increase, the disjunction will become more pronounced. Given the present structure of the discipline and the present curve of growth, we can look forward with confidence, if not with pleasure, to more research, more unread articles, less relevance of literature to life, more seeking out of neglected works, more coverage for coverage's sake, more minute specialization, more time-serving and ambition, less and worse teaching, less theory, less community, until we have indeed a "design of darkness to appall."

You have been patient to listen to these dyspeptic remarks; surely the problem is evident without my calling attention to it. On the other hand, you might with justice have expected a solution or two in compensation for hearing out the assault. The simplest and least practical solution is, of course, a change of heart. Even this may come, but perhaps not tomorrow or next Thursday. And for the meanwhile, I should like to offer some more proximate solutions, in brief, and in full knowledge of how difficult even they would be to effect.

First, let me insist that I consider research and publication to be good things, not only as they make works of literature available, but as they affect the researcher himself. I want to define research as disciplined reading and thinking with a view to discovery and publication as the submission of research to public review and criticism. Given these definitions, there can be no doubt that research and publication naturally tend to support intellectual well-being. Without them we shrivel or become cranky and delirious. They convert intellectual energies into tangible form, and afford both the pleasure of accomplishment and the sharp stimulant of criticism. Or they *should* do so: what I have been arguing is that in their present sprawling form they cannot and that we need to domesticate them once more.

To this end it would be well for new ambitious institutions and old ambitious institutions to say, and mean it, that excellent teaching is a legitimate form of research and publication. Because it is.

Again, presenting research to one's colleagues is a form of publication—one of the best, if the presentation takes place in a colloquium or seminar, and is followed by critiques and debate, rather than by respectful silence. Such colloquia should invite the attendance of colleagues outside the literary fields, as a hedge against parochialism. In the long run, the professional standards enforced by sessions of this kind will be higher than the somewhat nebulous ones that govern acceptance by journals, and the satisfaction will be correspondingly greater, not to mention the corporate intellectual life of the department and the institution. (It is shocking how little we make use of our colleagues *as* colleagues, beyond the routines of committee work.) And a department that is not nervous about its intellectual life will not need to rely much on external standards of acceptability.

Insofar as publication must continue through the medium of the learned journal, journals should encourage reverberations after the event itself, by welcoming rebuttal and counter-rebuttal. Indeed, they should print only articles with enough theoretical bite to initiate disagreement—but perhaps this is asking too much.

Along the same line, the profession should have a national review of scholarly books, comparable to the *New York Review* in intent and quality. Such a journal would submit the stream of publication to prompt, ample, and rigorous criticism and provide a forum for scholars who are willing to talk to each other, not merely note each other's books on index cards.

A review of this sort would go a way toward remedying the excesses of the scholarly and commercial presses, but not far enough. Though the words feel strange in my mouth, I think we are approaching a time when we will need some form of censorship—both of journals and of presses. At the very least, we must get them to make a distinction between specialist work and work that challenges our whole structure of ideas, the former to be printed in a uniform way and distributed mainly to libraries and information retrieval centers. And the commercial presses should make a further clear distinction between truly innovative work on the one side and introductions, summaries, handbooks, and textbooks on the other.

Our national organizations, notably the MLA and the NCTE, need to re-examine the purpose of their fraternal gatherings, as Howard Mumford Jones cogently argued in Chicago last December. Local and regional meetings devoted to unfamiliar activity of thinking, supplemented by small national meetings of specialist groups, might perform most of the intellectual functions—as opposed to social and administrative ones—that now somewhat inappropriately devolve upon national conventions. Similarly, we might consider a system of local and regional journals, whose best articles would be reprinted in a very few national journals.

And finally, perhaps by an act of superhuman self-denial we could relinquish the mind-forged manacles of our historical categories. Those of us whose work is genuinely historical do not need the categories, and for the rest—students especially—the historical sub-fields are simply a barrier to free development.

I began with concision, and I should like to end the same way though I have been anything but concise in the interim. We must humanize the *machinery* of literary study or risk sacrificing the humane value of the study itself.

I want to comment on some salient points of this critique (leaving aside the unpleasant irony that by making size the root of our problems, I left open the then-unthinkable possibility that economic strangulation would "solve" them through simple elimination of jobs, as is happening in 1975). First, the ills I identified were and are real enough: the unsuitable idea of knowledge, taken from science; blind specialization; lack of intellectual community; too much esteem for publication of research and too little for teaching. On the other hand, I made some supporting assumptions that I would not make now: that our main function was to foster literary culture and that we could do so by making some internal adjustments; that the essence of our work was the particular body of knowledge we professed; that literature in itself is a civilizing, moral force; and that any impedance of that force by professional structures must be perverse. Hence, I looked for changes—a new journal, more prestige for teaching, more forums for debate, regionalization of our organizations, less rigid divisions of the field—that we could ourselves accomplish, without changing our external relationships and, certainly, without changing society itself. I thought of the profession as self-contained and responsible to society only in that we were to preserve and increase literary culture, which could surely smooth the rough edges of philistine society. In short, I made assumptions—those, generally, traced by Raymond Williams in Culture and Society—*so familiar among literate people of the last 175 years that I was unaware of them as challengeable premises and thought of them as plain facts. Among other things, this book is an effort to examine them critically.*

In November of 1966, I was trying to cope with two disparate circumstances of which I made no mention in my lecture at NCTE. One was my new job in the administration of my college and the other was the war in Vietnam. My experience of both seemed unrelated to the subject of the lecture. But that was not so.

I had gone into administration that year, hoping to steer faculty and fellow administrators in the directions I pointed out at NCTE and after a lot of frustration working in these directions as a faculty member. Hundreds of hours of committee time and less than exhilarating results. Working from the "other side," I expected to have a more persuasive leverage (maybe even more power) and to further the interests I knew my faculty colleagues to share. But instead of finding them allies in the attempt to humanize scholarship, make the word "community" less empty, and strengthen liberal education, I met chairmen and others asking for increases in departmental size, trying to pull out of interdepartmental courses, proposing specialized Ph.D. programs, and asking for increased research benefits and reduced departmental teaching loads. Department competed with department, humanists with scientists, and everyone with the administration. And yet these were the same friends and colleagues who, over a drink or a cup of coffee, shared by and large my own views on the college and our work. There must have been influences upon their acts, other than the general ideas they expressed and presumably believed. And, of course, I began to see the same contradictions in myself. As I invoked the general welfare, I was often just advancing professional, academic interests.

Vietnam was a much more acute grief. By November, 1966, there was no day when I did not feel rage, anguish, and frustration over our government's actions. The gap between these feelings and the demands of business as usual became too great. I had already signed petitions and begun refusing to pay taxes; by the spring of 1967 I was organizing support for draft resisters (among the same faculty members whose academic politics I found so conservative!) and giving political speeches. But I wanted more integration. If humanistic culture really is a civilizing force, why wouldn't the college I worked for and the profession I worked in TAKE A STAND? So I pressed for motions in faculty meetings, for days to be set aside to discuss the war, for resolutions in MLA and NCTE, and for crash programs of all kinds to translate our moral views into political acts. And if I were giving a scholarly talk on language and literature, I would find a way to link it with Vietnam.

The futility of that kind of politics, except in making more trouble for the government, is now evident. But why? Why were these institutions unable to have the critical impact that their ideologies claimed for them? Why were universities unable to resist a government that was crushing the values of human freedom and of pursuit of truth, values that are the primary allegiance of the liberal university? Why couldn't literature professors enact the values we found in literary culture? The short answer, I now think, is that institutions don't exist in vacuums or in the pure atmosphere of their ideals. They are part of the social order and survive by helping to maintain it. A longer answer, giving substance to the short one, is the rest of this book.

II

Literature and the Rites of Passage

I mean to criticize a position that I will outline and simplify thus: literature—the best that has been thought and imagined and written— can serve the society in many ways. It tempers the hard rationality of science. It teaches moral and esthetic values in a world that otherwise aspires only to the material. It supports the individual person, against powerful leveling forces of a society of the masses. And it is an endless source of rich, vicarious experience, which permits us to imagine alternate worlds and criticize the present world. But for poets to be, as Shelley said, the legislators of the world, whether acknowledged or not, requires more than just giving literature a license to compete in a Darwinian cultural struggle, along with tin pan alley and television commercials and professional football. Most young people need to be formally initiated into literary culture—taught to appreciate, and even to read literature. English classrooms are the front line of culture. The support system they depend upon includes the recovery, preservation, and editing of texts; a scholarly provision of historical and linguistic understanding; and a critical effort in each generation to interpret and revalue literary works and relate their insights to the contemporary world. (Most poets themselves must be subsidized by universities.) It is in society's interest to train and pay enough teachers, scholars, and critics to ensure that literature exercises its civilizing influences.

People who hold these views assume that they can largely control the terms on which society accepts and finances the ministrations of literature. And they assume that the part of the work force that earns its living through teaching and studying literature will find no incompatibility between its interests and those of literature or, to put it more concretely, between its interests in literature and its interests in performing decent work for a decent living. Make these two assumptions, and it seems plausible that the literary profession can without much difficulty establish the set of practical arrangements that will best accomplish these admirable goals. Any flaw in these arrangements will then appear remediable: a failure of our own good will or practical ingenuity.

My own contrary opinion is that institutions built by teachers of literature are, like those of all groups, a compromise among our own needs, the needs of society as we see them, and the needs felt by powerful people and classes of people. Such institutions often betray the ideals of the professional group. It is not astonishing that the American Medical Association often has acted to limit *the availability of good medical care, or that fierce competition in law schools has encouraged some future attorneys to be unscrupulous and even* unlawful, *or that, in every age, some ministers of the Gospel have served the* secular *purposes of rulers and of rich people who endow ecclesiastical institutions. Should it be surprising to find that institutions built by teachers of the humanities sometimes* dehumanize?

Society has other uses for us than those we have generally chosen. It uses schools and colleges to sort out young people for various kinds of work. English teachers must do that and use literature to help in the sorting. Society needs help from the schools to justify its present divisions, including much inequality. There is pressure—indirect but heavy—on teachers of literature to join in this effort. The ruling classes want a culture, including a literature and a criticism, that supports the social order and discourages rebellion, while it sanctions all kinds of nonthreatening nonconformity. If we want to teach literature, we had better adapt it to this task, too.

How do these urgencies get transmitted to teachers and students of literature? I think that people are most malleable when they are advancing from one station in life to a higher one or trying to do so. The ideas that play a part in rites of passage make more of an impression than those ideas of smaller practical consequence. The values that inhere in rites of passage will be influential values. And the styles that are rewarded at initiation tend to become the styles of the initiates.

Literature, of course, plays a part in everyone's rites of passage, since everyone "takes" English in school. Teachers of literature help plan and administer the rites. Beyond that, teachers of literature have their own initiation ceremonies. My intention in the next three chapters is to look at the way teachers of English act at such times. Specifically, I want first to offer a "reading" of the Modern Language Association of America. It is the most influential of the professional organizations, in matters concerning literature; its meetings are a necessary stop for novices entering our profession; and they are the Mecca of an annual pilgrimage, at which thousands of teachers reaffirm values and folkways and discover how the leaders of the profession comport themselves. Chapter Three is about the Advanced Placement Program in English. Through this program and its climactic examination, teachers of literature play a part in selecting, from among high school students, those who will succeed in college and later. This selective process is often an intense one for the students, and I think that literary and cultural values made salient then are especially likely to stamp themselves on students' minds. In Chapter Four, I will look at the ideas about literature that have dominated graduate study for 20 years and, thus, have had a direct impact on the most critical rite of passage of our profession.

CHAPTER TWO

MLA: Professors
of Literature
in a Group

The principle behind this book is an examination of literary culture as American society has formally established it. This means paying more attention to how teachers of language and literature *profess* than to what they *say* about culture or about the role of literature. Any group of workers somehow confirms its identity and passes on its folkways. This it may do partly through an official organization—a guild or league or union or professional association or learned society. The shape of such an organization reveals something about what its members conceive their function to be and about what values they share. So it is worth taking a look at the largest organization of those people who profess language and literature in this country's universities: the Modern Language Association of America.

For me the wish to understand the MLA arose in 1968, when I became involved in incidents that are now part of its history. Since my relationship to the MLA, to that extent, is a personal one, I start with an incident that dramatized for me the ethos of the organization, its style of action, and its impact on its members.

I was standing in line to register at my hotel, having just arrived in New York for the 1968 meeting of the MLA, when an acquaintance

stopped to say to me, "Louis has been arrested." Louis was Louis
Kampf, head of the Literature Section, Department of Humanities,
Massachusetts Institute of Technology, and a friend of mine with
whom I was sharing a couple of rooms during the convention. His
arrest, on the first day of the convention, surprised me. More than
that: though I had been planning with Kampf and others an
attempt at a modest political insurgency at the MLA meeting, and,
though I had grown accustomed to the arrest of my friends,
colleagues, and students during the admirable years 1967 and 1968,
I found this arrest disquieting. It violated some immemorial
decorum, the nature of which I couldn't immediately identify.
Perhaps because others reacted similarly, Kampf's arrest became the
symbolic event, the charged event, of the three-day convention. The
facts were simple—indeed, stupid—enough. Some people from an
activist group, Kampf among them, were putting up posters in the
lobby of the Americana, one of the two main convention hotels. The
hotel guards objected, and tried to tear down one of the posters (it
bore Blake's words, "the tigers of wrath are wiser than the horses of
instruction"). Louis Kampf and others objected to the guards'
objections. The guards shoved. The poster defenders held their
ground. The hotel guards called the police. The police arrested three
men, including Kampf and two graduate students. (One of the latter
found out a few months later from his department chairman that the
FBI was investigating him; he asked his congressman why and
eventually discovered that their interest in him stemmed from the
battle of the posters at the MLA convention.)

Now, why did the hotel management act in such an extraordinarily edgy way, upon such slight provocation, given the kinds of
genuinely anti-social conduct hotels must be used to—say, at an
American Legion convention? (MLA meetings are sober occasions in
every sense except the literal one: at an earlier convention someone
overheard one hotel maid say to another, "I don't understand
professors—all that drinking and no fucking.") Again, why did
police remain stationed outside the Americana and the Hilton for a
day, until the MLA management insisted that they be removed?
Why did the reformers demand from the MLA a formal apology for

the arrest? Why did they hold a standing vigil in front of the platform at one of the large panels? Why did the MLA management operate for the following three days in a state of panic? Why did John Hurt Fisher, then executive secretary, an accomplished administrator as well as a mature scholar, accuse the reformers of *producing* panic, threatening violence, and planning the arrest in advance (none of which, to my knowledge, is true)?

The place to look for an answer, I believe, is not in the immediate antecedents of the events that ruffled the surface of the 1968 MLA convention. These were predictable enough, given the intrusion of politics into meetings of anthropologists, philosophers, psychologists, and other professional groups. Rather, one had best look to the nature of the MLA, to the part it plays in academic and literary culture, and to the needs it satisfies for its roughly 30,000 members. The feelings that attached to the scuffle in the lobby of the Americana cannot be attributed to the scuffle itself; such encounters are the daily fare of our society. It is the MLA, and its tribal function, that must be explained. When liberals and reformers found arrests and police to be profoundly incompatible with the MLA, and the establishment sensed an equally distressing incompatibility between lobby politics and the MLA, the two groups were demonstrating, in a perhaps unanticipated way, John Fisher's suggestion that the MLA is a "metaphysical union," a "fraternity held together by common values and interests."

In spite of the hostility that was driven to the surface by the Vietnam war, the siege of Chicago, and allied events, the membership of the MLA did indeed retain some fraternal and metaphysical ties. Though one group at the 1968 meeting was trying to preserve what the other was trying to alter or destroy, both seemed to know, as I shall try to illustrate, something about their corporate metaphysical life as literary scholars. They knew that their association with one another was mediated by a highly formal bureaucracy, which operated abstractly and legalistically, quelled dissent, and made action a breach of decorum—a disruption, to use the standard term of that era. They knew that the MLA is a meritocracy of scholarship and that those outside its elite could not expect to influence the course of its policies—this in spite of the obviously genuine intention of the secretariat to serve the whole membership. Both groups had also absorbed the ethos of professionalism, which insulates all such groups from challenge by outsiders. Again, they knew well that politics is to scholarship what drink is to driving. Finally, they had learned that culture is in old books and that it stopped some time ago. These are the tacit principles beneath the corporate structures we have built for ourselves. They bear examination, as does the question they raise: Why should the corporate face of the MLA accord so ill with the values to which an overwhelming majority of the members explicitly subscribe?

To start with what is least singular about this particular metaphysical union, but characteristic of all our bandings-together: when the band gets big enough, procedures supplant values, and people are absorbed in structures.

The first meeting of the MLA was held at Columbia on December 27, 1883, in a classroom. Forty teachers attended, and for three days they debated the role of French and German in the schools, the best methods of teaching these languages, the tyranny of the classics, and allied matters. In short, forty men came together to discuss with zeal the shape of contemporary linguistic and literary culture. In 1968, at the 83rd meeting of the MLA, there were more than 10,000 in attendance. They met in 67 sections (including English 8, 1750–1800; General Topics 5, Phonetics; and Spanish 6, Early Spanish-American), 67 seminars (including #58, Galdos' Perspective of Love; #36, The Literature of Exploration; and #24, Research on the Proust Manuscripts), two Forums, a General Meeting, a Business Meeting, and many others. By this time there were seventeen committees (program, research, honorary members, nominations, English Program, Materials Center, etc.). There was a special commission to study the MLA: it suggested that the Executive Council (the steering committee) should take a stronger hand in making policy, wondered if the MLA should change its name, and recommended that some MLA activities be decentralized.

This is the face the MLA presented to its members. How can one get past it and into any issue of significance? Not surprisingly, when the 1968 Business Meeting left its customary channels and, among other things, passed several openly political resolutions (no more war in Vietnam, no more draft, end repression of writers, eliminate anti-riot provisions from educational legislation), indignant members who mailed in suggestions[1] to John Fisher made straight for legal procedure. One member of the Executive Council wrote:

If I am right—if the Charter or the Maryland laws under which the Charter was issued forbid taking political stands—then the Business Meeting was clearly out of order. To endorse the actions of the Business Meeting would violate the Charter and would compromise the non-profit status of the organization. . . . If this line of approach should seem promising, a qualified legal opinion from the MLA lawyer would greatly strengthen the position of the Executive Council.

Another offered By-Law amendments—that resolutions not adopted by a two-thirds majority and those declared substantive (!) by the Resolutions Committee be submitted to the membership in a referendum. This was a common enough suggestion. Some went further, and asked that the procedure be instituted *retroactively:*

My suggestion is precisely this: that the Executive Council take the extraordinary step of declaring all votes taken at the business meeting in New York strictly provisional and void or suspended until or unless ratified by a mail ballot of the total membership. . . .

So much for legal procedure and due process.

(The Executive Council, more scrupulous than this correspondent, did not void the business legally transacted in New York, but it did take the unprecedented step of submitting the resolutions to the membership for an "expression of opinion." The general membership, lashing out, perhaps, against the invisible, omnipotent, and procedure-bound organization it had created, affirmed all four political resolutions, so that the MLA is now on record as having

1. These were circulated in the Executive Council and passed on to me by one of its members. All quotations from correspondence in this chapter are from the same source, or from letters written to Louis Kampf and passed on to me.

twice asserted that "The United States is waging an immoral, illegal, and imperial war in Vietnam," urged the immediate withdrawal of American troops, and called on colleges and universities to "refuse cooperation with the Selective Service System." This last made the Association a conspirator, but no criminal charges were brought, nor did the Government challenge the MLA's tax exemption.)

An organization grown large and impersonal tends to disaffirm in its methods the principles affirmed by its rhetoric. In doing so it damps the spirit of its members, deflects them from their original goals, and sanctifies procedures. When Louis Kampf taped up a poster in the Americana's lobby, and was taken into custody, he did something for which there was no authorization in the By-Laws. No wonder we quivered like school children before the ancestral wrath of a thousand deceased scholars.

Yet, more prosaically, the MLA is governed by only a handful of scholars. Nominations are made by a nominating committee of scholars, who naturally equate merit with their own style of achievement. When the members are allowed the luxury of a vote, they take the cue readily enough and vote for the best-known scholars. (How else does one become famous?)

This fact about the policy-makers of the MLA embodies a deeper truth about the metaphysical union, namely, that scholarship is far and away the most evident interest of the organization. Almost all the scheduled meetings at the annual convention address themselves to scholarly issues in scholarly "fields." Articles in the *Publications of the Modern Language Association—PMLA*, the official journal of the MLA—are overwhelmingly of a scholarly nature. The May, 1969, issue does include "the Barbarism of Virtue," an argument by Sidney Hook against political involvement of universities and professional societies (of which more later). The other articles are all scholarly, and a list of their titles is instructive as to the Association's channeling of its members' energies:

Der *Walpurgisnachtstraum* in Goethe's *Faust*: Entwurf, Gestaltung, Funktion.
The Damned Crew.
Cardenio, by Shakespeare and Fletcher.

Action and Suffering: *Samson Agonistes* and the Irony of Alternatives.

Fettered Fancy in *Hard Times.*

The Time Machine; or, the Fourth Dimension as Prophecy.

Poe and the Power of Animal Magnetism.

A Local Pride: The Poetry of *Paterson.*

Don Juan and *Le Misanthrope*, or the Esthetics of Individualism in *Molière.*

Functions of the Framework in La Fontaine's *Psyche.*

Arboreal Figures in the Golden Age Sonnet.

In the aftermath of the 1968 uprising came many reforms. One reform was a change in the editorial policy of *PMLA*, to make the journal of more general interest. But a 1975 table of contents would not contrast sharply with the above.

To be sure, the MLA has involved itself in non-scholarly matters—most notably, the reform of high school teaching in English and in foreign language and literature. Few members participate in these activities or even care about them. The MLA helped initiate summer institutes at major universities, with the aim of improving high school English teaching; John C. Gerber, filing a generally cheerful report on this venture, had to acknowledge that the institutes did not succeed in engaging university faculties more actively in teacher training:

Very few of the English departments involved seemed, at the time, to consider the Institutes an important departmental enterprise. In five departments even the chairman seemed indifferent. Occasionally our Evaluators encountered members of English departments who were not even aware of the presence of an Institute on their campus. Quite obviously, few of the twenty departments involved had made the Institutes a matter of departmental business. . . .[2]

This did not really surprise Gerber, though it annoyed him, and it should not have surprised anyone familiar with the folkways of the MLA and of American university faculties in language and literature. These indifferent chairmen and uninformed department members had learned early and well which way to cast their eyes: not

2. J. C. Gerber, *PMLA,* vol. 78 (September, 1963), p. 11.

down, toward the many millions of school kids, spending billions of hours in English classes, but *up,* toward the few whose work had shown its value by being published in *PMLA* and toward the even fewer whose scholarship had been further endorsed by their election to high office in the MLA.

To some, the emphasis on scholarship will seem so inevitable as to make the mention of it superfluous: what *else* would a learned society attend to? Yet most MLA members spend only a small fraction of their working time in scholarship. They have other interests that might well be given a place in the meetings and the journal. Volume I of *PMLA* (1884–85) did, in fact, include articles on "The Aims and Methods of Collegiate Instruction in Modern Languages," "How Far Should Our Teaching and Text-books Have a Scientific Basis?," "The College Course in English Literature, How It May Be Improved," and "The Realgymnasium Question" (on the democratizing of higher education in Germany and America). The MLA addressed itself to literary history and contemporary culture in about equal measure, as if the two could conceivably have something to do with one another and as if a young man or woman, aspiring to a literary career, might look for advancement through teaching and cultural criticism, along with historical scholarship.

But, by 1968, the symbolic and actual primacy of scholarship was indeed clear to anyone who looked. And this ordering of values naturally resulted in a kind of ruling class within the MLA and the profession. The best scholars were elected to office. Since scholarship is most at home in graduate schools, almost all of these men came from universities that grant the Ph.D.; one may surmise that most of the officers spent most of their time teaching graduate students. Again, since achievement in scholarship gives one professional mobility, most of the MLA leaders gravitated toward the prestige universities. Conversely, since it costs a lot of money to hire a scholar of distinction, only rich universities have, by and large, been able to afford MLA officers. From 1932 to 1969, the MLA was governed by only about 200 people—officers and members of the Executive Council. More than one-half of them were on the faculties of Yale, Harvard, New York University, University of California (Berkeley),

Columbia, Princeton, Chicago, Johns Hopkins, and Cornell. The chances of an excellent teacher from the University of Tulsa helping to govern the MLA were negligible; those of a cultural and political activist from Metropolitan Junior College in Kansas City were nil. And of course graduate students and junior faculty were also excluded, along with black scholars and all but a very few women.

The 1968 revolt changed the face of the MLA, but not its actual governance. Most immediately, Louis Kampf, caught up in a wave of celebrity after his arrest, was elected second vice president of the Association, and succeeded, by orderly steps, to the presidency in 1971; Florence Howe, another of the radicals, followed him in this sequence of offices two years later. And the MLA leadership itself responded to obvious unhappiness among the members by recommending constitutional changes. After parliamentary struggles (which may easily be imagined) had throttled interest in deeper reform of the MLA, the machinery ground out a new structure. The Business Meeting would no longer decide MLA policy; in exchange for this one annual shot at direct rule, the rank and file got a huge, 200-odd member Delegate Assembly. It meets for a few hours a year, allows much expression of opinion, and has no power. Power remains with the Executive Council, which is *advised* by the Delegate Assembly. Hence the presence in the latter of members from previously excluded groups may seem more cosmetic than revolutionary. And after a few people who would not have made it by earlier criteria were elected to the Executive Council, gravity returned to the proceedings, and the pool of candidates is again composed almost entirely of famous scholars from major universities.

This elitism is not the result of a conspiracy; the fact that it is unplanned only increases its power. Almost everyone seems to have found it *natural* that a rather large and extremely influential organization, with a budget of over $1,000,000, should be primarily responsive to the interests of the scholarly professoriate at just a handful of universities. Certainly that is what some of Louis Kampf's less enthusiastic correspondents were trying to say, after his election to high office, at the unruly Business Meeting of December, 1968:

Mr. Kampf:

I am curious to know whether, considering the infinitesimally small [sic] members-come-lately of the MLA who nominated you for the second vice-presidency of the MLA, you would really undertake to serve as president, assuming the unlikely possibility of two more such fluke elections as the last one. If so, I suggest that you have a look at the list of distinguished scholars who have been presidents of the Association. . . . If you do, I should think the membership should be given a list of your scholarly attainments.

Though I happen to be the particular infinitesimally small member (not come-lately, I confess) who nominated Kampf, what mainly interests me about this gracious writer is his ready assumption that democracy becomes invalid as soon as its principles conflict with the meritocracy of scholarship. (By the way, Louis Kampf had published an excellent and very scholarly study, *On Modernism*—an MLA Book Club selection—as well as a number of essays in cultural criticism, but these achievements, of course, left him still on the lower-middle reaches of the ladder of advancement.)

Another correspondent, this one from a distinctly non-elite university, voiced a similar distrust of popular movements:

I consider your "election" as 2nd Vice President as valid as that of Fidel Castro and Josef Stalin. . . . I hereby withdraw from the MLA until such time as its management is returned to the hands of Modern Language personnel.

This man knew his and Kampf's place. It would be pleasant to dismiss this sort of response as the inevitable squawk of the lunatic fringe, but unfortunately it represents, in all but tone, the widespread opinion of MLA members. Thus, a petition circulated by 24 distinguished scholars from Duke and North Carolina bemoaned the fact that 300 people (roughly the voting majority at the Business Meeting) were able to strike a political stance for the whole MLA, and asked the Executive Council to do what it could to reverse the votes taken in New York. I have already mentioned the aftermath of this effort; what bears comment here is that in the view of 24 scholars, and the many hundreds who signed their petition, measures taken by a majority of 16 scholars should have precedence over those taken by a majority of between 500 and 600 people voting at an open and legal business meeting.

The ideology that justifies scholarship as the finest manifestation of culture and of the disinterested quest for truth is of course not contemptible in itself. It can be defended as well as attacked. What I wish to note here is simply how comfortable this ideology is for the professors who have risen to the height of their careers and who, therefore, occupy ideal positions for inculcating ideology in younger aspirants to these same heights; and how comfortable it is to maintain the reputations of their universities; and so confirm their own wealth and power. Decades ago, in *The Higher Learning in America*, Veblen wrote that faculty members

are, by authority, expected to expend time and means in such polite observances, spectacles and quasi-learned exhibitions as are presumed to enhance the prestige of the university. They are so induced to divert their time and energy to spreading abroad the university's good repute by creditable exhibitions of a quasi-scholarly character, which have no substantial bearing on a university man's legitimate interests. . . .[3]

One needn't take so cynical a view. "Exhibitions of a quasi-scholarly character" do no doubt exist, but the genuine article exercises power enough. There is a ready equation of scholarship, its elite exponents, and the vested authority of the MLA. It is not surprising, therefore, that many conveners in New York, in December, 1968, felt vaguely that a scuffle at the MLA somehow constituted an assault on Truth—not by the police, but by those who were putting the posters up.

One of the major projects of the Modern Language Association is a large collaborative effort to provide sound texts of works by classical American writers. The Center for Editions of American Authors is managed by the MLA and funded by the National Endowment for the Humanities. Its work has been criticized (in the *New York Review*) by Lewis Mumford and Edmund Wilson, for being pedantic, unreadable, anti-literary, a boondoggle, etc. The MLA got up a booklet to refute Wilson (and more than incidentally to

3. T. Veblen, *The Higher Learning in America* (New York: B. W. Huebsch, 1918), p. 166.

persuade the National Endowment for the Humanities to donate $300,000 to the project). The tactic chosen by MLA participants in the counterattack was well signaled in a prologue by Gordon N. Ray (head of the Guggenheim Foundation, also a contributor to CEAA) —the MLA was pulling no punches:

The recent attack in *The New York Review of Books* on the Center for Editions of American Authors of the Modern Language Association of America raises complex questions of taste and emphasis. It must be obvious at the same time, however, that this attack derives in part from the alarm of amateurs at seeing rigorous professional standards applied to a subject in which they have a vested interest. Here, at least, the issue is not in doubt. As the American learned world has come to full maturity since the second World War, a similar animus has shown itself and been discredited in field after field from botany to folklore. In the long run professional standards always prevail.[4]

It is mildly amusing that Mr. Ray should be the one to cry vested interest. But what I mainly want to mark is the conclusiveness that is supposed to attach to the word "professional." If you can appropriate that word for your side, you have quite flatly won the argument, so Mr. Ray implies.

He is not alone, of course. The whole culture says with one voice that professionalism is good, and the literary academic man is no dissenter. The Duke-North Carolina petitioners recognized the clout that inheres in the word, so that when they came to their point (overturning the legitimate action of the Business Meeting, the attentive reader will recall), they said it this way: "We urge the Executive Council to affirm the professional character of the Association." That is to say, a professional group will not meddle in those matters that properly belong to other professionals—in this case, the military draft, the war, repression of writers, and threats to dissent on university campuses. This was a note often sounded in criticism of the 1968 meetings. To John Fisher:

I resent the fact that the MLA staff is doing nothing to prevent the Association from becoming a political rather than a professional organiza-

4. G. N. Ray, *Professional Standards and American Editions: A Response to Edmund Wilson* (New York: MLA, 1969).

tion. I resent the fact that there is now no national meeting at which I can talk about eighteenth-century Spanish literature without the fear that someone is going to ask me in what way it can be made "relevant" to Vietnam.

To Louis Kampf:

I think that you have killed the MLA unless something can be done to negate your power, illegally gained, or at least unprofessionally gained, which last, among the ladies and gentlemen of Academe, is about the same.

Clearly, professionalism ranks high in the value structure of at least some MLA members.

What are the professional standards that must be so jealously kept? It is hard to say, hard to find the theoretical essence of the profession, though in Chapters Eight and Nine I undertake an answer to this question. For now, it is enough to note that people in the profession really have no work in common, except teaching— and clearly, for the MLA correspondents, "professional" does *not* mean "having to do with the teaching of languages and literature." People do literary criticism, literary history, phonology, semantics, biography, bibliography, editing, poetics, cultural criticism, curricular planning, etc.; they also teach. There is no common core of knowledge, no "discipline," no theoretical framework, no central pragmatic problem to be solved. As in most academic fields, the profession of MLA members is simply whatever activities have grown up round certain academic subjects and have somehow become respectable. There are very few techniques that must be specially mastered and very few intellectual abilities that differ from the completely general ability to frame hypotheses and weigh evidence—that is, to be an intelligent human being. So "professional standards" means simply the standards of those who have achieved prominence in the profession.

The way to find the intellectual center of the profession is to go to an MLA meeting, attend sessions, try to get a job, read the professional journals, look at the résumés people in the profession prepare when they must advertise themselves—in other words, find out how people get on in the profession. I won't dwell on this matter, since I believe that the truth about the profession is much the same as the truth about most of the academic professions: when people mainly of good will and intelligence come together in a setting charged with power, money, and advancement, their "professionalism" defines itself in illiberal ways. The scholarship is narrow. Fields are limited in ever more exclusive, and so *safe,* ways: one is defined by the straitest jacket that can be wrapped round his humanity—not a critic, but a seventeenth-century prose man, or a Johnsonian, just as in other academic fields one becomes known as a county politics man or a specialist in fungi. The publication that will earn these epithets is *de rigeur*—or at least talk of such publication is. When I went round at the meetings a while back, looking for my first job, several interviewing teams from big-university English departments strengthened their profiles considerably by asking candidates, not what they were writing dissertations about, but what they were planning for their second books. Though performance doesn't usually live up to advance publicity, the lapses into print are frequent enough to inspire some uneasiness. Each annual MLA bibliography now includes about 30,000 items.

Since the Association has about 30,000 members, the figure would be reasonable enough if we were to share equally in the task of reading these books and articles; but, unfortunately, each professional is expected to read all the work in his field (one of the good reasons for ever-shrinking fields). Recall (Chapter One) my discovering that there were 75 books published in the modern field in one year. If no one except me "kept up" that year what did the field amount to? Not, certainly, a group of intellectuals who were maintaining a discourse about 60 years of literary culture. Rather, the field was a geometrically expanding archive, to be consulted by later aspirants to rank and influence so that they might prepare their own contributions to the glut of print.

The profession exists so that there may be a means of accreditation and advancement for people in the profession, not out of any inner necessity and certainly not out of cultural need or the need of individual teachers. Most individual teachers, I think, are what

William Arrowsmith called "conscript scholars"—people by and large of admirable sensibility who went into the field because they liked literature and wanted to teach young people, and who found that the way to convert these commendable tastes into an adequate living and the respect of others was to write what the profession seemed to want—but what it rarely read.

Bear in mind that most young people have their first direct experience of the MLA—first join it and first attend a meeting—and of the MLA's professional standards at the moment they enter the labor market for the first time, as full-time workers, cut loose from parental or governmental or university support. Messages concerning exchange values communicated at just this moment, and by just those men (rarely women) who have so visibly achieved comfort and power, are bound to get through, whether they bring pleasure or dismay. I should say that though the "slave market" (as recruitment at MLA meetings is called) is a frenzied and, lately, a cruel spectacle, I have never resented its existence. On the contrary, the function of low-cost employment agent seems to me one of the more honest, direct, and useful functions that the MLA performs, or did perform when openings still existed. But I deplore the values that are applied in the market, not through any devilment of the MLA, but because of the "profession," which after all is the metaphysical force that makes the MLA what it is.

Who stands to gain from this? Lots of people, I think; but for the moment let me dwell on just one group, professors themselves. Though the rites of passage into professional maturity may be painful, the blessings of professionalism are many, for those who make it through. For the successful ones, there are comfortable teaching loads, time off for special projects, sabbaticals, decent wages, respect, and independence from external control.

I once heard a good teacher from Carleton College, Wayne Carver, say at a conference, "We always describe ourselves as adventurers on the frontier of knowledge; but I think we're schoolteachers." That might not be a bad professional definition; at least it would give the emperor some clothes. But it's not likely to win wide acceptance, as long as professionalism affords us the one means of combining pleasure and virtue. And that is also why there will be many to cry "foul" at the first hint of unprofessional conduct in the lobby.

Political action is misconduct by definition, in the professional arena, as Sidney Hook and many others have said. Perhaps because Hook has become the Lone Ranger of the otherwise defenseless academic establishment, he was asked to address the general session of the 1968 MLA meetings, which he did with vigor. I have already mentioned his talk, "The Barbarism of Virtue," which appeared in the May, 1969 *PMLA*. In it Hook disputes a "novel-sounding set of doctrines about the nature of the university," chiefly that the university and the professional guild must engage moral and social issues in times of crisis. Lampooning the unctuousness of this dictum, he quotes, among others, me quoting Matthew Arnold quoting Bishop Wilson, all of us saying together (more or less) that culture not only seeks truth and beauty, but seeks to make "reason and the will of God prevail." This is "high-sounding nonsense," Hook says, for an attempt to make the university serve these sectarian ends will simply result in purging members of rival sects. Hook is being a little obtuse here, for he ought to have sensed that "reason and the will of God" was Arnold's quaint way (and mine; I won't speak for the Bishop) of saying "truth and goodness," and more important, that Arnold's emphasis was on neither of these terms, but on *"prevail."* Never mind. The point is simply that culture is a blend of theory and practice.

I think that the university is, too, and should be, though I am not ecstatic about its practice at the moment. But Hook means to deny this:

The primary goal of the university—or "mission" if one prefers a grander word—and of the scholar and the professional association of scholars is not the quest for virtue or power but the quest for significant truths, their transmission and critical evaluation by teaching and/or publication, and the promotion of programs of study, research, and teaching to further the goal.

This means no politics and no social action, though Hook would not exempt the scholar, in his role as *citizen,* from exercising social concern. And citizens, not scholars, must determine the uses of scholarship and the allocation of resources to one or another intellectual pursuit. For a scholar to take a stand *as a scholar* is for his mind to be conscripted, and the same holds true *mutatis mutandis* for a professional organization like the MLA.

This is essentially the view that prevailed inside the MLA, at least until 1968. Then there were rumblings in the MLA about social relevance, and John Fisher invited three speakers, including myself, to debate the issue. I said (and wrote—see *PMLA*, September, 1968), with a good deal less emphasis than I would now, that there was no point in discussing whether the MLA should exercise political rights, for it was in politics already, as is every organization, whether or not it takes a public stand. Hook sets aside this claim with a *reductio ad absurdum:*

To argue in this connection that the refusal of a university or professional association to take a position on a political issue is, in virtue of that very refusal, taking a political position is completely without merit, for it in effect says that the distinction between the scholar and citizen is a political distinction. Under certain circumstances the refusal that may have otherwise been avoided, might be characterized as a political action. But the responsibility of the citizen is not the responsibility of the scholar. Were the university or professional association to refuse to take a stand on a religious dogma or commitment on the ground that such avowals are irrelevant to the life of scholarship, would any person seriously contend that therewith the university or professional association was making a religious decision, and conclude that therefore religious neutrality was impossible? The logic of this argument would suggest that the university or professional association by refusing to take a position on everything under the sun actually takes a position on everything under the sun—which is absurd.

I quote because this did represent the MLA position rather well, and because it differs so sharply from any view of politics that I would find illuminating.

The analogy between politics and religion shows that for Hook, politics is a matter (a) of explicit political action, like voting, or (b) of having a "position" and speaking one's mind. I take politics to be any corporate action that seeks to affect the shape of society, whether

or not it is done within the framework provided for electing
candidates to public office, passing legislation, and the like. Politics is
the attempt to exercise power and serve interests. Groups and
individuals acting politically need not proclaim their "positions" or
even know them.

An example. One of the issues raised at the 1968 meeting of the
MLA was where to hold the 1969 meeting, which had been
scheduled for Chicago. Many members, however, thought that
Mayor Daley and the Chicago police had, by shedding so much
youthful blood at the Democratic National Convention, forfeited the
privilege of entertaining 10,000 professors of language and literature.
There was a ballot sent round to the members on this matter, with a
great deal of heated debate before, during, and after the December
meeting. In this debate the main issue was the appropriateness of the
MLA making a symbolic political gesture and thereby sacrificing its
political neutrality. But worried letters from the Chicago Convention
Bureau and Hilton Hotels Corporation made it clear that from their
point of view symbolic commitment is not the sole power the MLA
can exercise. They pointed, rather, to such very different effects as
the estimated $500,000 the hotels would lose if the MLA backed out
of its agreement and the temporary laying off of 4000 employees.
Though I am not sure what the MLA should have done in these
complex circumstances (what it did was move the 1969 meeting to
Denver), I think that it is clear enough what kind of political impact
either decision would have had, especially if multiplied a few hundred
times through like action by other organizations. Once the issue had
been raised, the MLA was in a position where it could not help
acting politically.

Such decisions are not made every day. But every day the MLA,
like all associations with a staff and budget, does allocate part of the
gross national product. In order to do so, it presumably makes social
decisions. It committed significant resources, many of them given by
the Rockefeller Foundation, to a Foreign Language Program which
had the clearly social result of almost doubling the percentage of
students studying foreign languages in high school. It lobbied
successfully for the establishment of a National Endowment for the

Humanities, and now that the NEH exists, the MLA petitions *it* for funds for the Center for Editions of American Authors; it uses its own funds to defend the CEAA against critics like Edmund Wilson and thus protect the source of income. The MLA helped steer large sums of money from the United States Office of Education into the improvement (that is, increased professionalism) of high school English teaching. It has helped fund work on computerized bibliographies, research information clearing houses, and other technological devices for information storage and retrieval, those regular companions of professionalism. And, of course, it has run its own house the way it has, thereby conditioning many thousands of young members for their roles as scholars.

Has the MLA pursued a single political course at all consistently? Mostly, it has pursued the politics of neutrality and guild interest, which means, basically, maintaining the status quo. There are glimmerings, however, of explicit political direction, over and above the easy alliances with USOE, NEH, Rockefeller, and the rest. The Executive Secretary's report in 1965 contains an interesting analogy: "I see no more likelihood of the MLA's taking this course [returning to the quietism of pre-1952 days] than of the United States going isolationist—and I fancy that the reasons are much the same. Neither the USA nor the MLA likes to contemplate the sort of world it would have to live in if it pulled back." Perhaps this remark gives some hint of what is meant when, often enough, an MLA resolution or report speaks ritualistically of the "national interest."

To follow the suggestion where it leads, one might go back to the early fifties, and the MLA's emergence into social activism (though not, of course, politics). In 1953, one finds Professor Bayard Quincy Morgan damning the shortsightedness of American educationists in striking German from the school curriculum after World War I and thus preventing us from understanding our enemy 25 years later. He made it clear that he regarded language study as no less essential in 1953—in fact, a matter of "the survival of the U.S.A. as a free and democratic nation." [5] The point is a little more explicit in another

5. B. Q. Morgan, "Unrecognized Disarmament," *PMLA*, vol. 68 (March, 1953), p. 40.

MLA address printed in the same issue of *PMLA*, this one by
Professor Hayward Keniston of Duke:

The world struggle in which we are involved is something more than a fight
for political power or economic hegemony. At bottom it is a conflict between
two different concepts of man and his society: the slowly won concept of
human freedom and responsibility on the one hand; on the other, the
ancient doctrine of statism and the relegation of the individual to an ant
role.
  Who are to be the leaders in this ideological war? Not the scientists; as
scientists they cannot be concerned with human values and ideals. Not the
social scientists, as long as they conceive their task to be the description of
social institutions and mechanisms, rather than the identification of
desirable individual and social goals. In the end, the only group that is
dedicated to the pursuit of ideas and ideals—the historian, the philosopher,
the priest, the man of letters, the artist, the scholar—in a word, the
humanist.[6]

Never did the war of ideas sound more attractive.

  Also in 1953, a blue ribbon committee of linguists, commissioned
by the American Council of Learned Societies, reported in *PMLA* on
the need for more language study. The United States had been
transformed, they said, from an insular to a world power. Then they
quoted an earlier ACLS report (by Mortimer Graves), which makes
the case quite plain:

The product of American industry spreads all over the world. Wherever
there is a paved road there is an American automobile; American oil is
produced wherever there is oil and used wherever oil is used. American
banks have branches and connections in every significant foreign city. . . .
No region is too remote to be the concern of American diplomacy. And all
too frequently American armed forces must ply their trade in lands and
among people whose very names would have been unknown to an earlier
generation.[7]

Prophetic words. Graves goes on to lament the failure of the

6. H. Keniston, "We Accept Our Responsibility for Professional Leadership," *PMLA*,
vol. 68 (March, 1953), p. 23.
7. M. Graves, "Language Study and American Education," *PMLA*, vol. 68 (September, 1953), p. 56.

scholarly world to prepare the United States for these responsibilities, and the committee comments, "the importance of language study in meeting this situation is clear."

Indeed it is. The MLA has understandably been at a disadvantage in competing with political scientists, biologists, chemists, and economists for a role in cold war diplomacy. But it is good to know that, at the time when American universities were wholeheartedly giving themselves to the war for men's minds and property, the MLA at least showed good intentions—rather, for instance, than directing its zeal against Senator Joseph McCarthy, whose name is absent from all of the *PMLA* pages given over to ideological war and the cause of freedom in the year 1953.

(His name might well have been mentioned by one of Louis Kampf's correspondents:

. . . Whenever any American can not exercise his right to travel and be secure in his person because of the threat of violence and disruption by any other group of "Americans" such as your "New University Conference" then I believe it necessary to request the Federal government's aid. Therefore, all the information from MLA on violence and the threat of violence—along with your statements and those of the President and the Executive Secretary of MLA—have been sent to the House Committee on Un-American Activities and the U.S. Justice Department.)

For the MLA and the ACLS there were occasional pats on the back from public officials—e.g., Congressman Brademas and Commissioner of Education Earl J. McGrath—including a burbling speech by Hubert Humphrey, in 1966, which asserted that with the establishment of the NEH, "the President and the Congress have gone officially on record as holding that the strengthening of the humanities *as such* is in the public interest" (italics HHH's). And there was non-negligible assistance to scholarship from various government agencies. So perhaps it is not surprising that when the MLA's first Vietnam resolution was passed in December, 1967, it declared the merit of the war itself to be "a matter of contention," but said there was no doubt that democratic institutions could survive only if education were kept up and expressed particular concern about "the insufficient funds for programs in the Humanities, in relation to the resources available for the war effort." Since this resolution clearly answers to the interests of scholars *as scholars,* Sidney Hook would presumably not find it offensive. Nor would the MLA establishment. But if lobbying in Washington is non-political, the exemption plainly does not apply to lobbying in the Americana Hotel.

In his now famous essay on "The Responsibility of Intellectuals," Noam Chomsky pointed out that:

Intellectuals are in a position to expose the lies of governments, to analyze actions according to their causes and motives and often hidden intentions. In the Western world, at least, they have the power that comes from political liberty, from access to information and freedom of expression. . . . The responsibilities of intellectuals, then, are much deeper than . . . the "responsibility of peoples," given the unique privileges that intellectuals enjoy.[8]

Of course literary intellectuals are not quite in the position Chomsky describes, and I would not have dwelt so long on the relatively feeble politics of the MLA were it not for the insistent claim that the MLA must not, and does not, play politics.

It seems to me that the special responsibility of literary intellectuals and scholars has to do with precisely the center of their vocation: literature itself. Academic humanists often speak of themselves, a little grandly, as the preservers and transmitters of literary culture, and I have no quarrel with that design. What should be questioned is the *means* of preservation and transmission.

It might be to the point here to mention that the literature we are to preserve includes works by Milton, Voltaire, Rousseau, Swift, Goethe, Byron, Blake, Shelley, Carlyle, Shaw, and others of that rebellious ilk. Beyond that, I think it is accurate to say that every good poem, play, or novel, properly read, is revolutionary, in that it strikes through well-grooved habits of seeing and understanding,

8. N. Chomsky, *American Power and the New Mandarins* (New York: Vintage, 1969), p. 324.

thus modifying some part of consciousness. Though one force of literature is to affirm the value of tradition and the continuity of culture, another, equally powerful, is to criticize that which is customary and so attack complacency. That second side of literary culture is extremely valuable in the way Chomsky has in mind, since it ensures a difficult time for barbarism posing as humanity, for debasement of values, for vapid or devious rhetoric, for hypocrisy in all forms.

How have we preserved and transmitted it? A distinction is necessary. The critical force of literary culture must have played some role in the personal-political lives of literature professors this past decade. I admire the many teachers of literature who, like many poets, spoke out early against our government's conduct in Vietnam, and I would like to think that their humanistic training and practice helped them see and oppose injustice. But in our institutional efforts to preserve and transmit culture, I see only a denial of the critical spirit. Our computerized bibliographies, our fragmented "fields," our hundreds of literary journals and 30,000 books and articles, our systems of information storage and retrieval, our survey courses and historical pigeonholes, our scramble for light loads and graduate students, our 67 sections and 67 seminars, our emphasis on technique and procedure, our hierarchy of scholarly achievement, our jealous pursuit of social neutrality and political vacuity—in all this I see a retreat from criticism and a movement into more comfortable ways of life.

John McDermott has argued persuasively that technology, rather than being the neutral and willing servant we like to think it, is fundamentally "systems of rationalized control over large groups of men, events, and machines by small groups of technically skilled men operating through organizational hierarchy." [9] If this is true, how might we curtail its capacity to limit our freedom—not to mention to destroy the biosphere and the like? A hopeful answer is that culture would serve its critical function and do something to

9. J. McDermott, "Technology: The Opiate of the Intellectuals," *New York Review of Books* (July 31, 1969).

retrieve civilization from the hole that capitalist technology has dug. This is why it is no small matter to find that the largest organization devoted to the furtherance of literary culture has acted as if its aim were to imitate technology, rather than control it. Of course criticism has *not* succumbed. Nor has the careerist frenzy, which we seem determined to create, managed to overcome the lively humanity of most MLA members. These are cheering signs. But I would be more cheered if there were another vehicle for the aspirations of literary culture than that leviathan, the MLA, which, as John Fisher says, is pretty much what its members want it to be.

The MLA member who turned Louis Kampf in to the Justice Department and HUAC offered this parting shot: "I'm afraid my stomach is not strong enough to contain you and your cohorts." Kampf himself, in Theodore Roszak's *The Dissenting Academy*, wrote that "The MLA's power lies in its strong stomach, in its capacity to digest almost everything. . . ." [10] Well, the MLA did digest Louis Kampf and the rest of us cohorts, without more than a mild stomach-ache, and with few important changes in the professorial body politic. Institutions like the MLA are durable and likely to go on advancing the professional image of members with only temporary interruption by war, famine, and the taping-up of posters in hotel lobbies.

10. *The Dissenting Academy* (New York: Pantheon, 1967), p. 51.

CHAPTER THREE

Advanced Placement
on the Ladder
of Success

One way to get at a society's ethos is to see how it selects, at various stages of life, its favored people. I mean those people whom it perceives as having unusual talent or merit, by reason of which they are unusually valuable to the society and deserve more than the common share of its rewards. In America, the years from sixteen to eighteen are critical, because people that age are scrambling for position in the important and intricate hierarchy of colleges and universities. Of course well before this point in an American student's life, he (not she) may have been marked for success and a share of power by being born into a wealthy family and sent to one of the traditional private schools. But America can use more than this hereditary elite, and universities are its main instrument for selecting other elites. Of students in these age groups, close to 40 percent will go to some kind of college. Only 10 percent or so will go to colleges that are regarded as selective and whose names on a curriculum vitae are a special badge of merit. And on the order of 2 percent will be recognized at those elite institutions as somehow *ahead* of the rest.

That recognition comes through a variety of means—scholarships, prizes, honors, etc. One that is both important and easy to examine is the Advanced Placement Program. Like the College Board exams that well over a million students take in competing for entrance to elite colleges, the Advanced Placement exams are sponsored by the College Entrance Examination Board (CEEB) founded by the prestigious eastern colleges in 1900, which now represents almost all colleges and universities that admit students competitively. The Advanced Placement and the College Board exams are administered by Educational Testing Service (ETS), "an independent, nonprofit agency" which "provides all technical and operational services for the examinations." [1] Actually, ETS does much more than this language implies, and, in particular, it plans, writes, pre-tests, and amends the examinations. Anyone who has worked, as I have, on an ETS exam will agree that ETS has far more influence on the test than has the CEEB. The CEEB is a rather formless organization with a staff of modest size; the ETS is the nation's (and doubtless the world's) largest tester of human beings, and a big outfit even by corporate standards: its gross annual income is over $50 million.

The ETS has come under a lot of criticism in the last few years—for racial bias, for ethnocentrism, for secrecy, for elitism, for sheer bulk. In my own view, this criticism is understandable but misplaced. The purpose of this chapter, however, is not to join the battle around ETS and its operations, but to look in some detail at the one of those operations that bears most directly on literary education in America.

For Advanced Placement is more than a test. Any student can, to be sure, pay the fee and take the test; but most who do so have spent from one to three years in a special high school or prep school course, so that in their senior year they have done "college-level studies" in their Advanced Placement fields. Needless to add, when the schools design their Advanced Placement courses, they pay close attention to the examination, which is the payoff for students, as well as to the model syllabi that CEEB prepares. In the "Acorn Book," as it is informally called, where these syllabi and example tests are printed,

---

1. *A Guide to the Advanced Placement Program, 1969–70* (New York: College Entrance Examination Board, 1969), p. 11.

CEEB says that the "course descriptions are . . . not designed to tell schools what they must teach, but rather to explain what form of advanced preparation is most likely to lead to a student's advanced placement in college." [2] Nevertheless, it is easy to imagine the influence that ETS and CEEB have on schools trying to win for their best students the honor that goes with a high score on the Advanced Placement exam, not to mention the actual skipping of elementary courses that follows a good score in most colleges.

The Advanced Placement Program has on its side all the pieties that go with a competitive academic system and with a meritocracy based on individualistic ideas:

The basic tenet of advanced placement is that all students do not have similar abilities and interests that develop at the same rate in all subjects. As some students require a slower pace if they are to learn effectively, so the stronger students should be permitted to proceed at appropriately greater speed and depth. (Acorn Book, pp. 3–4)

Obviously, it is hard to object to the fostering of excellence. And individual treatment for students may be welcome, against a background of mass education. In short, the values of rigor, flexibility, and individualism underlie Advanced Placement.

Along with these explicit goals, I think, come hidden assumptions that are more dubious, even in terms of liberal academic doctrine. Most obviously, Advanced Placement endorses the idea of stratification itself. The very term "advanced placement" implies a scaled sequence of achievements along which a student may make faster or slower progress. The literature of the program is full of buried metaphors—placement, credit, level, grades—that preserve this root idea of our educational system. In short, for all the emphasis on intellectual accomplishment as its own reward, the actual mechanisms and language of Advanced Placement bespeak a more mundane system of rewards—in fact, a ladder of success leading to wealth and power, on which Americans climb to very different levels.

2. *1970–72 Advanced Placement Course Descriptions* (New York: College Entrance Examination Board, 1970), p. 2. (The cover of the book bears the insignia of an acorn and oak leaf.)

And indeed, studies of kids who have had Advanced Placement work show that they continue to advance smartly in the accepted ways: they perform well (mostly A's and B's) in the advanced courses they place into at college; they tend to major in the subject of their Advanced Placement work or in a closely allied subject; they maintain high academic averages; they go on to graduate school in an overwhelming proportion; and, presumably, they reach the top of the ladder fastest, to take their place in time among the professional and intellectual elite of this country, an elite that will determine the intellectual and cultural pattern of the society a generation hence. It may be worth noting, too, that "nearly all of the students" interviewed in 1967 in a follow-up on Advanced Placement "were involved in some way with their culture—trying to improve and enrich it, or at least to understand it. Almost none of them were militantly rejecting it or withdrawing from it." [3]

To these chosen ones, the Advanced Placement Program opens doors and makes promises—not explicitly, but effectively nonetheless. Through the examinations, through the methods of grading them, through their use for placement in college, through their influence on teachers, through Advanced Placement literature and through conferences of school and college teachers, through Advanced Placement courses in the schools, through the very criteria used in selecting high school students in the first place, messages are communicated to the Advanced Placement clientele—messages about studenthood, about teacherhood, about knowledge and culture, above all, about what kind of performance society rewards. What particular messages is our Advanced Placement establishment in English communicating?

First, it is telling students how to behave—on the test and in life—if they want to get on well. Several injunctions are heard sharply and persistently.

A good student attends to details, is careful and exact. "Write a carefully planned essay," "give specific examples," "read the passage

---

3. Patricia Lund Casserly, "What College Students Say About Advanced Placement," *College Board Review* (Winter, 1968–69), No. 70, p. 18.

and all the questions carefully before you begin to write your answers," "be specific in your illustrations." If the student should fail to pick up this message; if, for instance, he should read the directions carelessly, he will indeed get into trouble. Witness the guidelines for graders of the essay portion of the 1969 AP test in English:[4]

> Behind this question lie several elements which should be kept uppermost in mind in scoring the responses:
>
> The student is asked to consider "why" the character has or has not been made to change
>
> The student is asked to deal with "important characters"
>
> The student is warned against merely describing the character or summarizing the plot
>
> The student is confronted with the question of appropriateness of choice in starting to frame his response around a particular author or work

The original question was brief:

> In some novels and plays the experiences of an important character change him; in others the experiences of an important character leave him almost unchanged.
>
> In an essay, apply this statement to a novel or play by one of the authors listed below *or* by an author of comparable literary excellence. Consider why the character has or has not been made to change. Do not merely describe the character or summarize the plot.

But this language is to circumscribe the student's answer fairly tightly. Is he expected to have any notions of his own about character and experience? Perhaps, but the injunction to "apply this statement to a novel or play" is not likely to bring them out. The examinee will focus, if he knows what's good for him, on technique, on the internal structure of the work, on the fictive world as a separate creation; the range of askable questions is small indeed. It rules out such matters as why literature gets written and read,

---

4. This is a mimeographed document called "Advanced Placement Examinations, May 1969; English Sample Answers," distributed to a conference at Brandeis University at which I gave a talk that was the starting point of this chapter. I should stress that these guidelines were not for publication and, doubtless, would have been more formally and sometimes more diplomatically phrased if they had been intended for a general audience.

whether it changes anything, whether it conveys beliefs, how it rises from and acts upon its culture, what it does to its readers. A test cannot do everything, to be sure. But this one invariably puts the technical and formalist questions, where it might ask at least some of the other sort.

History—the flow of life from which literature comes, and *to* which it gives direction and meaning—is relegated to the "background." As the Acorn Book says (p. 60), an Advanced Placement student

studies the work, itself: its use of literal and figurative language; its characters, action, and themes. From his observation of details he moves to a consideration of structure and meaning. He may use the historical context as background for his understanding of a work of literature.

The student who learns this emphasis is well on his way toward a slot in the profession. His high school courses also taught him how to use the work of others, "properly acknowledged," and thus, "how scholarly papers are written." And the examination gives him the opportunity to "demonstrate his mastery of the competencies described in the course of study." He has entered a reassuring world of fact, detail, questions that have answers, and skills that can be mastered.

Another hidden injunction: Be docile. The student can hear this one between all the lines I've been quoting. He is not to develop his own, possibly contrary, reading of a work, but simply to validate or invalidate someone else's categories. That he should object is improbable, as the guidelines say more than once: "In the unlikely event that he may criticize the question or challenge the worth of the passage, he may still receive a top score if he writes perceptively and knowledgeably about the question or passage." Unlikely indeed, given the instructions the student gets. And one may wonder about the handsome openness of the sentence I just quoted—elsewhere, the guidelines grant that some students may challenge the question, but go on to say, "when you encounter such belligerent responses, please take them to your table leader." This is ominous. In spite of the conscious hyperbole in "belligerent," the point remains that Advanced Placement graders are not to reward criticism of the test's assumptions. The very criteria for channeling students into the program suggest a fully socialized pupil: he should be ambitious, have his parents' approval, sport a good record, have the support of his former teachers, and successfully manage an interview with his prospective teacher.[5]

Another thing a student is supposed to be is objective. The Acorn Book says that his Advanced Placement English course will teach him how to read *and respond* to works of literature, but if the descriptive material and the examinations are any indication, the Advanced Placement Program actually teaches the students *not* to respond to literature, not with his feelings. His concern must be with "organization of the elements of the poem," with "particular uses of language" that express a contrast, with the function of minor characters, with the way structure, imagery, and sound contribute to the whole meaning of a poem—"Your feeling about the poem is important," he is implicitly told, "only as the outcome of careful reading." His role is that of the neutral instrument, recording and correlating the facts and drawing conclusions. If any need or interest *other* than the formalistic drove him to read the work, or indeed, if something within turns him *against* the work, he will quickly learn to suppress these unwelcome responses. They are not among the competencies that will move him a step up the ladder. To his reading of a poem he is supposed to bring the techniques he has mastered, and only those. He is, in other words, alienated in very nearly the Marxian sense. And, of course, the ideal student is of the middle class. Docility, care, tidiness, professional ambition, the wish for objectivity, these are all qualities valued particularly by the middle class and encouraged in its young.

If the student has every chance to absorb these messages, the teachers are no less favored, though naturally they are less impressionable. Their role is complementary to that of the student. They are to transmit skills and competencies, to preserve the value of orderliness, and to keep literature from abrading middle-class

5. *A Guide to the Advanced Placement Program 1969–70* (New York: College Entrance Examination Board), p. 18.

assumptions—even when the literature itself means to do so. It's true that, according to the Acorn Book, the teacher "functions in a sensitive and responsive manner, . . . helping the members of his class to assume much of the responsibility for their own learning." That is safe enough in an Advanced Placement classroom, for both parties know well enough within what boundaries learning is to be held and what kind of "responsibility" is in the student's best interest.

The Advanced Placement ethos domesticates student and teacher. It does the same for literature. Literature is, of course, part of culture and part of history. It comes out of specific times and social conditions, and it helps to create the future. Like all art, it tends toward the rebellious and iconoclastic. The poem disrupts the routine perceptions of everyday, and makes us see the world with new vision. Literature is disconcerting, it can even be subversive. But none of this will be apparent to the student or teacher socialized by the Advanced Placement regime, which takes its stamp from the formalism that came out of Richards and Brooks and Warren. Let me characterize an archetypal work of literature, as someone from an alien world might infer it to be, if he had only Advanced Placement publications to go on.

1. It would be regular, finely structured, above all—built around contrasts, parallels, balances; all its elements (choice of words, phrasing, sentence structure, figurative expressions, tone, imagery, etc.) orchestrated to express a theme.

   (Yet we all know and value open forms, Shandean, dadaist, high romantic, which seek to *admit* discontinuity and absurdity, the irrational and the incomprehensible.)

2. The ideal work is an artifact of language. Its units are verbal ones, its lines of structure are relationships of words or blocks of words, or at most, static feelings that relate to one another.

3. In the archetypal work, self is abstracted into *character*, a set of attributes. Thus, the student is asked to say (writing about Pope's *Moral Essays*, Epistle II, "of the Characters of Women") how Chloe's character is established (not felt), whether the character

of an important figure in a novel or play has been made to change, what the functions of minor characters are (e.g., as foils to main characters, instruments in the plot, etc.), how the setting reflects the state of mind of a character. A character is a counter in the game of structure. This means that the student is trained to translate person into structure, and that is natural, since, as we have seen, his preferred strategy for reading is to depersonalize, to deny his *own* selfhood.

(In this frame of reference, what will happen to the *felt* idea of the hero—as against the hero-as-chesspiece? How can a student trained to read this way feel Raskalnikov or Elizabeth Bennett or Meursault or Pip as an alternate self, in whom he vests his whole sense of identity for a fictional while?)

4. In the ideal work, feeling is transformed into *attitude,* much as person becomes character. Of a Mark Twain passage: "What attitude (or set of feelings) toward the speaker is developed in this passage?" Of Edwin Muir's poem about Ulysses: "What is the poet's attitude toward the situation he describes . . . ?" "Decide on the attitude of the wife to the husband." "Consider the poet's attitude (emotional response) toward the central concerns of the poem." "Analyze the speaker's attitudes toward God." An attitude is static, balanced, a fixed relationship with something. It is easily held in check and calls neither for action nor for change.

(One can trace this diminution of feeling back to I. A. Richards and his *Principles of Literary Criticism*, where he sees poetry as coping with emotions but bringing them into equilibrium. In the vocabulary of New Criticism, ambiguity, tension, and irony all tend to work in the same direction—toward the neutralization of feeling by freezing it into an artifact of eternity. More about this in Chapter 4.)

5. Yet if the work is finally passionless and abstract, its reference is nonetheless to the individual psyche, not to society. The student focuses on a character, on the poet's attitude, on the individual's struggle toward understanding—but rarely, if ever, on the social forces that are revealed in every dramatic scene and almost every stretch of narration in fiction. Power, class, culture, social order

and disorder—these staples of all literature are quite excluded from consideration in the analytic tasks set for Advanced Placement candidates.

(Hence, it is natural that the question on Chloe's character completely ignores that personality's obvious derivation from and dependence upon a decadent and brittle society. "Virtue she finds too painful an endeavor, / content to dwell in decencies forever." Decency is what society perceives, externally, as virtue, rather than virtue itself. Chloe is prudent, does what she ought, is reasonable, attends to decoration, to minor contractual ties with other people—e.g., favors and debts. The student who wrote the best of the sample essays went considerably beyond the question—he perceived the difference between the way most people see Chloe and the way she really is, and was able to speak of "social capital." But naturally enough, he could not see her as the product of a corrupt social order or begin to say *why* she was able to make social capital in her ways.)

6. The work of literature that emerges has almost no intellectual content: the same process of distillation and attenuation that turns people into characters and feelings into attitudes turns ideas into *themes*. A theme is an idea, with the verb and the direct object taken away: age, time, innocence, human fallibility, and the like. The Advanced Placement work of literature contains themes, and it may even contain issues, but there is no suggestion that it may actually contain an idea or press a claim. It is intellectually bloodless.

[In one of the sample exams there are two paragraphs by Santayana forecasting the violent end of society, as "brute humanity" (the people who control industrial power) threatens to overthrow "polite humanity" (the people who make high culture). Almost any bright and socially minded student today could see that this is a questionable opposition: that polite humanity may be just the other face of brute humanity, that culture may *aid* in bringing about doomsday, and that Santayana's rhetoric covers up the superficiality of his thought. The student is asked to write about Santayana's *rhetoric,* to be sure, but only as "devices" by means of which he makes his points. The ideas themselves are apparently unchallengeable givens, or worse, empty shells to be painted with rhetoric, neither better nor worse than their negations.]

7. The composite work of literature is tame. It will not cause any trouble for the people who run schools or colleges, for the military-industrial complex, for anyone who holds power. It can only perpetuate the misery of those who don't. It is, therefore, an excellent thing for the Advanced Placement student to assimilate and internalize.

[One sample question comes dangerously close to trouble. It speaks of characters who violate "the laws, the conventions, the rules of conduct of a society" (Acorn Book, p. 72). But the student is immediately given an exhaustive list of purposes the author may be furthering by such portrayal; those purposes are: (1) to arouse our sympathy for the character; (2) to divide our interest sharply between sympathy for the character and desire to support the principles of the society; (3) to arouse our satiric mirth at the character; and (4) to laugh with the character at the conventions that are being violated. Were one speaking of literature in another context, a fifth purpose might occur: to arouse revolutionary consciousness. Since the writers endorsed in this same pamphlet, for Advanced Placement use, include Blake, Byron, Shaw, Lawrence, and Orwell, it would have been appropriate, though perhaps dangerous, to mention this possibility.

Again, two questions mention comedy, and one even suggests that comedy is social. But that same one also says that comedy shows us man's *humanity,* implying that its social force must be wholesome. So it is, I believe; but the rubric ignores the nearly universal plot of comedy, namely the welcome overthrow of the archaic and repressive values embodied in an older and tyrannical generation, by a youthful generation that stands for intuitive decency, freedom, and love. Will the student ever notice, on his own; the subversive side of comedy? of laughter?]

8. And of course, having eliminated *overt* social and ideological content, the ideal literary work of the Advanced Placement test smuggles back in all the usual class and cultural biases, disguised as eternal literary values. There is a select list of authors and works, mostly by white men of the middle or upper class. (This has changed somewhat since 1970, but only in response to the pressure of the newly aroused groups that constituted the "movement.") If a student goes outside this exemplary list, he is to stick with works of "recognized literary merit." Not only is his range of reflected cultural experiences extremely limited; any perceived connection between the Great Books he studies in class and the flow of literature all around him is simply taboo. He will not think of Keats and Hemingway as in any way related to pop lyrics, jokes, television commercials, films, popular fables and myths, and the thousand uses that the culture around him—both spontaneous and canned—makes of imagination and fiction. High culture is evidently quite apart from this vulgar surge and, hence, not to be used to make sense of the passing scene. They are simply two pheonomena of different orders. The student can hardly be blamed if he concludes, consciously or unconsciously, that culture is something in old books, something to which one is given access in the course of those same rites of passage that lead ultimately to comfort, security, and power. But meanwhile, his training *in* high culture, if the Advanced Placement materials are any indication, guarantees that he will learn nothing from it about whence that power derives or about how to use or redistribute power. The concepts he has learned to use are a mystification: they conceal the true relationships of things.

So the society implied by the apparatus of the Advanced Placement examination in English is a neat hierarchial one, in which the student carefully follows directions, the reader consults his table leader when he encounters an unruly examinee, the teacher steers his charge toward those ideas that will be safe for him, and the writer makes elegant formal structures that display technique and use "devices." In this society all contradictions are held in balance, and no emotion exceeds its proper limit. This is what Marcuse calls "total administration."

Out there in American society, familiar contradictions exist. Cities are fearful encampments. Highways and automobiles, made for easy commerce, have become a social menace. The richest society in history is, as I write, unable to find work for something like one member in ten of its labor force. Our use of land and air and water continues to threaten land, air, water, and people. The war to "protect" South Vietnam went on ruining it, at American expense, though no longer with American soldiers or American political opposition.

The voraciousness, the callousness, of America's assault on land and people follows upon a tradition of voraciousness and callousness that goes back to our first arrivals, when freedom-loving settlers made the perfectly casual assumption that they could use the land however they liked, expelling and murdering and cheating the Indians, and importing a slave population, from still another continent, to be brutalized and exploited.

In those times, we now clearly understand, verbal culture helped to rationalize and moralize our ancestors' depredations. To what extent does the culture of *this* time—so much more managed and bureaucratic—to what extent does our verbal culture serve to blind us to the nature and effect of our deeds? What I have been suggesting here is that at a crucial moment of his initiation into the cultural establishment, the Advanced Placement student in English sees his elevation on the ladder of success identified with a prophylactic view of literature—literature as pure structure, literature as the mummy case of feelings and ideas, literature removed from the stream of culture.

I used to wonder why it is that society pays English teachers so much money to do what by and large is fun: teaching fine literature. I now think that our function is extremely valuable: namely, to ensure the harmlessness of all culture; to make it serve and preserve the status quo. The university profession of English plays a part here. The examining committees of ETS are composed of college and school teachers; in my experience the college teachers tend to influence the school teachers more than the other way around. And this is also true at Advanced Placement conferences, not to mention the impact on schools of what the colleges will and will not allow for college credit and advanced placement.

The most recent critique I have read of ETS deplores its bias, its arrogance, its unrestrained "power of the gatekeeper," and recommends government regulation, beginning with an antitrust suit against the rather incestuous league of ETS and CEEB for restraint of trade.[6] Yet Steven Brill, the author, also quotes a Duke faculty member who cites the willing cooperation of professors with ETS because of the "prestige and money" in it. And Yale's Dean of Admissions told Brill, "I guess we're reasonably satisfied with things as they are. And besides, there's no pressure to improve it" (p. 79). Like the College Boards, the Advanced Placement program fits in nicely as a part of "things as they are." It brings together, without any real conflict, the university teacher's ideal of professional standards and the larger society's need to identify the elect among its youth.

It would be naive, anyhow, to expect the "gatekeeper" in a stratified society to let in the unwashed. Brill joins those who criticize ETS tests because "black and brown and poor people don't do well" on them, and he refers to an ETS study showing that

there is a direct, continuous correlation between family income and S.A.T. (Scholastic Aptitude Test) scores: high school seniors coming from wealthy families have higher median board scores than seniors from middle-income families, who in turn have higher median scores than those from low-income families. (p. 70)

But of course: that's what the tests are supposed to do. I sympathize, though not politically, with the annoyance of one ETS official who told Brill:

Our tests predict how a student will do—what his grades will be. If a student is culturally deprived, that means his grades won't be as high when he gets to college or law school. Our tests only reflect that.

6. Steven Brill, "The Secrecy Behind the College Boards," *New York*, vol. 7 (October 7, 1974), No. 40, p. 82.

And the President of ETS, William Turnbull, said "Criticizing us on that basis is like criticizing the Toledo Scale Company because some people are fat" (p. 70). Brill doesn't like the analogy, but I think it reasonable. You can't expect a testing company to make tests that inaccurately select those who will be successful in society. And to the extent that English teachers cooperate in making tests, it is predictable that they will enact the same values.

Similarly, IQ tests, which are charged with predicting success in school, *have* to find some way of predicting that black and brown and poor children will not generally succeed, since the structure of our society guarantees that result. Hence the supposedly astonishing revelations of Herrnstein, Jensen, and Shockley are in fact quite circular and empty. And most of the enraged opposition to these racist ideas is misdirected, like Brill's opposition to ETS. It is short-sighted to let criticism rest with demanding that IQ tests be color-blind or class-blind, and it is short-sighted to ask that College Boards and Advanced Placement programs place as many poor and minority people among the elect, since society will un-elect them soon enough. We should understand what we are up against: not tests that are arbitrary, but a class society that requires such tests. No attack on these rites of passage can be finally successful unless it overturns bourgeois culture, itself, and the rule of our dominant classes.

CHAPTER FOUR

Teaching and Studying
Literature at the
End of Ideology

The last three chapters diagnose what Herbert Gold once called "happy problems," problems of the overweight rather than of the starving. Our classrooms filled up during the fifties and sixties, as students left the sciences and sought insight through the arts. Teachers and even critics of literature acquired more prestige than they had had within living memory. With prestige came fast promotions, good salaries, low teaching loads, many graduate students, research factories, hundreds of new journals, computer-assisted bibliographies and concordances, fellowships, easy publication, textbooks, royalties, consultantships. Yet almost at the height of this prosperity the feeling spread that something had gone sour in the profession, some teachers came to suspect that literary culture might indeed be "irrelevant," and essays like the one reprinted in Chapter One of this book began to appear.

Unfamiliar prosperity and expansion tested the ideals of the profession. As new institutions like the Advanced Placement Program in literature were constructed, and as old ones like the MLA were radically altered, the idea of literature as a civilizing force could be held up against concrete social forms—of our own making, and with literature at the center—that seemed very defective as

reflections of civilization. Humanist, humanize thyself. To understand how wide a discrepancy existed between the workings of the
profession and its articulated values, it will be useful now to look
straight at those values. Specifically, I shall analyze the pre-eminent
set of ideas that American literary humanism adopted and developed during the post-war period. Such an analysis will not only
make clear the hopes we had for literature and for ourselves; it will
also describe the climate of ideas in many or most graduate
departments of literature. These ideas were the cultural myths that
graduate students subscribed to; they were the accompaniment to
still another rite of passage, that from student of literature to teacher
of literature.

To place these ideas in perspective, I shall discuss at some length
an early expression of doubt, an essay by Lionel Trilling called "The
Two Environments," written in 1965.[1] When it appeared, it drew a
good deal of interest, mainly, I imagine, because it challenged some
favorite premises of literary education, premises that Trilling himself
has worked from, along with many of the rest of us. When we have
had to justify the presence of literature in the curriculum, Trilling
says, we have slipped easily into the vocabulary of the "whole-man
theory" (p. 213). That is, we have held the study of literature "to
have a unique effectiveness in opening the mind and illuminating it,
in purging the mind of prejudices, and received ideas, in making the
mind free and active." The result is "an improvement in the
intelligence . . . as it touches the moral life" (p. 212). This argument
has proved remarkably durable since Matthew Arnold gave it its
best-remembered articulation, surviving innumerable challenges of
the Auschwitz-commandants-read-Goethe variety. It has convinced
not only teachers of literature, who after all need this kind of
reassurance, but students in large numbers who want to read and
live by modern literature, in particular. I think that Trilling is right
in saying that for them "an involvement with modern literature goes
with an insistent . . . concern with morality" (p. 220). This concern

1. In Lionel Trilling, *Beyond Culture: Essays on Literature and Learning* (New York: Viking
Press, 1968), pp. 209–33.

fixes on the sense of style, and on the cultural and moral values that inhere in style and are heightened in literature and by literary study. Literature really is criticism of life, and students and teachers of literature have been the conscience of the culture to an extent that might have satisfied even Arnold—whatever he might have thought of the concrete directives of that conscience.

But, as Trilling rightly observes, the very success of literature has changed the terms of Arnold's plea. To oppose the philistines then, or even in Sinclair Lewis's time, was in effect to oppose *the* culture. That is no longer so. Now, Trilling says, "the student is at liberty to choose between two cultural environments" (pp. 226–27). One, still, is philistine culture, and the other defines itself by opposition to the philistines. But as we and our students find this second environment more peopled and more comfortable, the opposition to philistines itself becomes one of two established parties. About the time Trilling wrote, these parties came into sharp intellectual and stylistic opposition to one another—as was revealed by the continuing fuss about long hair, drugs, and sex, by the vogue of books like Reich's *The Greening of America* and Roszak's *The Making of a Counter Culture*, and by the voyeurism of timelifenewsweek. Yet both parties have eaten from the same board throughout their quarrel. That last is my observation, of which more later. Trilling's is that the second environment has lost some of its critical nip, that it carries in it a "trivializing force," which dissipates real cultural debate into "transcendent gossip." For this reason, he says, "those few teachers . . . who do not think that preparing students for entrance into the second environment is enough to do for them in the way of education, may one day have to question whether in our culture the study of literature is any longer a suitable means for developing and refining the intelligence" (p. 232).

So much has happened since 1965. After our unpleasant awakening to the dissonance of external events, a rereading of Trilling's essay is a strange experience, punctuated with phantom exclamation points and asterisks not in the original.

But my subject in this chapter is what happened before 1965, not after, and I have spread out the content of Trilling's essay at such length because it seems to me an extraordinarily telling account of trouble within the academic literary culture. Telling, because Trilling's distress has its origin in the very success of our profession. Teachers of literature have had some part in creating a large, audible, sensitive, and highly moral adversary culture, which is what we meant to do, yet I imagine that even in 1965 Trilling was not alone in harboring doubts about this achievement. Needless to say, those who have looked at other indicators of professional health have been a good deal less equivocal than Trilling. And anyone can think of a dozen more recent examples of self-doubt or rage, directed at the management of academic literary culture: the MLA insurrection of 1968, Florence Howe's election to the second vice-presidency in 1970, the black studies movement, the attempt of the jobless to organize in or against the MLA, the Anglo-American Seminar on the Teaching of English,[2] the rebellion of graduate students in many universities, and so on. That the profession has been self-critical is not surprising, but that the critical mood set in at precisely the moment of amplitude and prestige bears comment.

In 1948, Stanley Edgar Hyman began his survey of contemporary criticism by judging it "quantitatively different" from—*better* than— any previous criticism. Looking ahead, he ventured that "the immediate future of criticism should be even greater, and a body of serious literary analysis turned out in English of a quality to distinguish our age." [3] The sense of vistas opening was a common experience. I started college in 1948, and I recall the excitement communicated there by teachers of literature who would have agreed with Hyman's prognosis for criticism. And to be in graduate school in the fifties, even in the dim Eisenhower years, was to feel a part of a fresh intellectual movement and a renewal of the vitality of literary study. We expected that the teaching of literature, too, would increase in quality and importance; Hyman saw "democratic

2. A critical discussion of English in the schools, held at Dartmouth in 1966 and reported informally in Herbert J. Muller, *The Uses of English* (New York: Holt, Rinehart & Winston, 1967).
3. Stanley Edgar Hyman, *The Armed Vision: A Study in the Methods of Modern Literary Criticism*, rev. ed. (New York: Random House, 1955), p. 5.

possibilities for modern criticism," which, by making its method widely available, would train more people as capable critics, "in most cases not professionally, but in their private reading and their lives. And the vested interests *that* possibility menaces are much bigger game than the priesthood of literary criticism" (pp. 11–12). There it is: We were confident then that we could challenge philistine culture and the hierarchical society by extending the influence of literature.

The question, then, is what happened to us—people who read and taught literature in universities—that in achieving pretty much what we set out to achieve we built a cultural situation that many of us find so distressing? My way toward an answer will run first through a reconsideration of some things that New Criticism meant, taking full advantage of hindsight. For the New Criticism was the central intellectual force in our subculture during those years. Then I will quickly examine some of the counterforces, looking for the cultural foundation of the arguments brought against New Criticism. Finally I will try to relate this phase of our literary history to some wider cultural concepts. I hope it will be clear along the way that when I say "we" and "us" I intend no condescension to those whom I think benighted but hope to convert. I am, rather, making an effort to understand some of my own intellectual history and to let these past two decades teach me something now that I failed to learn at the time.

At the outset of any retrospective on the New Criticism, it should be acknowledged that this school made its greatest impression on our day-to-day lives and work, not through the literary and cultural theory with which many of the chief figures occupied themselves, but through the style and method of close reading displayed in a relatively small number of essays, primarily by Cleanth Brooks, William Empson, R. P. Blackmur, and the I. A. Richards of *Practical Criticism*, and in the sacred textbook, *Understanding Poetry*. These essays taught us how to write papers as students, how to write articles later on, and what to say about a poem to *our* students in a 50-minute hour. Surely we absorbed the cultural values inherent in close reading—exactness, sensitivity to shades of feeling, the need to see pattern and order, the effort to shut out from consciousness one's own life-situation while reading the poem, and to pry the words loose from their social origins—surely we absorbed these values as we imitated the models before us. But when we thought about what we were doing, especially when that was attacked, we would draw upon the rationale and the theory supplied by the New Critics. A theory becomes influential when called into play in defense of practice. So the theoretical talk of the New Critics is a convenient place to look for the ideas that support—that license—the work of students and teachers of literature. I want now to arrange some of those ideas in a convenient row (more convenient than is quite justified by their original development), leading from the poem itself out to the whole social and metaphysical context.

Start with the familiar notion that the poem is a self-contained whole, autonomous. This premise is often disparaged now, as it was 20 years ago, for seeming to absolve poetry of moral responsibility, for sponsoring a decadent aesthetic of art for art's sake. But that is much too simple a charge: the pages of the New Criticism are bound together with moral fiber, almost strident in urging a social mission for literature. To see what is really at stake in claiming the autonomy of the poem, it is best to consider what the New Critics themselves meant that proposition to deny.

They were denying, first, that poetic language has reference to reality in the same way as prose, and that literature competes with science. The "heresy of paraphrase" is that you can take a message away from a poem, or mine the poem for its content, leaving form behind. Richards even allowed himself to say that "the greatest poets . . . refrain from assertion." [4] Second, the organic idea of poetry denies that the poem should be read as an avenue to the poet's intention or as a part of his autobiography. And third, the New Critics meant to deny the "affective fallacy" that the poem is its psychological effects on the reader.

4. Ivor A. Richards, *Principles of Literary Criticism* (New York: Harcourt, Brace & World, n.d.), p. 276.

The intent of this ontological position is not to divorce literature from social and personal reality but to make the relationship an indirect one—of which more later. The New Critics know that poems are related to life, but they want to let the poem create its own mimetic life before seeing how it fits the world outside. And they know that the poem is not an object. As Wimsatt scrupulously says, "The poem conceived as a thing in between the poet and the audience is of course an abstraction. The poem is an act." [5] But for criticism, Wimsatt goes on, and for critical reading, the poem "must be hypostatized," detached from its origins and effects and from the stream of history. In brief, this is a point about how to experience and criticize literature. Wimsatt and the others ask us to relax our pragmatic and empirical muscles while reading a poem, to let the poem have its own way, to accept its world in a passive mood. Poetry is different from other uses of words, notably the use of words in science, in the view of the New Critics, and requires a different state of consciousness.

It is a familiar observation that that state of consciousness excludes (willing suspension of disbelief) those modes of reality testing appropriate to scientific discourse. It particularly excludes looking for a one-to-one correspondence between propositions and parts of the external world. Less explicit but equally important is the separation of literary experience from action. In this the New Critics are with Auden: "Poetry makes nothing happen." More sharply, in Richards's account of poetic experience the function of the poem is precisely to block any overbearing impulse to action, by bringing the "appetencies" into balance. Eliot would put it otherwise, but he and all the rest would agree that the sphere of a poem's operation is the sensibility, not the will.

Furthermore, though poems, as Wimsatt says, unquestionably are acts, both in their making and in their uttering, the New Critics make almost nothing of this. Wimsatt expresses the standard position, that "both speaker and dramatic audience are assimilated

5. William K. Wimsatt, *The Verbal Icon: Studies in the Meaning of Poetry* (New York: Farrar, Straus & Giroux, 1958), p. xvii.

into the implicit structure of the poem's meaning," [6] so that action is only an artistic fiction rather than a dynamic in which the poem participates. By this account Yeats is not really, through "Easter 1916," taking sides in the rebellion, but putting forth an artistic hypothesis. Kenneth Burke, at some distance from the central group of New Critics, is the exception. He treats poems as "strategies" which, like all symbolic structures, produce "frames of acceptance." "Acceptance" here is not equated to passivity; rather, frames of acceptance "fix attitudes that prepare for combat"; they define a *we* and a *they*.[7] Burke allows some conflicts, at least, to be real, not fully containable by some arrangement of attitudes, and he sees poets and poems as participating in those conflicts. Given the wide currency of Burke's ideas, it is noteworthy that the New Critics never built on this particular idea. It accorded badly with their attempt to theorize a state of mind peculiar to literary experience.

The specialization of the mind is assumed by the aesthetics of New Criticism, too. Murray Krieger is right in holding that though the New Critics do not have an explicit theory of the unique aesthetic experience, they both need and imply one.[8] And Eliseo Vivas, much influenced by New Criticism, developed the appropriate theory. The aesthetic experience, in his familiar phrase, is a state of "intransitive, rapt attention," [9] in which we feel all meanings and values to be in the art object rather than in the world beyond the object. Emotion and perception, as well as the intellect, need a separate set of rules for the right apprehension of literature.

I have been stressing the fragmentation of self that is strongly implied by the New Critics. Yet *their* composite theorizing explicitly stresses reconstruction of the whole person. Their argument runs thus: In return for the discipline of intransitive attention, of blocking

6. *Ibid.*, p. xvi.
7. Kenneth Burke, *Attitudes Toward History*. I quote from an excerpt in Kenneth Burke, *Terms for Order: Studies in Evaluation*, ed. Stanley Edgar Hyman (Bloomington: Indiana University Press, 1964), p. 70.
8. Murray Krieger, *The New Apologists for Poetry* (Minneapolis: University of Minnesota Press, 1956), p. 129.
9. Eliseo Vivas, "Problems of Aesthetics," in *Creation and Discovery: Essays in Criticism and Aesthetics* (Chicago: Henry Regnery Co., 1955), p. 146.

interpretive instincts, setting action aside, and restraining all stock responses, the reader has a total and unified experience. For Brooks the main task of the poet is to "unify experience," and so "return to us the unity of the experience itself as man knows it in his own experience." [10] Though the almost ritualistic iteration of the word "experience" shows where Brooks's wishes would lead him, the passage hardly explains why one would read a poem. What is so defective about the original, unmediated experience that we must resort to poetry to recapture it? Ransom, interpreting Eliot, gives a clear answer: "In action . . . the situation as a whole engages us too completely; . . . it is when this situation exists for imagination, not for action, that we are freed from its domination and can attend to its texture." [11] This is a crux. As I have already suggested, most of the New Critics would have agreed that action impedes the deeper flow of understanding and the refinement of emotion, and that wholeness of experience, paradoxically, is most available to us when we abstract ourselves from action and let consciousness reign. Most comment on this special and intuitive knowledge of experience, held out as the main reward of poetry, has followed the New Critics' explicit distinction between poetry and science—poetry treats an "order of existence . . . which cannot be treated in scientific discourse." [12] But I think that the deeper message is in the continuation of Ransom's statement: poetry, he says, recovers the "denser and more refractory original world which we know loosely through our perceptions and memories." The "original world" can best be known by being out of it. The truest experience is abstract experience, well distanced by poetry.

Poetry lets us "realize the world" [13] for another reason as well. The world is infinitely complex, Brooks and several of the others insist. To see it clearly requires selection and ordering, both important activities of art, whatever theorist you read. But at this point one

10. Cleanth Brooks, *The Well Wrought Urn: Studies in the Structure of Poetry* (New York: Harcourt, Brace & World, n.d.), pp. 212–13.
11. John Crowe Ransom, *The New Criticism* (Norfolk, Conn.: New Directions, 1941), p. 156.
12. *Ibid.,* p. 281.
13. John Crowe Ransom, *The World's Body* (New York: Scribner's, 1938), p. x.

should ask why the selection and ordering that any of us performs just in the course of being awake, or that science offers, are inferior to the selection and ordering achieved by art. The answer is clear in the reasons the New Critics give for setting such extraordinary value as they do on irony, ambiguity, tension, and paradox, in critical practice: these devices are important for their "resolution of apparently antithetical attitudes," [14] which both daily life and science leave in dissonance. This idea has its origin, for the New Criticism, in Richards's *Principles of Literary Criticism*, where a "balanced poise" of the attitudes plays a central and almost therapeutic role. Richards supposes that our cultural sickness is an imbalance of attitudes and impulses and that poetry can set us right by helping us achieve a state of equilibrium. The more discordant elements drawn into this unity, the more effective the poetry—for this reason Richards praises tragedy as "perhaps the most general, all accepting, all ordering experience known." [15] And Brooks says that the good poems manage a "unification of attitudes into a hierarchy subordinated to a total and governing attitude. In a unified poem the poet has 'come to terms' with his experience." [16] Now, putting together these suggestions with Eliot's famous diagnosis of a "dissociation of sensibility" in the modern world, I see a sequence of this sort: The world is complex, discordant, dazzling. We want desperately to know it as unified and meaningful, but action out in the world fails to reveal or bring about a satisfying order. The order we need *is* available in literature; therefore literature

14. Brooks, *Well Wrought Urn*, p. 157.
15. Richards, *Principles of Literary Criticism*, p. 247. It is worthwhile speculating if this is not one of the reasons for the extraordinarily high value our culture sets on tragedy. Georg Lukacs points out that bourgeois theories of tragedy see this mode as arising from "the terrible side of life" (Schopenhauer), and so degrade specific historical tragedies into occasions for the "universal human tragedy" [*The Historical Novel*, trans. Hannah and Stanley Mitchell (Boston: Beacon Press, 1963), p. 122]. But I don't think that Lukacs is right in crediting this fondness for tragedy to belief in the "futility of life in general," though that phrase no doubt does justice to Schopenhauer. More recent bourgeois ideas of tragedy stress its integrative force, its ability to reconcile and bring about acceptance. The New Critics' theory of poetic structure may explain why—and why we have so many books with titles like *The Tragic Vision* and *The Tragic Sense of Life*.
16. Brooks, *Well Wrought Urn*, p. 207.

must be a better guide to truth than are experience and action.[17]

But the specific truth to be got from literature is less clear than the desire for it; and the particular values that poetry advances are nebulous. Not that we can remain puzzled to know what values the *critics* hold—these are plain enough, especially among those half-dozen New Critics who are Anglicans or Catholics. But all of them are surprisingly reluctant to ascribe their particular values to poetry. Obscurity sets in when they address the subject; as when Richards looks to poetry for those "most valuable" states of mind that "involve the widest and most comprehensive co-ordination of activities and the least curtailment, conflict, starvation and restriction," or when Wimsatt writes that "Poetry, by its concreteness and dramatic presentation of value situations, whether it inclines to a right answer or to a wrong answer . . . has the meaning and being which makes it poetry. This is the poetic value." [18] These formulations don't take us far. The reason for the difficulty may be seen in another comment of Wimsatt's: that the Arnoldian view of poetry as criticism of life is defective because "so much" of poetry "is in one way or another immoral" that no one ethic can accommodate all the great poems.[19] This is more helpful. The value of poetry transcends the values of individual poems and poets, and lies not in urging one or another moral view but in embracing ("coming to terms with") ethical complexities. A proper reading of poetry neutralizes and flattens out not only impulses toward action but perhaps even those toward moral judgment. Poetry, capital P, can prefer no one value system or course of action, but accepts and comprehends all values, all actions, and in fact everything that makes up reality.

Richard Foster, in a helpful book on the New Criticism, argues that most of these critics have a quasi-theological bent. They are the

17. In an essay called "Art for Art's Sake," E. M. Forster said quite openly what I take the New Critics to be saying more confusedly or obliquely: ". . . order in daily life and in history, order in the social and political category, is unattainable under our present psychology. Where is it attainable? . . . The work of art stands up by itself, and nothing else does. . . . It is the one orderly product which our muddling race has produced." [*Two Cheers for Democracy* (New York: Harcourt, Brace & World, 1951), pp. 91–92.] The parallels between Bloomsbury and the New Criticism are often close.
18. Richards, *Principles of Literary Criticism*, p. 59; Wimsatt, *Verbal Icon*, p. 98.
19. Wimsatt, *Verbal Icon*, p. 89.

proper heirs of Matthew Arnold in substituting poetry for religion as man's "ever surer stay." [20] It seems to me that in spite of their talk about the decline of culture and sensibility, the "ever surer stay" they offer us the assurance that we *can,* after all, "come to terms with experience"—by containing it, by striking balanced attitudes, as a successful poet does, and emphatically not by acting to change the society that gives rise to our experience.[21]

Not only is this a passive solution, it is, also, importantly, a personal one. The New Critics see poetry as serving the individual reader, and only very indirectly as amending the flawed society. In fact, many of the formulas they offer of desirable social goals are so abstract as to call into question the seriousness of their interest. When Richards says that our sickness is being cut off from the past and that myths and poetry will "remake our minds and with them our world," [22] when Tate says that the man of letters is "to attend to the health of society *not at large* but through literature—that is, he must be constantly aware of the condition of language in his age," [23] and that "the end of social man is communion through love"; when Eliot says in *After Strange Gods* that the function of literature is to combat liberalism;[24] when Ransom says that "the object of a proper society is to instruct its members how to transform instinctive experience into aesthetic experience" [25]—I find it easy to believe that

20. Richard J. Foster, *The New Romantics* (Bloomington: Indiana University Press, 1962), esp. Chap. 2. That the New Critics do so is undoubtedly one cause of the cultural situation Trilling describes in "The Two Environments." By the time Trilling wrote, a generation of college teachers trained to New Criticism had acted as missionaries for literature, not as the attainment of a gentleman, but as an alternative to the religious life.

21. It is interesting to note that Richards, probably the most influential founder of the movement, tied his work to a number of social causes: improving international communication, spreading literacy, creating basic English, improving university teaching, and so on. But the social aims yielded, among his followers, to the other side of Richards's intentions, the subjective and therapeutic.

22. Ivor A. Richards, *Coleridge on Imagination* (New York: Harcourt, Brace, 1935), p. 229.

23. This in defending his vote for Ezra Pound to receive the Bollingen Prize; *The Man of Letters in the Modern World: Selected Essays, 1928–1955* (New York: Meridian Books, 1955), p. 266. The quotation that follows is on p. 22 of the same book.

24. T. S. Eliot, *After Strange Gods* (London: Faber & Faber, 1934).

25. Ransom, *World's Body,* p. 42.

they are thinking, not about the whole of any society, real or imagined, but about the style of life available to a comfortable man of letters within society. If so, it doesn't really matter how the society is organized, short of totalitarianism, since the man of letters can cope. "If modern man wishes to save himself as a human being in an abstractionist society, say all the New Critics, let him turn to literature and the arts." [26] But for "modern man" we had better substitute "the literary intellectual," for to whom else is this solution readily available? Murray Krieger holds that the social mission of criticism, according to the New Critics, is "to affirm the uniqueness and indispensability of art's role in society." [27] This has to mean society *as it is;* for Krieger the issue is how we defend poetry within the status quo, and primarily *to* those who have any say about "art's role in society," the classes with power or influence.

Now, against any substantial analysis of society, all of this is a parlor game, and the social pieties of the New Critics themselves are the sort of horn-tooting that you might indulge in while asking the National Endowment for the Humanities for some money. Why are these generally sophisticated men so very inept when they discuss society? I think it is partly because everything in their ideology turns them away from politics. They see art as freeing man *from* politics by putting him above his circumstances, giving him inner control, affording a means of salvation, placing him beyond culture. [28]

It will be obvious that this is an angled shot of the New Criticism. I have deliberately tried to draw out those implications of the New Critics' work that will serve my present purpose, and my account has been critical. Now I want to reiterate the perspective from which the criticism is leveled. I can myself understand if not accept Foster's labeling the New Criticism the "chief movement for literary humanism of this century." I think that the New Critics were

26. Foster, *New Romantics*, p. 44.
27. Krieger, *New Apologists*, p. 5.
28. I have not mentioned R. P. Blackmur in this essay, partly because of the difficulty I have in understanding his later essays, but it is at least clear that those later essays urge the transcendental uses of literature I am stressing.

sensitive and well-intentioned men, whose practical influence on the academy was good. I do not hold them to blame for the recent crisis of confidence in academic literary culture, much less for the viciousness that is widespread in American society. To go looking for the villain among critics and English teachers is, in my view, completely to misconceive the task of cultural analysis. Plainly the New Criticism, like its opponents, was a relatively minor cultural force. It did not create the academic literary scene of the fifties and sixties, but merely presented itself as a timely instrument to serve purposes of our own and of the larger society. A few words about that.

Many aspects of the New Criticism answered to our needs, but the one aspect I wish to single out is its flight from politics. Trilling said of intellectuals today that "we all want politics not to exist." [29] This is particularly true in America, where the social pressures that drive people to conscious politics have rarely existed for long; for us "there has always seemed a way out." [30] Americans have generally been able to move on when a situation calling for politics arose—across the frontier, to a suburb, into technologically ensured privacy. What has increasingly governed American public life is what Philip Slater calls the

Toilet Assumption—the notion that unwanted matter, unwanted difficulties, unwanted complexities and obstacles will disappear if they are removed from our immediate field of vision. . . . Our approach to social problems is to decrease their visibility: out of sight, out of mind. This is the real foundation of racial segregation, especially in its most extreme case, the Indian "reservation." The result of our social efforts has been to remove the underlying problems of our society farther and farther from daily experience and daily consciousness, and hence to decrease, in the mass of the population, the knowledge, skill, resources, and motivation necessary to deal with them.[31]

29. Trilling, *Beyond Culture*, p. 164.
30. Irving Howe, *Politics and the Novel* (New York: Fawcett World Library, 1967), p. 164. Howe is explaining why political ideas have never shaped up so clearly here as in Europe and why the tradition of the political novel is correspondingly thinner.
31. Philip Slater, *The Pursuit of Loneliness: American Culture at the Breaking Point* (Boston: Beacon Press, 1970), p. 15.

In America we use technology and production to shut out social ills, and so to evade politics at whatever cost.

Academic humanists in the fifties had special reasons for wanting politics not to exist. McCarthy had made activism improvident for college teachers at the start of the decade, and, in any case, the cold war had reduced ideology to seeming inevitabilities of free world and iron curtain, while drastically narrowing the range of domestic political positions available and pretty much guaranteeing that support for Adlai Stevenson would seem the most daring political act within the bounds of realism. At the same time, technological advance and the rapid increase in production kept before us a vision of steady improvement, and made radical social change seem both remote and disturbing. What those of us who studied and taught literature particularly needed, therefore, was a rationale for our divorcing work from politics, for lying low in society.

Kenneth Burke wrote an analysis of such tranquil historical moments, back in 1937, that is worth quoting apropos the fifties:

The ideal conditions for thought arise when the world is deemed about as satisfactory as we can make it, and thinkers of all sorts collaborate in constructing a vast collective mythology whereby people can be at home in that world. Conflicts are bridged symbolically; one tries to mitigate conflict by the mediating devices of poetry and religion, rather than to accentuate the harshness.[32]

In such a period, ironic "frames of acceptance" are bound to be wanted. The New Criticism was such a frame, already built and ready for use by the end of the war.

Some homelier truths are also worth recalling. Academic salaries in this country touched bottom at the end of the forties, in terms of purchasing power. I well recall that as I came to graduate school in 1952, those leaving Harvard with Ph.D.'s counted $3,000 a good salary. Professors were poor; I thought of entering the profession as tantamount to taking vows of poverty. But economic conditions gradually improved for us through the decade, for demographic and

32. From Burke, *Attitudes Toward History*, quoted in Hyman, ed., *Terms for Order*, p. 77.

political reasons (universities, recall, became an instrument in the cold war—the battle for men's minds). A new, distinctly less ragged style of life became possible, and with it an almost-earned upper-middle-class self-image. As we were switching from beer to booze and buying second cars, few felt any hard economic interest in politics. The social change that was carrying us along was quite satisfactory. And with this frame of mind, the New Criticism accorded well.

So far I have virtually equated theory of literature in the postwar period with the New Criticism. In so doing I have of course greatly oversimplified the actual situation in universities, both by omitting the other schools and by slighting the polemical and contentious side of the New Criticism itself. I will not make up this deficiency. To do so would require roughly equal time for philologists, literary historians, Chicago critics, and so on.

Instead I will say just enough to suggest that in the terms I have outlined, the opponents of New Criticism offered no real alternative to it.

What kept the English department busy before New Criticism arrived was, of course, philology and literary history. Philology, whose territory was not deeply invaded, never really entered into battle with the New Critics, but literary history very much did. It could not help doing so, since the New Criticism challenged its right to control the curriculum and the budget. To be sure, the challenge came more in the form of physical presence than of doctrine, though Ransom did attack English faculties for being "mere historians," unable to recognize a good new poem when they saw one, much less deal with the texture of literature. In any case, the mere historians were embattled, and those of us who were in graduate school 15 to 25 years ago will remember their grumblings and disparagings. Douglas Bush handed down the official indictment in a 1949 MLA talk. According to his bill of charges, the New Critics ignore historical context; they therefore make damaging errors; they glorify technical method and assume that "literature exists for the diversion of a few sophisticates"; they are "aesthetes" who "create a moral vacuum." Poetry deals with morality and so should criticism.[33]

But in spite of the high feelings and the real antagonisms that split the profession for a while, the division was not deep. Bush would bring morality back into criticism—by siding with one or another ethic drawn from the past, as we know from his other writings and their championing of Christian humanism. Such free-swinging uses of the past do not bring criticism into any closer touch with the concrete moral situation of the present than the New Criticism. The distance, with Bush, is simply of time rather than of abstraction. As I have said, the New Critics did not lack for moral sentiments.

As for the dispute about method, the scholars and the critics had after all a common intent: to get at the ethos of a work or a poet, to mediate his wisdom (his coming to terms), with empathy for all systems of thought, in the dispassionate way of the intellectual. The scholar would do this by coming at the work from outside, the critic by exploring its interior. Either method will suffice to withdraw the work from *our* history and politics. So scholar and critic have long since realized their community of interest, in a setting where differences of method—specializations—are a positive professional asset rather than a contradiction. It reduces anxiety if one can succeed as a scholar *or* as a critic, and leave half the "field" to another guild of experts with whom one is no longer in competition.

The other collective assault on the New Criticism came from Ronald Crane and the Chicago critics. They bore down on the New Critics' attempt to see all poems as importantly alike and as distinct from prose or from science. The Chicago group would dwell more on the various genres and subgenres of literature, those traditional forms that shape individual works. In other words, for the criticism of a given poem it may be more helpful to say at the start that it is an elegy than that it is a poem. I reduce this doctrine to such a minimum, not to imply that no significant philosophical issues were at stake (there were some), but to show that the issues for teachers of

33. Douglas Bush, "The New Criticism: Some Old-fashioned Queries," *PMLA*, vol. 64 (Suppl., Part 2, March, 1949), pp. 19–21.

literature were once again primarily those of method. Almost everything I said about the ethos of New Criticism applies equally to Chicago Aristotelianism. In fact, in the elaborate taxonomy of literary works that Chicago promised, in the prospect of a well-ordered and infinitely large body of practical criticism, and in Crane's plea for "much inductive theoretical research . . . into problems both of general poetics and of the specific poetics of literary forms," [34] the Chicago critics were even better equipped for the professional decade than the New Critics. And needless to say, their call for a "pluralistic" criticism, one that would take systems of thought as premises for inquiry rather than as competing doctrines, promised to reduce values to methodological preferences and make an unthreatening place for them in the professional life.[35] My contemporaries in graduate school might recall maneuvering their way through first an Aristotelian paper on a narrative poem, then a myth-and-ritual job on a Restoration comedy, and on to a synthesis of Brooks and Lovejoy applied to several metaphysical lyrics. At many universitites the graduate course in literary theory laid these methodological riches out before us and left us free to make the choice appropriate to the critical occasion. If the Chicago critics had not come so much later onto the stage, and if they had offered more easily adaptable styles of practical criticism, they might well have stolen the scene, for their ideas met the same needs as did those of the New Critics.

Of the other attacks on the New Criticsm, most were even less abrasive. Mark Spilka, in an article whose subtitle was "A New Critical Revision," praised the movement for "its promise of something like objective certainty about subjective truths," but accused it of partly losing this aim in a self-defeating formalism, succumbing to the methods of science in an effort to defeat science.[36]

34. Ronald S. Crane et al., eds., *Critics and Criticism: Ancient and Modern* (Chicago: University of Chicago Press, 1952), p. 19.
35. On this matter of values, the case of Yvor Winters is instructive: Winters relentlessly kept his values out in the open, and partly as a result of this has had less influence than any of the other major New Critics—except among his own students, who tend to remain fervently loyal. Values were to be kept in their place.
36. Mark Spilka, "The Necessary Stylist: A New Critical Revision," *Modern Fiction Studies*, vol. 6 (Winter, 1960–61), pp. 284, 297.

About the same time, Roy Harvey Pearce, arguing that language
itself embodies history, pled for a more historical understanding of
literature. Yet Pearce had no particular view of the meaning or
direction of history, such as to put us and our literature in dynamic
relation to it; rather, he appropriated history as "an indefinite series
of examples of what we would possibly have been were we not what
we are." [37] Such a view preserves the New Critics' denial of our
particular historical being and their attempt to set us above history
as "users" of the past. Probably Hyatt H. Waggoner expressed the
consensus of academic literary people at the end of the fifties when,
in registering some complaints against the New Criticsm, he
nonetheless called it "the best criticism we have or are likely to have
for a long time." [38] And studies like Krieger's and Foster's represent
further stages in the domestication, adjustment, and assimilation of
what was at the outset a moderately iconoclastic body of criticism.
The waters were fairly calm.

Moreover, those few who did frontally attack the New Criticism
often did so on premises that would exclude almost *all* criticism. Very
early Mark Van Doren set himself in opposition to a criticism
"obsessed with a desire to be scientific about poetry," and so destroy
its beauties: "The poem is a bird that threatens to escape the net of
analysis, so that the net grows ever wider, and tougher with
interwoven analytic threads." [39] Although this was and is a common
complaint, it can easily be recognized as an attack on thinking, not a
call to a better mode of thought. And though Karl Shapiro, when he
excoriated New Criticsm 20 years later for being concept-ridden,
dogmatic, and abstruse, avoided Van Doren's misty nostalgia in
favor of a gritty plainness, he shared Van Doren's preference for
intuition and a hegemony of taste. The critic's real job, he can only
say, is "discriminating between" works of literature, without apparently employing any system of concepts.[40] These are aristocratic

37. Roy Harvey Pearce, "Historicism Once More," *Kenyon Review*, vol. 20 (Autumn,
1958), p. 588.
38. Hyatt H. Waggoner, "The Current Revolt Against the New Criticism," *Criticism*,
vol. 1 (Summer, 1959), p. 224.
39. Mark Van Doren, *The Private Reader: Selected Articles and Reviews* (New York: Henry
Holt, 1942), p. xiv.
40. Karl Shapiro, *In Defense of Ignorance* (New York: Random House, 1960), p. 12.

positions, rooted in the pride of the natural-born critic (and, usually, poet) who needs no shared ways of thinking, and whose advice to teachers would no doubt be "look into your guts and write—if you dare." It is not surprising that such views made little headway against the New Criticism, which at least aimed toward a democracy of critical ideas, available to all.

Meanwhile, there were a few explicitly political critiques of the New Criticism. The most influential, perhaps, was the argument offered in 1949 and 1959 by Robert Gorham Davis, and revived many times since, that the New Criticism implies a "reactionary position in politics and a dogmatic position in theology." [41] Though this is a bit closer to my own view, I hope I have made it clear that it won't hold up. There are indeed many remarks by Eliot, Tate, Ransom, and others praising monarchy, aristocracy, the ante-bellum South, etc.[42] But the criticism and literary theory, in sharp contrast to these political manifestos and asides, are square in the middle of the bourgeois liberal tradition.[43] The explicit politics of these men is a pseudo-politics. It constitutes an enabling mythology that ties their criticism to social yearnings and nostalgia but not to any possibility of action or affiliation. And it has little or nothing to do with the implicit political content of their writings about literature. In implicit politics, all the competing criticisms of the fifties were pretty much the same. At the risk of vulgarization, I would say that the main political effect of our theorists was to help emplant literary criticism, along with its producers, tightly and securely within the network of bourgeois institutions.

41. Robert Gorham Davis, "The New Criticism and the Democratic Tradition," *American Scholar,* vol. 19(Winter, 1949–50), pp. 9–19, and American Scholar Forum, "The New Criticism," vol. 20 (Winter, 1950–51; Spring, 1951), pp. 86–104, 218–31.
42. To conduct the assault on this level quite properly invites the kind of response Tate offered to Davis: that Eliot voted Labor, that an American New Critic voted for Norman Thomas, that Tate himself voted for FDR, etc. (*American Scholar,* vol. 20, p. 87.)
43. As is, after all, appropriate to their social origins. Read the first chapter of Louise Cowan's *The Fugitive Group: A Literary History* (Baton Rouge: Louisiana State University Press, 1959), for an account. Myths of the Old South don't apply well to this amiable collection of middle-class college boys, the liberal heirs of nineteenth-century capitalism.

In the postwar period, as American universities underwent enormous growth, a much larger segment of the population came into these institutions than before. This meant that market conditions required a great increase in the professoriat. One consequence was the new academic prosperity to which I have already alluded. And along with the prosperity came unaccustomed prestige, as intellectuals and technocrats were brought into the making of national policy, not as in the past because of their social backgrounds but for their expertise. In short, the university was a place where large numbers of people were trying to cut loose from their social origins and join an intellectual elite. And a new elite of this sort needs a set of myths to justify its status to itself and to the larger society.

Here a general principle of ideology is helpful: a privileged social group will generalize its own interests so that they appear to be universal social goals ("What's good for General Motors . . ."). In America, in the fifties, the bourgeois intellectual needed assurance that his privileges were for the general good. For example, a critic and teacher of literature whose work is fun and respectable, but who sees little evidence that he is helping to ameliorate social ills, or indeed serving any but those destined to assume their own positions in the ruling class—a teacher in this dubious spot will welcome a system of ideas and values that tells him that politics and ideology are at an end, that a pluralistic society is best for all, that individual freedom is the proper social goal for rich and poor alike, and that the perfection of self can best be attained through humanistic intellectual endeavor. And this is what the New Criticism and its rival theories had to offer. The tacit ideology has its proper place in bourgeois culture; its main features are practically inevitable, given the position of critics and teachers in this capitalist society.

Bourgeois culture rests on the idea of freedom.[44] In our society, people interact mainly through the market, and this medium tends to obscure all social ties except those mediated by commodities, the

44. Through this part of the discussion I am drawing on Christopher Caudwell's *Studies in a Dying Culture* (London: John Lane, The Bodley Head, 1938) and *Further Studies in a Dying Culture* (London: John Lane, The Bodley Head, 1949).

cash nexus. An example: the patent law is our way of dealing with useful knowledge. It regularizes and makes legal the private ownership of ideas, for a time, and emphasizes their cash value, but ignores the social origin of all inventions—the shared knowledge that underlies them—and also the sometimes devastating social consequences of their use.

It is easy in a free-enterprise system to ignore one's total dependence on other people and especially easy for the affluent. Their relationship to other people is indirect, effected through money. Possession of means gives them frictionless control over other people's labor, and such control feels like freedom. The affluent can do as they please, up to a point, and it is natural enough for them to conclude that their well-being *derives* from freedom. It is but a short step to elevate freedom into a universal social goal, not seeing that the kind of freedom they enjoy can't be made universal because it depends on the servitude of others: on the other side of the cash nexus is someone whose choices are fewer and who does not feel free.

Though bourgeois culture declares its allegiance to freedom, the security of the well-to-do demands that there be close limits (law and order) to freedom of action by the powerless. Hence, the ideologue settles on freedom of *thought* as fundamental, and he is willing to allow everyone that freedom so long as it does not lead to "disruption." The university perfectly embodies this notion. Our dogma is academic freedom, which in practice means that you can think and write what you like, but as your speech approaches to political action you are more and more likely to find yourself without a job. Universities are supposed to remain neutral, stay politically pure, as are other academic institutions like the MLA.

The literary wing of the academy wholly subscribed to these doctrines through the fifties, as I hope I have sufficiently shown, and developed its own version of them. Literature was divorced from particular ideologies and identified with a pluralism that would help preserve individual freedom. The doctrine of diversity is often advanced, even in the midst of doctrinal wars ("I disagree with what you say but I will defend to the death your right to say it"), by the Chicago critics and by their opponents. Even an often dogmatic man like Tate finds it natural to say, in the midst of controversy, "nobody knows what criticism is relevant to a democratic society. I like a lot of free play. I think that people ought to find out the truth wherever they can." [45] It is easy to translate this into the implied language of the powerful: "You are entitled to your opinion, and it won't affect my actions one whit."

As a corollary of this stress on freedom, the bourgeois intellectual sees art and aesthetic values as independent of social process. Caudwell points out that beauty can only be a construct generated by culture, a "specific social product." [46] But since the bourgeoisie relies for its comfort on the discomfort of others, it has good reasons for cloaking or ignoring the realities of social process and it looks away from labor and economic activity to find beauty. Art is, in brief, a means of freedom from society. And that seems to me the best explanation of the way our criticism has justified literature: as freeing man by setting him above his circumstances, by letting him "come to terms" intellectually, but taking him out of the present and making him one with "the tradition." All the schools of criticism agree that literature is a very special and separate thing, whose privileged cultural position needs defending—against science, against politics, against commercialization, against vulgarity, against nearly the whole social process.[47]

The other cardinal principle of bourgeois culture is that we must prefer thought to action—in fact, abstain from all social action except the pursuit of our individual economic goals in the market, and voting for candidates for public office. I have pointed to the distancing of action by the New Criticism. In part, the preference for

---

45. Allen Tate, in American Scholar Forum, "The New Criticism," p. 87.

46. Caudwell, *Further Studies*, p. 87.

47. Stated at this level of generality, the goal of postwar criticism is much the same as that of most English criticism since the spread of literacy through the industrial revolution. This was Arnold's aim and that of his contemporaries, with partial exceptions like Morris and Ruskin who sought the interpenetration of art and the reality of daily labor. But to hope for a vital literary culture among the working class was to hope against the economic stream, for reasons made clear enough by Martha Vicinus's *The Industrial Muse: A Study of Nineteenth-Century British Working Class Literature* (New York: Barnes and Noble, 1974) and by Q. D. Leavis's *Fiction and the Reading Public* (1932; reprint ed., New York: Russell & Russell, 1965).

contemplation is due to a natural wish for protection against social upheaval. But it is also surely the case that we prefer thinking to action because thinking is the mark of our separation from and economic superiority to those who do physical labor. As Caudwell says, thought is "favored socially to the extent to which it separates itself from action, because it is just this separation which has generated its superior status as the mark of the ruling, 'cunning,' or administrative class." [48] In our technological time, the university is built on precisely this distinction. That is why the cliché used by its enemies is "ivory tower." It is where the administrative class learns to think, where the scientific foundations of technology are laid, and where ideology is built to sanction the distribution of power and wealth. In this last task the American literary profession has cooperated, in part by insisting that the means to personal well-being and wholeness is through withdrawal from social action and the achievement of all-embracing states of mind. That is where the New Criticism pointed us, and where most of us, under the banner of humanism and the advancement of knowledge, gladly went.

Where else we might have gone, under different historical circumstances, it is profitless to guess. Marxism did, of course, offer a logical alternative: criticism written as part of a world revolutionary movement. Marxism could connect literature and goals for action, thus rebuilding somewhat the whole person. It could bridge the seeming gulf between high culture and the lives of ordinary people. And it could use literature as an agent of liberation, rather than of bourgeois freedom, which depends on exploitation. But that is another story. Given how American academic intellectuals were functioning in the forties and fifties, Marxian criticism was bound to be excluded from among the possibilities for respectable discourse about literature.

A few words of recapitulation. After the war, the academic literary profession in this country set an exciting course for itself: to revive literary culture and disseminate it widely and democratically, to the

48. Caudwell, *Further Studies*, p. 117.

general benefit of society. This project was, as Richard Foster said of the New Criticism, "perhaps the most extraordinarily successful of all consciously waged literary revolutions." [49] And its legacy has been in many ways admirable. To quote Foster again, education in English departments trains students to be "more alive and catholic" than an earlier generation. They and we constitute a "coherent and meaningful literary culture," which has advanced a "religiously felt resurgent humanism." In all this the socioliterary history of the last 25 years has indeed nearly fulfilled Arnold's wishful prophecy. Yet many of us are deeply dissatisfied with where we have arrived, with the elitism at institutions like the Advanced Placement Program and the MLA, the vestigical disdain for the unwashed, the "second environment" of which Trilling spoke.

I think that in retrospect we can see the origins of our present malaise in the core of our earlier beliefs. We wanted to move out of social action; we wished politics out of existence. But as Georg Lukacs says, "everything is politics"; every human thought and act is "bound up with the life and struggles of the community." [50] The denial of politics could not continue forever. For one thing, external events caught up with us and disturbed the great bourgeois peace of the fifties—the war in Vietnam, the uprising of oppressed peoples here and abroad, [the destruction of the biosphere through unchecked forces of the free-market economy] No walls built around the free play of intellect could exclude these world-historical events.

But, also, the very humanism we learned and taught was capable, finally, of turning its moral and critical powers on itself. Not directly. First, the humanism saw the inhumanity of the society outside the university—and credit to it for doing so. No one can tell exactly how much the values and perceptions of literary culture, as diffused among the young, helped make *visible* the war on Vietnam and, at home, racism and poverty. But there can be no doubt that those living in the "second environment" were among the first to wake

49. Foster, *New Romantics*, p. 22. The quotation that follows is on p. 28 of the same book.
50. Georg Lukacs, *Studies in European Realism* (New York: Grosset & Dunlap, 1964), p. 9.

from two decades of political sleep. From the burning of draft cards
to the perception of humanism's role in maintaining class privilege
and exploitative consumerism is not, perhaps, very far. I would like
to think not, because I take seriously Caudwell's prediction, made 40
years ago: "Humanism, the creation of bourgeois culture, finally ~~of course.~~
separates from it." [51] It "must either pass into the ranks of the
proletariat or, going quietly into a corner, cut its throat."

51. Caudwell, *Further Studies*, p. 72.

English 101 and the Military-Industrial Complex

"English" is reading and writing, literature and composition. I have been analyzing some uses that our profession makes of literature. In this section, with the great help of a chapter by Wallace Douglas, I take up composition.

In a sense to be explored later, literature is the subject that the profession chose, but composition is the subject that created the profession.

Writing took on new functions in nineteenth-century America. Complex industrial firms needed a corps of managers who could size up needs, organize material, marshal evidence, solve problems, make and communicate decisions. Government and other bureaucracies had similar need for exposition and argument and allied skills. Writing was no longer mainly a private and public art, but a tool of production and management.

Simultaneously it was becoming the primary means of communication to a newly literate public.

Rhetoric and oratory had always been college and university subjects. American universities now brought them down to pragmatic earth in the shape of composition and the daily or weekly theme. And English departments formed around the task of instructing an enlarged university population in these matters. I simplify. But the underlying proposition seems secure: compositioon took the place it has in the university curriculum because of structural changes in society and in the productive system. Not surprising, then, that the goals of Freshman English, however they were adorned with academic and cultural ideology, should be framed in response to needs of the industrial state and its governing class. English teachers, granted, often show esthetic contempt for the language of businessmen, bureaucrats, advertisers. Yet the "theme" we teach students to write is as much an invention of such philistines as of English teachers. And the attitudes we encourage students to have toward language—toward order, correctness, tone, dialect—have been and still mainly are an academic version of attitudes deeply held by those outside the academy.

The exchange is reciprocal. The leaders of industrial society let English teachers know—indirectly, to be sure—what kind of writing they want; and English teachers help teach the next generation of leaders what kind of writing to want.

A huge and complicated subject, with many dangerous passages. It is easy to overstate the importance of instruction in writing, which after all is in some ways notoriously ineffective. It is easy to oversimplify connections. And it is easy to sound conspiratorial. Yet for all these doubts and hedges, I am certain that the values and folkways of freshman English have important subterranean links to the values of industrial society, and that seeing these links is essential to understanding our profession. The next three chapters are an initiative in that direction, far from a seamless argument but also far better than ignoring the subject. (The initiative will come nearer to completion with Wallace Douglas's book, now in progress, on the history of freshman English.)

We explore three aspects of the subject here. In Chapter Five, Douglas follows the evolution of rhetoric at Harvard, from the ancient form it had at the beginning of the nineteenth century, through the innovations of Channing, to its embodiment after Eliot in the institution of freshman English, driven now by a very different set of motives and values. Chapter Six leaps to the present moment, almost exactly the hundredth anniversary of freshman English. In this chapter I look at some inheritors of the Channing-Eliot conception—writers of textbooks for use in composition courses—and of their underlying premises about writing and its place in the world. And Chapter Seven follows the trajectory of that hint, glimpsing the kinds of composition that are in fact written and highly rewarded in our world. They provide a mirror within which to see, however dimly, another image of freshman English and of the values that attend on literacy in America.

CHAPTER FIVE

Wallace Douglas
Rhetoric for the Meritocracy:
The Creation of
Composition at Harvard

In 1925, in a review of Charles S. Pendleton's *The Social Objectives of School English* ("a sight-seeing bus touring the slums of pedagogy"), Mencken noted—gleefully, I judge—that first of all in Pendleton's list of 1581 "objectives" there stood "the ability to spell correctly without hesitation all the ordinary words of one's writing vocabulary." [1]

In 1928, in a dissertation on the history of the teaching of composition in teachers colleges, a scholar called Leon Renfrew Meadows put this forward as one of his conclusions: "Independent thinking and clear, forceful, correct expression were strongly emphasized by our early teachers and writers in the field of composition." As evidence, Meadows offered the thought and practice of Simon Kerl, who published a "composition and rhetoric" in 1869. Kerl, it seems, thought well of themes on "birds, bees, ants, wasps, flies, bugs, and spiders." And indeed Meadows reprints an example of such a theme.

1. H. L. Mencken, "The Schoolma'm's Goal," *Prejudices Fifth Series* (New York, 1926), pp. 141–6, at p. 143. Pendleton published his own book in Nashville, in 1925. The review appeared in the *Mercury* in March 1925.

Insects generally must lead a truly jovial life. Think what it must be to lodge in a lily. Imagine a palace of ivory and pearl, with pillars of silver and capitals of gold, and exhaling such a perfume as never arose from human censer. Fancy, again, the fun of tucking one's self up for the night in the folds of a rose, rocked to sleep by the gentle sighs of the summer air, with nothing to do when you wake up but to wash yourself in a dew-drop, and fall to eating your bed-clothes.[2]

Accuracy in mechanical matters, a more or less specialized means of expression, and some evidence of originality, imagination, or independence in thinking (perhaps even to the point of eccentricity) —I suppose most English teachers today would agree that these about exhaust the aims they set for students. And few among them will argue about the rightness of those aims, still less about their meaning. After all, most English teachers are traditionalists, especially about themselves and their work. And even the most uninformed among them are likely to have some dim belief that their object and practices in teaching composition, or "good true writing," [3] are warranted by an ancient foundation in the work of, say, Isocrates, if not of that greater one than he, Socrates himself. Some may even call up the early humanists, whose command of Standard Written Tuscan, which they must have been taught, perhaps enabled them to make their livings as writers of letters.

I am willing to see a connection between many practices of current composition teachers and those that can be inferred from the works of any of the great rhetoricians. But I find it very difficult to go beyond that fact, obvious enough in itself, and to say that composition is, as it were, rhetoric under another name; or that it would be, if only it were to be transfused with discussions of invention (or at least the *topoi* and *loci communes*), voice, and audience.[4] And I do not even see anything very interesting in

2. Leon Renfrew Meadows, *A Study of the Teaching of Composition in Teachers Colleges in the United States* (New York, 1928), p. 10, citing Simon Kerl, *Elements of Composition and Rhetoric* (New York, 1869), p. 22.
3. Marlene Griffith, "Thoughts on Teaching Writing," *College Composition and Communication*, vol. XXV (December, 1974), 368–73, esp. p. 370.
4. Cf. W. S. Howell, *Eighteenth-Century British Logic and Rhetoric* (Princeton, 1971), p. 443n., on "attempts to make the ancient theory of topics available to speakers and

questions that concern a possible relation between rhetoric and composition, or in those that concern a reversal of history that might transform composition back into rhetoric or just make the alleged connection more apparent. The interesting questions are those that ask why and how rhetoric in its truncated and debased modern form[5] has been able to survive, and indeed flourish, as the study of written composition, or as practice in the production of written compositions and communications. After all, it is not immediately apparent what contribution to the education of *vir bonus peritus dicendi* is made by "the ability to capitalize speedily and accurately in one's writing." [6]

A beginning to an answer for such questions can be made by looking into the developments in the theory of rhetoric and oratory that seem to have occurred between the establishment of the Boylston Professorship at Harvard (1803) and the Inaugural of Charles William Eliot (1869), especially those that are embodied in the Boylston lectures of the great Edward Tyrell Channing, who held the office from 1819 to 1851. In my discussion I shall treat the Statute of the Boylston Professorship as marking the initial assimilation into the academic tradition of certain ideas in eighteenth-century rhetoric that seem to me to be essential, constitutive elements in the idea of composition. Channing's Lectures can be seen as a nearly final stage in the long devolution of classical rhetoric, or—more usefully here—as a second stage in the development of the idea of composition, one in which the already attentuated ties between rhetoric and that part of one of its parts, composition, were finally dissolved—or at least one in which the reasons necessitating

---

writers [or anyway to students of freshman composition] of the twentieth century." The seventeenth- and eighteenth-century rhetoricians, he says, got rid of it; and "rhetoric should not accept it today without proclaiming it an aid only to the slow and the dull." It is conceivable, of course, that its modern proponents already value it for precisely that fact.

5. That is, reduced to a study of style, supported by study of various grammatical rules. Cf. Adams Sherman Hill, *The Principles of Rhetoric* (New York, 1895), p. 1: "The foundations of rhetoric rest upon grammar; for grammatical purity is a requisite of good writing."

6. Mencken, p. 143.

such a dissolution were set forth—and the concept of practice in "writing" was introduced to the academic community and its supporters, and introduced with a social objective to boot. Eliot completed the development, in the Inaugural, first, by refining the social objective that Channing had imagined and, second, by opening the curriculum to the study of the mother tongue, with which, as things turned out, Channing's practices in writing were to become so inextricably entangled that in many cases "composition" has meant little more than study of the mother tongue, or of a selection of dialectal items regarded as defining Good or Appropriate or Standard or Prestige English.

Money for the Boylston Professorship was left to Harvard by Nicholas Boylston, a Boston merchant, who died in 1711. The bequest was paid in 1772, but for some reason nothing was done about a professor until 1803, when, apparently under threat of being sued by a nephew of Boylston, the Corporation appointed a committee to draft a statute for the office. The Statute was received by the Corporation in April 1803 and approved by the Overseers in July. Apparently it was largely the work of Eliphalet Pearson, the Hancock Professor of Hebrew and Oriental Languages. This need not be cause for surprise: since 1785, instruction in English grammar and composition had been in the charge of the Hancock Professor, perhaps, as Morison suggests, because study of the mother tongue was then thought of as but a "humble handmaid to homiletics." [7]

Pearson divided the work of the professorship into private and public lectures: the first consisted of instructing and drilling the undergraduates in the stylistic bases of speechmaking and perhaps in some of the preliminaries of the art itself; the second consisted of a more or less ceremonial account of the history and theory of classical rhetoric, as it was conceived in the eighteenth century, for the benefit of upper classmen and graduates resident in the neighborhood. In

7. Paul E. Ried, "The Philosophy of American Rhetoric as it Developed in the Boylston Chair of Rhetoric and Oratory at Harvard University" (Ohio State Dissertation, 1959), pp. 20–24 passim. See also Dorothy I. Anderson and Waldo W. Braden, eds., *Edward T. Channing, Lectures Read to the Seniors in Harvard College* (Carbondale, Illinois, 1968), p. xiv. On the status of English: Stanley E. Morison, *The Development of Harvard University, 1869–1929* (Cambridge, 1930), p. 98.

the public lectures, the professor was to expound such ancient matters as the "parts" of rhetoric, the kinds of speeches, and the topics, but also such relatively up-to-date matters as the "connection [of rhetoric] with the powers of the mind natural and acquired" and the "qualities in the speaker, in his style and in his delivery, indispensably requisite to form an accomplished pulpit orator." [8] For my purposes, however, Pearson's work in the Statute is most interesting because (perhaps consequent upon the moment) it seems to call for, or at least to allow, attitudes and practices out of which could develop the assumptions about young people, language, and discourse that underlie the modern school subject of composition. Evidence on that point can be found in Pearson's general charge for the Professorship and his rules for the private lectures.

After some preliminaries about requirements in character, piety, and acceptance of Christian doctrine; an educational rule that the Professor should "labor to advance the interests of general science and literature"; and a rule of academic governance that the Professor should "religiously observe the will of the founder and these statutes, except as far as the same may be duly repealed, altered or suspended" by appropriate authority;[9] Pearson set about constructing what amounts to a course outline, complete with a teaching objective. The "principal duty" of the Boylston Professor, Pearson said, was to be

to instruct the students of the several classes in the nature, excellence, and acquisition of the important art of Rhetoric in its most extended and comprehensive sense, or in the theory of writing and speaking well, that is, with method, elegance, harmony, dignity and energy.[10]

I think that that statement reflects the tendency among the rhetoricians of the eighteenth century to generalize "rhetoric" to

8. Ried, pp. 199–200.
9. *Ibid.*, p. 199. Since 1937 the Boylston Professorship has been held by Robert Hillyer, Theodore Spencer, Archibald MacLeish, and Robert Fitzgerald, apparently without any substantial change in the Statute. In the long, complicated, and rather odd history of rhetoric, this conversion of a professorship of rhetoric and oratory to the uses of poets is surely one of the strangest events.
10. *Ibid.*, p. 199.

mean, in George Campbell's phrase, the "art or talent by which the discourse is adapted to its end." The origin of such a definition as Campbell's seems to have been in the hopeless inability of neoclassical rhetoricians and literary critics to analyze the extension of the term "discourse," [11] itself probably a consequence of their common-sense perception that all the forms referred to by "discourse" occur in "the same medium, language." So Campbell's definition cannot be supposed to contain an implied "rhetorical," to limit "discourse" and perhaps carry us back to the three kinds of speeches of ancient rhetoric, or some other such tidy distinction. Like it or not, we have inherited from the eighteenth century a "comprehensive sense" of "rhetoric," which makes it refer to a "grand art of communication, not of ideas only, but of sentiments, passions, dispositions, and purposes," or an "art by which men operate on the minds of others." [12]

Such modernity is not, however, characteristic of Pearson's whole course of study. In much of it, he seems to have depended on the conservative, or even dated, work of John Ward, who lectured at Gresham College between 1720 and 1758. Certainly the phrase in

11. Cf. George Campbell in the Introduction to *The Philosophy of Rhetoric* (ed. Lloyd F. Bitzer [Carbondale, Illinois, 1963], p. xlix): "Poetry indeed is properly no other than a particular mode or form of certain branches of oratory. . . . The same medium, language, is made use of; the same general rules of composition . . . ; and the same tropes and figures. . . ."

12. *Ibid.* In books II and III of the *Philosophy*, which compose two-thirds of the work, Campbell sets forth the principles according to which language is adapted so as "to convey our sentiments into the minds of others, in order to produce a certain effect upon them." In general, it seems to me, Campbell sought his criteria in the expectations in style and usage that could be posited for a general (his word is "promiscuous") audience, such as would be found in "a christian congregation in a populous and flourishing city, where there is a great variety in rank and education." Addressing such an assembly requires the greatest attention of the speaker, so that "whilst on the one hand he avoids, either in style or sentiment, soaring above the capacity of the lower class, he may not, on the other, sink below the regard of the higher. To attain simplicity without flatness, delicacy without refinement, perspicuity without recurring to low idioms and similitudes, will require his utmost care" (pp. 102, 139).

I take it that that passage is the ultimate source for the once popular doctrine of appropriateness, and also of Professor Gorrell's persistent attempts to make rhetoric into the study of the reasons for various linguistic and stylistic choices that are made to achieve different "effects." See his latest explanation in *College Composition and Communication*, XXVI (February 1975), pp. 14–19.

the general charge in which Pearson defines "writing and speaking well" seems to reflect Ward's summary of Cicero on speaking well,[13] and Pearson could well have put together the outline for the public lectures from the chapter headings in Ward. It is even possible to find passages in which Ward, like Pearson, seems to add a *scribendi* to Quintilian's definition of "rhetoric" as *Scientia bene dicendi*, as if in anticipation of Campbell's extended sense of the term. One of these comes in the second lecture, at a point where Ward is trying to explain the difference between rhetoric and grammar so as to establish style as the province of rhetoric. Ward summed his argument up with this interesting sentence:

For tho rhetoric is said to be the art of speaking well, and grammar the art of speaking correctly; yet since the rules for speaking and writing are the same [i.e., when the formation of sentences is being considered], under speaking we are to include writing, and each art [rhetoric and grammar] is to be considered as treating of both.[14]

The unexpected connection of speaking and writing is simply a result of Pearson's need to explain why "style," a word coming from *stilus*, an instrument for writing, can be applied to oratory. And so it is hardly possible to construe Ward's "writing" as meaning "pieces composed to be read," as would be necessary if the sentence were to be used as a source for Pearson's synonomizing of "rhetoric" and "theory of writing and speaking well." In general, as a matter of fact, Ward seems to use "writing" in connection with transcribed speeches and to make a fairly obvious point:

Many things appear well in speaking, which will not bear a strict scrutiny. While the hearer's attention is obliged to keep pace with the speaker, he is not at leisure to observe every impropriety or incoherence, but many slips easily escape him, which in reading are presently discovered. . . . And therefore it is not without reason, that Cicero recommends to all such, who are candidates for eloquence, and desirous to become masters of a good stile,

13. On Ward as Pearson's source, see Anderson and Braden, *Channing*, p. xv. It may also be worth noting that Ward, like Pearson, omits "memory" as one of the parts of rhetoric.
14. John Ward, *A System of Oratory Delivered in a Course of Lectures* . . . (London, 1759), I, 23; II, 110 ff.

to write much. This affords them an opportunity to digest their thoughts, weigh their words and expressions, and give every thing [sc. "idea"] its proper force and evidence; as likewise by reviewing a discourse when composed, to correct its errors, or supply its defects; till by practice they gain a readiness both to think justly, and to speak with propriety and eloquence.[15]

No doubt the passage encapsulates a justification of composition work, a favorite among teachers, but writing up a speech in order to check its errors and infelicities is not at all the same thing as making a written composition.

The proper conclusion seems to be that, in his general charge, where he made writing a subject of study equivalent to speaking, rather than merely one of a number of "methods of improving Eloquence," [16] which is the way it appears in Ward and in the stipulations on the subject matter of the Boylston public lectures, Pearson was anticipating the modern schoolbook view of rhetoric as the "science" of discourse in general. In the body of the Statute, however, especially in his directions for the private lectures, or undergraduate study, Pearson stuck pretty close to the older view of rhetoric as the study of the styles appropriate to the various forms of public spoken discourse, in which state, of course, rhetoric had been the staple of the exercise-work in the Latin grammar schools for several centuries.

In the private lectures, then, the Boylston Professor was to set forth for "his pupils in a familiar manner the principles and rules of his art"; but it was to be "his particular care to aid their application of them in practice in suitable exercises assigned by him for this purpose." In the freshman and sophomore years, the first of these objects was to be taken care of by study of some of the classics of rhetoric, in the first year with the texts in the original language, "assigned portions of which [the students] shall recite or render to him in English," in the second year with the texts in English and the recitations in the "vernacular." In the junior year, the lectures were to have "the purpose of forming [the students'] style," in the senior

15. *Ibid.*, II, 117–18; see also I, 317.
16. Ried, p. 201.

year, that of "cultivating a correct and refined taste in style." [17]

The "suitable exercises" that were to test the effectiveness of, or at least were to go with, the instruction in theory, were to be of three kinds. First, in the freshman year, the Professor was to "instruct and exercise [the students] in the Arts of reading and speaking with propriety." Then, in the sophomore year, he was to hear the students in practice (and I suppose memorized) speeches of various sorts. In addition, in alternate weeks, during the first part of the year, he was to "inspect and correct their written translations of elegant passages of Latin or Greek assigned by him for that purpose"; "in the latter part of the year," he was to work on such "specimens of their own composition, as their progress in letters may permit." Presumably, the "specimens of their own composition" would also have been in Greek or Latin. In the junior year, the same sort of activity seems to have been intended: first, composition-sentences that put into practice the principles and illustrated the figures that were discussed in the lectures and textbooks, until the latter had been got through, then compositions that were, in some sense, the students' "own." In the senior year, the compositions, which were to be frequent, were to have the same purpose as the lectures, that of cultivating "a correct and refined taste in style"; "this important end" was to be accomplished by the Professor's "pointing out the good and bad qualities and peculiar features of their compositions." [18]

Since in the junior and senior years, instruction was to be from textbooks in English, Pearson must have supposed that the composition exercises would be too. But Pearson's only explicit concern for composition in or of the mother tongue is expressed in connection with the public lectures. One of the responsibilities of the Boylston Professor, Pearson said, in what sounds like something of an appendage, should be to "examine and compare the properties of the Ancient and modern languages, particularly of the English, with reference to composition" or, that is, the structuring of sentences—"the several members, words, and syllables, of which they consist, in

17. *Ibid.*, pp. 199, 200.
18. *Ibid.*

such a manner, as may best contribute to the force, beauty, and evidence of the whole." [19] But he was to do so "either in distinct lectures [in the public course], or as opportunity may present during his course." And it was not until 1810 that instruction in the composition of the English sentence (and presumably the composing of English sentences) was formally made a duty of the Boylston Professor. The study of English grammar remained with the professor of Hebrew.[20]

In Pearson's "suitable exercises" there are, no doubt, traces of whatever activity the *grammatici* of the ancient tradition used to develop *hellenismos* and *latinitas* in their small pupils. And there may be something remarkable in the fact that a collegiate subject—or, anyway, activity—should have been conceived largely in terms of the primary and elementary stages of the ancient rhetorical curriculum. Pearson's class exercises, it seems to me, can, or even must, be seen as deriving from the attitude, perhaps more general than we like to think, that is expressed in Quintilian's "Without elocution, invention and disposition are useless, and like a sword in a scabbard," [21] or the perhaps cheerful remark that he makes right after the one about the uselessness of invention and disposition without elocution:

This [elocution] is therefore what is principally taught; this no one can arrive at, but by the help of art; this requires study, practice, and observation; this is the exercise of our whole life; by this one orator excels another; this gives one kind of eloquence the preference to another; what is either commendable, or culpable, in oratory, is found here.[22]

Professor Howell, following Quintilian, has a very nice statement of the reasons for the popularity of elocution in European grammar schools during the sixteenth and seventeenth centuries. It is perhaps not quite so intentionally sardonic as I have taken it to be, and I hope that readers who know his generous and kindly works will not

19. *Ibid.,* p. 201. Cf. Ward, I, 336.
20. *Ibid.,* pp. 24–25.
21. Quoted in Ward, I, 304.
22. Ward, I, 304. He seems to qualify Quintilian on pp. 305–6.

fault me for the way I use it. The reasons for the popularity, Professor Howell thinks, are not hard to conceive.

It was more obviously within the capacities of lower school children to be able to identify the tropes and figures of style in the poems of Horace or Virgil and in the orations of Cicero than it would have been for them to comment upon the state of the controversy in one of Cicero's forensic speeches or to show how Cicero had derived one of his arguments from such a topic as adjuncts or contraries. The tropes and the figures, in the Latin and Greek terminology that was assigned to them in textbooks on rhetorical style, must have appealed mightily to the mentality of the pedagogue. Here were long lists of definitions that students could be made to memorize in Greek and Latin and to illustrate from the classics as passages were translated aloud and facts of style and grammar noted. Here also was material to serve as a point of reference for student writers. They could be instructed, for example, to develop their Latin theme on one day in terms of such figures as repetitions and contraries, and on another day in terms of such tropes as irony or allegory.[23]

The passage helps us to see what was behind Pearson's bare directions in the Boylston Statute and, incidentally, suggests the one true connection between modern composition and ancient rhetoric.

Professor Howell suggests that, in addition to whatever convenience they might have afforded the teacher, such exercises would have had the practical vocational value of "cultivating the student's verbal aptitude in the Latin language, at a time when he could use that language only in the world of learning but never in the world of everyday life . . . ."[24] I don't doubt that the pedagogues would have found some such justification for their drills; after all, they still do. But surely today it is possible to see that their words would have been warranted only if some considerable number of their pupils had been headed toward "learning" not "life." But even in the seventeenth century children who were being schooled seem to have come from sufficiently different backgrounds and to have had sufficiently different "career goals" for Locke to complain about the "ado [that

23. Howell, *Logic and Rhetoric*, p. 106. Cf. Richard L. Graves, "A Primer for Teaching Style," *College Composition and Communication* XXV (May 1974), 186–90.
24. *Ibid.*

was being made] about a little Latin and Greek, how many years are spent in it and what a noise and business it makes"—a fact he regretted all the more because the learning of Latin ("being nothing but the learning of words, a very unpleasant business to young and old") was expected of children "who, after they are once gone from school, are never to have more to do with it as long as they live," and therefore must be "whipped to it." [25] Whatever their influence on the stylistic taste of the learned and literary communities, the exercises in Latin grammar and composition could have meant to most pupils only tedium so intense "that only brutality could induce children to put up with it." [26] Discipline and conspicuous consumption are likelier explanations than direct vocational training, which is not to say that the two former are not, in their way, vocational.

But, it will perhaps be said, since the exercises suggested by the Boylston Statute would have been in English—some of them, that is—they would have meant neither boredom nor inutility. Perhaps, though the statement does seem somewhat to beg the question. Anyway, it is less the popularity than the nature of the study of elocution that interests me. The Boylston exercises resemble, if they are not based on, a version of rhetorical studies that had been narrowed for school purposes, rather than in any direct response to Ramistic theories, and that had dominated lower schooling for many hundreds of years. Ramus may have reduced the verbal "parts" of rhetoric to elocution only, the schoolmasters have gone further and, in that worried search "for suitable exercises for the practice of writing," which Bain called "a prime consideration with the teacher," [27] have gradually transformed ancient elocution into little more than practice to achieve purity in diction, perspicuity in sentence structure, and proper ordering, which gives a discourse its appropriate style.

25. John Locke, *Some Thoughts Concerning Education*. The passages come in Parts Seven and Nine. I have used an abridged edition, ed. F. W. Garforth (Woodbury, New York: Barron's Educational Series, 1964), pp. 129, 196, 200.
26. Cf. Lawrence Stone, "The Massacre of Innocents," a review of various books on the concept of childhood, *New York Review*, vol. XXI (14 November, 1974), pp. 25–31, esp. pp. 30–31.
27. Alexander Bain, *English Composition and Rhetoric* (American edition, revised; New York, 1869), p. 5.

In essence, it seems to me, the schoolmasters, on whose practice Pearson proposed to construct a university subject (and did!), conceived their "objective" to be that of establishing in their pupils a style and lexicon more or less specific to oratory, or—I really think this is more accurate—to public conversation in polite society. Ward may acknowledge this in his explanation of the values that support or indeed control his discussion of barbarisms and solecisms. He will, he says, use different criteria than the grammarians, for whom "all words are esteemed pure, which are once adopted into a language, and authorised by use." Such a standard will not do for oratory (or conversation), in which "neither all words, nor all expressions are so called [pure], which occur in any language; but such only as come recommended by the authority of those, who speak or write with accuracy and politeness." [28] "Politeness" is worth note, as is the figure in "comes recommended," which seems to derive from social or business letters of introduction.

Ward next suggests "that we should speak agre[e]ably to the common usage of the tongue, that everyone may understand us," avoiding the difficult and affected. Then he sketches a theory of the sociology of usage. The learned, he says, often drop usages they themselves have introduced; they come to think of them

as mean and sordid, from a seeming baseness contracted by vulgar use. For polite and elegant speakers distinguish themselves by their discourse, as persons of figure do by their garb; one being the dress of the mind, as the other is of the body. And hence it comes to pass, that both have their different fashions, which are often changed; and as the vulgar affect to imitate those above them in both, this frequently occasions an alteration, when either becomes too trite and common. But besides these sordid words and expressions, which are rendered so by the use of the vulgar; there is another sort first introduced by them, which is carefully to be avoided by all those, who are desirous to speak well. For the vulgar have their peculiar words and phrases, suited to their circumstances, and taken from such things, as usually occur in their way of life.[29]

Here, Professor Howell says, Ward was discussing "the social

28. Ward, I, 308–9.
29. *Ibid.,* I, 309–10.

dynamics that lead people of the middle class to seek to improve their conversational manners, and that lead people of the upper class to make that improvement difficult." He is also, of course, *mutatis mutandis,* discussing the social values and function that are realized in the teaching of composition. If the literary style is, in Professor Howell's harsh phrase, "the offspring of learning and politeness," and to be regarded as having "dignity" (sc. "worthiness") when it can be seen as more or less sharply opposed to "ordinary, vulgar speech," [30] it is hard not to conclude that the purposes of composition, as it came to be conceived in the latter days of rhetoric, was the acquisition of certain linguistic forms of relatively narrow currency, which today would be said to represent good or appropriate English, but which in more candid times could be described, simply and without apology, as signs of social rank.

But, as may be indicated by Ward's shift from the learned to the polite and elegant, and by Professor Howell's introduction of "people of the middle class," ranking systems change, as do their designations; and with them must change also the content of school subjects associated with the ranking systems. Such a change can be seen, I think, in the differences between the ideas of rhetoric and composition that are found in the Boylston Statutes and those set forth by Edward Tyrell Channing in his *Lectures Read to the Seniors in Harvard College* (1852).

In their public lectures, John Quincy Adams (1806–1809) and Joseph McKean (1809–1818), the first two of the Boylston Professors, seem to have followed Pearson's directions quite closely. If one is generous, perhaps the same can be said of Edward Tyrell Channing. In his *Lectures,* Channing went through at least the kinds of oratory (giving three of six lectures to the "eloquence of the pulpit"); and, though in a somewhat peculiar fashion, he also followed Pearson's direction to "divide [rhetoric] into its constituent parts." For Channing these were, first, "to analyze the style or method of persuasive address" in "any form of composition, any use of language

30. Howell, *Logic and Rhetoric,* p. 108.

that aims at power over the heart"; second, "to instruct a man in
finding and arranging the arguments, the reasons, the proofs by
which he is to maintain his great, his leading proposition"; third, "to
instruct in speaking"; and fourth, "to teach the principles of
composition, or, generally, of a good style, in the popular sense of
that phrase." The list certainly notices disposition, elocution, and
delivery; and, with "finding . . . arguments," Channing may have
intended a reference to the topics, if not even to invention as
Aristotle conceived it.[31]

In explaining the nature and subject of rhetoric, as Pearson had
directed, Channing may have gone further than even Campbell in
extending rhetoric "beyond the supervision of orators and speakers."
For Channing rhetoric is simply but extensively "a body of rules
derived from experience and observation, extending to all communication by language and designed to make it efficient." Having thus
extended the meaning of "rhetoric," Channing had to devise, if not a
definition, at least a set of specific characteristics for "oratory." To
do this, he first went back to the ancient idea of persuasion: "to bring
men, by whatever modes of address, to our way of thinking, and then
make them act according to our wishes." Then—and this may be his
essential contribution to whatever theory there is to govern the
practice and values of the modern teacher of composition—he set
about to distinguish the situation of the modern orator. In other
words, he proposed to infuse the old definition with a new content
derived from or based on the circumstances of what he called "a
modern debate." I think he began from a renovated conception of
"audience," though he may have begun from new ideas of proof and
argument, for which he sought support—practical, if not theoretical
—in the characteristics of a new audience. At any rate, in his
exposition, it was with the audience that Channing began.[32]

"A modern debate," he said, "is not a contest between a few

31. Ried prints outlines of the lectures of Adams and McKean. For Channing, see
Edward T. Channing, *Lectures Read to the Seniors in Harvard College* (Boston, 1856). The
passages in this paragraph are from pp. 32, 33, 35, 39, 40. For Pearson's direction, see
Ried, p. 200.
32. Channing, pp. 13, 17. This was his Inaugural Lecture.

leading men for a triumph over each other and an ignorant multitude; the orator himself is but one of the multitude, deliberating with them upon common interests, which are well understood and valued by all." The orator, he continued,

does not come to a raw, unprepared audience, brought together to receive opinions for the first time, from him, upon questions they are to decide, and to give themselves up rashly to any one who will flatter their weakness, consult their prejudices, or minister to their taste or passions. They are not assembled to be the subjects upon which he may try the power of his eloquence, but to see what eloquence can do for the questions. The subject is more thought of than the author, and what he says must come from the subject rather than from his art. The excitement he would produce must follow and mingle with conviction, not take the place of it;—the splendor that surrounds him must be the natural light of truth, not the false brilliancy that startles and blinds.[33]

In his discussion of the "modern debate," Channing was in fact rejecting Aristotle's basic conception of rhetoric as a study dealing with matters of opinion, "things about which we deliberate, but for which we have no systematic rules," and the techniques for arguing about such matters before an uninformed audience, "such hearers as are unable to take a general view of [a complicated argument, or follow a long chain of reasoning]." As a matter of fact, he seems to have taken occasion, perhaps in passing, to reject also Aristotle's distinction between artificial and inartificial proofs. In short, Channing's intention was to develop a modernized rhetoric, the assumptions of which would validate "the purity and elegance of [Cantabrigian?] style in composition and elocution," and perhaps also "the uniform set and drift of opinion in matters literary, political and religious, which [had] so long marked the highly cultivated, but small and rather removed society of which [Harvard and Cambridge were] the centre." [34]

Channing, in the last nine lectures, took a remarkably literary approach to his subject, which seems to hover between the grounds of

33. *Ibid.*, p. 17.
34. Aristotle, *Rhetoric*, I, i (1354a); I, ii (1357a). R. H. Dana, Jr., "Biographical Notice [of E. T. Channing]," in Channing, pp. vii–xx, esp. p. xiv.

taste and the acquisition of the style of public discourse in an age characterized by "the stable foundation and ample protection of government, the general diffusion of knowledge and of a spirit of inquiry," and a tendency, in free countries, anyway, "to make the security of individuals and of the state rest on laws and institutions, and not on popular caprice or the power of any one man." The implication, which is spelled out in the first part of the first lecture, is that classic oratory and rhetoric, rising in countries that did not enjoy such conditions, had lost their efficacy, since they no longer answered to the needs of the society.[35]

In this new world of free governments, the orator's audience could be conceived, at least by Channing, as

men who are slow in receiving and abandoning opinions, who are too wary, conscientious, or wilful to be easily and suddenly operated upon, and who are, at the same time, so intelligent and thoughtful, that they cannot wholly escape the power of just sentiments, however unwelcome they may be.[36]

Whether that is to be read as an apotheosis of the Yankee or only of the Cambridge intellectual may be questioned. At any rate, the existence of such an audience, Channing said, might be supposed to have "modified and given a peculiar character to eloquence without impairing its efficiency." The new style in eloquence is more "temperate," less given to appeals to "transient impulse," less dominated by "imagination and passion," the once "turbulent masters" of public discourse and action. Where once the orator thought of himself as putting on arms "for the fight of eloquence," or of proving himself "a man-at-arms in the war of pleaders," now he must think of himself as something of a schoolmaster. The eloquence of the modern orator works not by producing an "obvious," and immediate, "effect on the decisions and conduct of men," but more by exerting "a growing and permanent influence over [their] character and opinions." Channing concludes that the new style in eloquence

35. Channing, p. 13.
36. *Ibid.,* p. 19.

aims at making men think patiently and earnestly, and take an active part themselves in giving efficacy to another's arguments or persuasions. It has only to secure a lodgement for truth in the mind, and by and by the truth will quietly prevail.[37]

In that whole argument, Channing retained the terms and details of what might be called an oratorical image of public discussion; that is, one of a man addressing a public assembly. Indeed, at one point in his general comparison, Channing used the ancient categories to speak of the modern courtroom orator who is "thwarted by the cold vigilance of judges, or the restraining formalities of practice," of the legislator whose influence is limited "because parties are bound down to an arbitrary course of political opinion and conduct," and of the preacher (who can stand for the epideicticist), who himself must deal with an audience that, on the basis of results, may be thought of as being also, even though improperly, "on guard against the power of an orator." So far, then, Channing's revisions in the theory of rhetoric can be seen as affecting only the surface characteristics of one part of rhetoric, eloquence or style; but the result is significant beyond even the modifications in taste and composition required by Channing's notions of "a good style, in the popular sense of that phrase." [38]

For Channing had in mind, and working in his argument, an image of quite another sort of public discourse or "opinion-forming," as we would say. "We have now," Channing said,

many other and more quiet ways of forming and expressing public sentiment, than public discussion in popular assemblies. Opinions are now constantly coming to us from other men and all parts of the world, through many channels, and we are thus able to instruct ourselves, and to think liberally and independently on all subjects, and especially on the opinions that are most current at home, and which the ancient orator might have appealed to with unresisted and terrible power.[39]

That "and more quiet ways" is a splendid touch. And if there is

37. *Ibid.,* pp. 13, 19, 20, 21.
38. *Ibid.,* p. 18.
39. *Ibid.,* pp. 16–17. On "home opinions," see pp. 3–4.

any doubt that Channing was thinking of print media, it can be settled by noting his strictures on the civic responsibility of the classical republican. "It was not for him," Channing said, "to acquaint himself with distant nations for the sake of correcting his false notions or enlarging his narrow views . . . ." I take it that Channing cannot have been expecting that any great number of his fellow citizens would be able to better the basis for their votes in town meetings by the broadening effects of travel. And the next sentence makes his meaning clear: "It was not for him [the classical republican] to read and reflect . . . ." [40] So I think it is safe enough to take "quiet ways" as referring to print and "many channels" as referring to an increase in the number, significance, and influence of journals of opinion.

Channing's argument assumes a public discourse that has been relieved (if that is the word) of all its mediate ("relatively ultimate") ends, such as moving and pleasing, and, with them, most of the mnemonic and attention-holding devices of style that ancient theory had collected. Presumably these were to be replaced by what I suppose might be called devices of instruction. The general end of discourse remained, however: "to bring men, by whatever modes of address, to our way of thinking, and thus make them act according to our wishes." It is hard, reading his comparison of ancient and modern oratory, not to feel, at least occasionally, that Channing had not got into his notions about oratory all the consequences of his belief in the high bourgeois myth of a society that tends "to place the security of nations and of every individual on the broad foundations of laws and institutions, and to make it the interest of the highest as well as the humblest citizen to respect and trust in them" and of his consequent belief in an audience that expects to form opinion and perhaps act, on the basis of information intended to narrow the probabilities under discussion. [41]

But there is, all the same, a point in Channing's argument that, it seems to me, radically revises the ancient concept of the rhetorical

40. *Ibid.*, p. 3.
41. *Ibid.*, pp. 13, 15.

situation. Evidently, Channing supposed the ancient orator to be a "despot," who could "save freedom or destroy it" by "appealing to any principle of human nature which would aid him" to manipulate the feelings, vindictive or generous as the case might demand, of those assembled before him.

A modern orator, however, must deal with a quite different sort of audience, the one that had been brought into being by the expansion in the numbers and the influence of the "quiet" media of print and the opening of the American market place of ideas to "opinions" (how the old terms persist!) from men the world around. In an informed audience, or at least one seeking to be informed, the members are able to think "liberally"—that is, objectively, disinterestedly—and "independently"—that is, as individuals. It was Channing's straightforward and rather simple conclusion that, therefore, and because of the growth in the mechanisms of the state, we now "see the audience controlling [the orator]." But the truly radical point in Channing's revision of rhetoric is in his view of the orator and of the relation between orator and audience, which had to—or at least did—follow his awareness of the importance of print as a medium of public discourse. In the new meaning, orators become men trafficking in information and perhaps ideas, and they must think of themselves as no longer addressing the ears and through them the emotions and prejudices, but now rather as putting their words before the eyes and gaining through them access to the knowledge and intelligence of an audience conceived of as individuals and able, therefore, to submit the words of the *writer* to consideration and judgment.[42]

This is a quite radically new view of rhetoric, it seems to me. Its paradigmatic image is that of a man thinking, of a man whom "increased knowledge" has made "more contemplative," less likely to turn to public occasions for "excitement," who "feel[s] the most deeply when alone," who is not insensitive to the imagination and the passions, but who is always tempering them with judgment. Channing's somewhat Platonic effort to preserve the dynamics of

42. *Ibid.*, pp. 3, 4, 16.

ancient rhetoric by calling up the judgment is a valiant one, surely.
But what one sees, or at least what I see, is a man in a study—the
house is in Brattle Street, I think, and the hour is that all too magic
one between dark and daylight, when, unnecessarily, night is
lowering—who is contemplating the information, ideas, and opinions in some interesting journal "devoted to literature, art, and
politics." [43] It's all very solitary, very romantic. Or perhaps, more
accurately, and with less of the sort of literary flourish to which
Channing took such exception, it is a vision of economic man and of
the ineluctable, or at least automatic, controls of the free market, as
they could be transferred to the market place of ideas and the
commerce of public discussion.

As I have said, the relation between rhetoric and composition is an
obscure one at best, even when rhetoric is transformed into
communication theory, as Channing may almost have done. But in
the long evolution of ancient composition (the study of the structuring of sentences) into modern (the production of whole, if practice,
pieces in various forms of more or less public discourse), the
collocation of Channing's ideas that I have been analyzing has an
important place. Without question, the modern school and college
subject of composition has been shaped by the theory of rhetoric
adopted by Channing. I do not mean that composition would not
have come to be what it now is, if Channing had not held the
Boylston Professorship. After all, his ideas are but extensions,
clarifications, or perhaps just simplifications of general tendencies in
eighteenth-century rhetoric, which others could have articulated for
the academic tradition quite as well as Channing. Nevertheless, the
facts are that Channing was the Boylston Professor, and, in the
public lectures required of him, he did at least adumbrate an idea of
rhetoric as the study of written communications. Furthermore, his
pedagogical theory—as a teacher of composition—does seem to have
been derived from his idea of a new medium of discourse and the
style appropriate to it.

43. *Ibid.,* p. 21. The description of the journal is from the early issues of *The Atlantic
Monthly.* It is, of course, an anachronism to use it here; still, it seems to fit the point.

In the history of the teaching of composition, Channing's pedagogy may be more important than all his pulling and hauling to make "rhetoric" take in periodical essays and articles. In fact the middle seven of his last nine lectures constitute a handbook of "methods" in composition that is at least as good and up to date as any we now have. I know of no earlier work that is quite like these seven lectures.[44] That may say something about the state of our art or mystery, at least it explains the significance of Channing.

The base or root concepts of Channing's pedagogy are those oddities of modern schooling, the teacher of writing and the "good writer" in his pupilage. How pupil becomes writer, whether by growth or making, is of course the central question of the theorist. About it, however, Channing disclaimed any knowledge. Grammars, rhetorics, and dictionaries can be listed, exemplary authors named, lectures summarized, and "the method of conducting the critical exercises in composition" described. However "insufficient" may be the explanation that would be provided by such a list, at least it shows what Channing thought to be his "teaching materials," the tools of his art.[45]

Though, like many modern teachers, clothing, perhaps protecting, himself with the mystery of an art, Channing seems to have been not at all unwilling to say where evidence of a teacher's success or failure must be sought. That is in what a man does "when he passes from the rudiments at school to responsible writing in the real work of life."

In other words, having in his first chapters described a rhetoric that had social and practical value because of its tie to written, published communication, Channing now was asserting a similar value for the school subject of composition, which he was creating out of the *elocutio* of the old rhetoric, as a practice necessary to all expecting to enter a working public life that he saw as being increasingly dependent on the written and printed word.

But, unfortunately for his argument, Channing had said that the

44. Coleridge's description of Bowyer's tastes (*Biog. Lit.,* c. I) sounds very much like Channing's, with apparently similar results for their teaching techniques.
45. Channing, p. 185.

creation of a "good writer" is inexplicable not only by the teacher, but also by the product: "The young man himself could not explain the process by the most severe inquiry into the growth of his mind, and of the now fully developed power of execution." He had also seemed to associate composition with some sort of "rudiments" in schooling. The remarks reflect, if they are not actual consequences of the always dubious status, professionally, of one who must necessarily, often in spite of himself, be concerned with the "concrete enduring entities" of students as such, rather than with the "very abstract entities, the products of logical discernment" [46] that constitute the "subjects" of advanced education.

Channing's answer seems to me a sort of cry in a wilderness of uncertainties and does little to lessen the unhappy effect of "rudiments." Teachers, Channing argued, using the Victorian obfuscatory abstraction,

can say truly that part of their instruction was most definite, and, though humble, it generally accomplished what it proposed. Perhaps they hope[47] that more was taught than forms and proprieties, and that they led the mind to feel that there was some bond between the forms and proprieties and its own action. The process, after all, may have been more than mechanical.

"The instructer [sic]," Channing added, knowing so little of how a good writer is made, "will not try to show a single point of its [the writer's preparation] efficacy beyond the most humble of its offices." [48]

The passage makes Channing an early defender of the composition teacher as a dealer in minimum essentials and mechanics; and I guess one would have to look far for another defense as effective in its loftiness. But Channing, who was, after all, a writer before he was turned into a teacher, is really more interesting theoretically than that passage makes him out to be. He has an extraordinary section on the behavior of writers when composing that, had it been

46. Alfred North Whitehead, *Science and the Modern World* (New York, 1948), p. 80. The quotation is from Chapt. V.
47. I think that "hope" should probably be "may hope."
48. Channing, pp. 186-7.

attended to by composition teachers, including Channing himself, would have generated a pedagogy far removed from those rudiments that Channing found so troublesome.

Channing began this discussion with the remark, "There is something worth our notice in the state of our minds when writing or when previously meditating upon our subject." Of course he was writing before the advances of the depth psychologies, and so at first the remark may seem innocuous enough. But as Wordsworth knew, the associationist psychologies had depths of their own, and Channing was, in fact, preparing to ask a question about the relation between the regnant, conscious mental faculties (that would have been his word) and the sensations that are "felt in the blood, and felt along the heart" and that come "into [the] purer mind" only secondarily.

His question was whether the "mental action" in writing or planning for writing is to be thought of as voluntary or not. His first answer is the straightforward one of the practical man or the teacher.

I have always been accustomed to prepare myself for the work. I can recognize certain habits and methods which I generally follow and which I know that I formed for myself. If a man is not a master in an occupation like this, what is meant by such expressions as the mind's deliberate discoveries, its creative power, its reliance upon its own efforts in the absence of foreign aids and motives? [49]

But at least sometimes, when he thought man-writing, Channing could be aware of "the mind's perpetual activity and flow of thought," which, though subject to direction by the will, is not dependent upon it. Indeed, in a kind of illustration of his own principle, Channing's thought here, or perhaps the force of a figure he had borrowed from Josiah Tucker, carried him to a picture of composing in which the will seems hardly to exercise even direction. In this passage (a long mediation, as it were; no doubt the Greeks had a word for it), Channing gave a writer's answer to his question about control.

49. *Ibid.*, p. 188.

How much does he [the writer] set down which he anticipated when he began to reflect upon a subject? After his work is done, how much does he find to be the result of previous design? He may begin with a prominent idea, which it is his purpose to lay open. Very soon unexpected relations spring up and gather round it, till sometimes the original subject becomes subordinate. A deeper and more comprehensive truth is discerned. His first scheme will be an embarrassment to him, if he has not set about his work with the feeling that it is never wise or safe, in entering upon a course of meditation, to say precisely whither it shall lead him. He thinks it will never do thus to commit himself as to the result. The incipient motions of thought, doubtful and [im]prudent as they may be, may even acquire heroic energy, and his subject will dilate with his capacity and warmth.

Then—it is almost as if he had suddenly been reminded that he was, or was supposed to be, talking about a school subject, and perhaps to an audience who might be involved in determining not merely its shape but even its existence—Channing interjected a denial of the obvious accusation.

This is far from being a sign of an ill-disciplined mind, or of one ignorant of its strength and resources, and borne into mere extravagance by a weak surrender of itself to a passing influence. It is the natural experience of some men in the healthiest condition. In others, constitutionally more cool, or habitually more guarded, the course of ideas will be slower and less unexpected, but not essentially unlike.[50]

Probably not much of a course outline could be built up from this genial (in Coleridge's sense of the word) and plastic conception of composing. Yet I wonder whether teachers could not, if put to it, devise situations in which students could have that kind of experience of composing. Channing, who seems to have conceived of students as writers *in posse* (part of the time, anyway), continues with a suggestive vignette of a student "meditating upon his regular exercise in original composition, with little to say, and that, as he thinks, very poor."

He cannot take hold of anything definite and encouraging. Even his reading upon his subject distracts him with its variety of information and

50. *Ibid.,* pp. 188–91.

opinions. But let him once preserve, in the best words he has at command, some one idea which flits before him, and immediately a neighboring thought shall come to the light, and then others with ever-multiplying relations and an ever-increasing distinctness. He might have this idea floating about in his mind for hours as a subject of meditation or reverie, without any adequate conception of its bearings; but now, in a fixed, visible form, it seems to put his mind in order, and prepare it for manful enterprises which it had shrunk from before.[51]

That hardly sounds like even the genesis of a thesis sentence, let alone an outline for a five-paragraph theme. And one can question whether such a scene can be accommodated to a system in which learning is punctuated (indeed, defined) by marking periods fitted out with points of sequence, increment, and development, as a chart for growth and ranking. And, indeed, as is suggested by that daunting phrase "manful enterprises" and its apparent corollary of growth therefor, perhaps it could not have had much of a part in Channing's own procedure. For in a subsequent lecture, on the habits of a writer, Channing announced, embracing contradictions, I guess,

One thing which the writer has to do for himself, and in which all depends upon himself, is to acquire such self-command that he can give his whole attention to a subject, so that he shall be in a way to comprehend it perfectly and be able to put down his thoughts freshly as they occur, without losing a step in the longest train. This self-control must be a principle and a habit . . . .[52]

Here Channing was probably thinking more of a writer with a job to do, and that one with relatively limited terms of reference, rather than of a student having to fix up an assignment on a topic, such as the "Comparative difficulties of abolishing war, slavery, intemperance, etc.," or "Consider Whately's Doctrine, that the operation of reasoning is in all cases the same—also the universal application of the syllogism." Nevertheless the sense of the disciplined writer, of the discipline in writing, gave Channing what composition needed if it

51. *Ibid.*, pp. 240–41.
52. *Ibid.*, p. 208.

was to become a fixed element in the college and school curriculum; that is, an end in discipline or vocation that would remove from it, or at least conceal, all taint, every stigma of its connection with the creative, the feeling, with "the unproductive literary dreamers, who seem to think that rare gifts set them above conscience and rules, and that the delicate structure of their minds requires them to keep aloof from the rude encounters and intimacies of daily life." [53]

What Channing had done in this passage was to give composition an end beyond that of becoming "skilful in composition." Properly regarded—that is, as being a "duty"—writing, Channing said, even though doing it in college makes it seem like "a mere literary exercise,"

will prepare us in a degree for active life, by giving us habits of self-denial, industry and close study, a general and ready command of our faculties, a clear, direct way of thinking on all subjects and occasions, a promptness and decision in our opinions, and a natural and precise method of expressing them. A man who writes much and with consideration is doing himself an incalculable good in respect to every other study. Thus what to one seems absolute drudgery and to another an amusement or refinement, may be made a means of forming good intellectual habits generally, and a generous preparation for the varied calls of life.[54]

When Eliphalet Pearson charged the Boylston Professor with the duty of instructing Harvard students in "the important art of Rhetoric in its most extended and comprehensive sense," and then defined the "art" as "the theory of writing and speaking well," he was incidentally including in the Statute ideas that were to become important elements in the creation of the modern school subject of composition. If we assume, as I think we must, that Pearson's "comprehensive" came from Campbell, then we can say that the Statute contained the notion of a general theory of discourse, call it "rhetoric," if you will, though "communication," Campbell's second term, seems more specific to his meaning. And such a theory of "discourse-in-general" seems to me to have been the somewhat illogical pre-condition for the modern concept of "good writing,"

53. *Ibid.,* p. 209.
54. *Ibid.,* pp. 209–10.

perhaps a rather Platonic ideal, which is at the heart of composition teaching, though realized, if at all, only in such universals as "correctness," "vigor," "vividness," or "economy," none of them being attached to any specific kind, medium, audience, or role, except insofar as any particular composition teacher will have some particular examples from which to draw some signs of "good writing." Furthermore, if we assume, as I think we can, that Campbell's analysis of "communication" to include among its objects "sentiments, passions, dispositions, and purposes," as well as "ideas" is also within the ambience of the Statute, then I think we can say that at the time the Statute was being drawn, there were already present in rhetorical theory ideas that would open the way to the peculiarly personal kind of "theme" that used to be, and perhaps in some places still is, characteristic of composition-work.

Channing's contribution to the development of composition begins in his attempt to purge "rhetoric" of its ancient connotations of public controversy carried on by members or clients of a ruling class before an uneducated, uninformed, and untrained audience. How far the audience and orator of ancient rhetoric may, even whimsically, be associated with the famous distinction in the *Poetics* between the "men of consequence" and the "no-accounts," I do not know. In any event, Channing saw that, if the art of which he was a professor were to retain any credibility, it would have to be given an image more in keeping with the actualities of a society where opinion was more and more coming to be formed by the report and the article, rather than by the debate. To do this, he first changed the locus of the oratorical situation from the public assembly to a generally private room, the medium from the spoken to the printed word, and the agent from the orator to the writer. At this stage of the argument, Channing must have thought to himself that if orators had needed training, so would writers. The training he devised was determined in part by the school-related developments that had already reduced rhetoric pretty much to the study of style; in part also by Channing's own awareness (the result, perhaps, of his editorial experience) that most of what was even then still being studied under the heading of "style" might once have been appropriate to the needs of the ancient oratorical situation, but was, if anything, dysfunctional in the situation he had just invented. Hence his earnest efforts to expunge from the papers of his students all the stylistic elaborations which, originating in the oral situation of the ancient orator, with that postulated audience of inattentive traditionalists, were now become a bother to the cultivated readers of his own class. But considerable though Channing's feat was in finding a subject, or at least an occupation, in the teaching of writing, still something more was necessary to establish it as a school and college subject: namely, a social purpose. This Channing found, ingeniously, in just that training in the rudiments of public discourse in which composition is entangled and by which it is to a great extent defined. Such training, Channing asserted, is not simply a means to acquiring skill in composition, it is also a quite direct preparation of the work habits and thought patterns that are needed to function in any of the "varied calls of life."

Who knows whether even that would have been enough to assure a place in the academic community to so odd an enterprise as one which, seemingly, was intended to prepare young men of the propertied classes to be able to write, in the honorific sense. But the question is moot. For, in the event, Channing's subject of writing was swept up in the imperial plans of Charles William Eliot, gained a new and more certain means of determining those with proper habits, and thus became a fixture in the schools and colleges of the United States.

It was "on the raw and cloudy afternoon of Tuesday, October 19, 1869," in the First Parish Church, before galleries "quite filled with ladies" and a main floor that "held many distinguished people," that Eliot delivered his Inaugural Address. The Address is well known, of course, among English teachers interested in their history because of Eliot's complaint about "the prevailing neglect of the systematic study of the English language" in the schools of the United States. But the significance of Eliot's complaint, and especially its bearing on the development of composition, can hardly be understood unless it is seen in connection with his vision of the social function of the Harvard he was preparing to create, the Harvard in which, after

1872, when Eliot appointed Adams Sherman Hill to the faculty to begin improving both the students' use of English and also the place of English, the subject, in the curriculum, modern composition came into being as a more or less collegiate subject.[55]

The basis of Eliot's educational reform was his recognition of a deficiency in the values and attitudes of the American people; or, to be quite accurate, the deficiency he saw was in the training system that the American people had developed for sorting themselves out. "As a people," he said, "we do not apply to mental activities the principle of division of labor; and we have but a halting faith in special training for high professional employments." Here Eliot was, apparently, using Adam Smith or the Mancestrian factory to defend Harvard's (not his) upper division electives against the uniform course of study, which was, he noted, "still the prevailing system in American colleges," and which still seemed "to most Americans a very proper and natural thing, even for grown men." But more, far more, than the course of study was on Eliot's mind; and in his next sentence he moved out of the Yard into the world of class and ethnic and regional rivalries. He complained that the American people (or anyway those of them in New England) held the "vulgar conceit that a Yankee can turn his hand to any thing," and they "insensibly carry [the conceit] into high places, where it is preposterous and criminal."

> We are accustomed to seeing men leap from farm or shop to court-room or pulpit, and we half believe that common men can safely use the seven-league boots of genius. What amount of knowledge and experience do we habitually demand of our law-givers? What special training do we ordinarily think necessary for our diplomatists? [56]

It seems to me that this passage in the Inaugural Address reflects an awareness in Eliot of something gone wrong with the stratification

55. Hill was in Eliot's class (1853), so he, too, would have had his rhetoric from Channing for a while; and he seems to have carried on Channing's fierce defense of a plain style. Perhaps he got his devotion to grammar and good usage from Francis James Child, who succeeded Channing, or it may have come from his newspaper work.

56. Nathan M. Pusey, ed., *A Turning Point in Education.* The Inaugural Address of Charles William Eliot as President of Harvard, October 19, 1869 (Cambridge, Mass., 1969), Introduction, p. v, pp. 8, 9. See also p. 21. Hereafter "Eliot."

or licensing system of the society. Things might not yet have been falling apart into mere anarchy. But still in only thirty-seven years Boston was to find itself with a Mayor called Fitzgerald, whose parents had emigrated from County Wexford in the Forties, but who was rearing his family in the relatively Pierian precincts of Concord. "They" defeated him two years later, by the way, with the candidate of the Good Government Association. So the center seems to have held, more or less, until well after Eliot's most active years. That it did depends, in part at least, on what Eliot did for the best by his reform of Harvard.

Eliot's reference to men leaping from "farm or shop to court-room or pulpit" suggests that he had in mind only an increasing professionalization of the gentlemanly (in the American sense) professions, for which indeed "special training" and perhaps even "knowledge and experience" might be argued to be necessary. But of course the whole point of Eliot's new Harvard was that it was to be a growth industry, as we say; and that meant students for whom the curriculum of the gentlemanly professions, the "one uniform curriculum" of the colonial colleges, would be irrelevant, as we also say. One of Eliot's solutions, of course, was to expand and specialize (departmentalize) the old curriculum. But even expanded and specialized, for what specific jobs can undergraduate education, of the liberal sort, be supposed to train? Or how can training that is by definition liberal be said or supposed to be job-specific? Surely Eliot cannot be thought to have intended to turn Harvard College into a teacher training institution or a mechanism for the self-perpetuation of the ancient disciplines as collegiate departments.

Eliot found an answer to this interesting problem in a brilliantly percipient redefinition of the qualities of the college-produced elite. Speaking about Harvard's openness to "students in all conditions of life," and of the support the University could give poor students of "capacity and character," Eliot added that "the recipient must be of promising ability and best character."

The community does not owe superior education to all children, but only to the *élite*,—to those who, having the capacity, prove by hard work that they have also the necessary perseverance and endurance.[57]

57. Eliot, p. 15. Note the italics and accent for *élite;* evidently the word hadn't yet been naturalized.

No doubt "capacity" and "promising ability" carry some of the connotations of that intellectual rigor and challenge to which academic meritocrats are nowadays paying such deferential attention. And Eliot may indeed have thought that scholarships—"the coveted means of intellectual growth and freedom"—provided the recipients and (due to the "beneficent mysteries of hereditary transmission") their descendants the "Capital" of "personal culture" that outearns all other. But a capital of personal culture is not quite the same thing as the skills, whichever they are, that are said to flourish under the challenge of intellectual rigor. And the sequence of Eliot's argument suggests that in his view scholarship students had to come up to the University with a sort of primitive accumulation of value-producing character traits. Indeed Eliot saw the very "process of preparing to enter college under the difficulties which poverty entails" as precisely the test of whether "worthiness" of character exists. Presumably he expected the course of study to offer still further occasions for such testing.[58]

But of course sons of the poor, entrants to the elite by right of Harvard's certification of their character, of their "perseverance and endurance," constituted only one sector of Eliot's college-produced elite. In addition to the "poor scholars and preachers of duty" who "defend the modern community against its own material prosperity," there were the men who came to Harvard from "refined homes," bringing with them "good breeding, gentle tastes, and a manly delicacy." [59] For these others, these more truly Harvard men, who perhaps may be thought of as entering the College by an almost prescriptive right, Eliot seems to have had a rather different notion of the function of the course of study; that is, a different notion of the qualities of character that Harvard was to certify them to possess.

For these men Eliot mentioned no test of worthiness. For them he saw no creation of capital in culture. Presumably that had been accumulated for them, since from "early life" they had "enjoyed the

58. *Ibid.,* p. 16. Locke too thought that a properly furnished mind had some sort of capital value.
59. *Ibid.,* p. 16.

domestic and social advantages of wealth," and no doubt the self-expansionism of capital could be felt operating in them as in the system at large. At any rate, for these men the college experience was to provide a kind of moral superstructure, a set of driving principles: "openness and activity of mind, intellectual interests, and a sense of public duty." "The country," Eliot added, with Arnoldian concern, "suffers when the rich are ignorant and unrefined. Inherited wealth is an unmitigated curse when divorced from culture." [60]

It is in the conclusion of this paragraph that Eliot's transforming vision of the university is best seen in all its power and force. In that summation Eliot presented the Harvard experience as one that converted poor and rich, or anyway those who had endured and demonstrated their "capacity and character," their open-mindedness and "sense of public duty," into one body, "the sons of Harvard." To characterize them, Eliot, more or less predictably, went back to the ancient concept of aristocracy—one of its versions, anyway. He was not, he was careful to say, using the word in the sense of "a stupid and pretentious caste, founded on wealth, and birth, and an affectation of European manners." He was rather thinking of an aristocracy of achievement:

—the aristocracy which excels in manly sports, carries off the honors and prizes of the learned professions, and bears itself with distinction in all fields of intellectual labor and combat; the aristocracy which in peace stands firmest for the public honor and renown, and in war rides first into the murderous thicket.[61]

Of course the passage makes Eliot sound like a practice run for Theodore Roosevelt, or at least for the figure that legend has made him. But it is necessary to remember that the basis of those oddly corporeal achievements was "openness and activity of mind, intellec-

60. *Ibid.,* pp. 16, 17.
61. *Ibid.,* p. 17. Does "public honor and renown" contain some sort of veiled reference to fears of municipal corruption if government should fall into the hands of unassimilated groups?

tual interests, and a sense of public duty." Eliot seems to have conceived the task and accomplishment of Harvard training as that of developing in its students, or at least some of them, a set of habits and interests, which, while not turning them from "the patrimony of knowledge"—the ethical and cultural lore with which collegians pre-Eliot were furnished so that they could carry on in recognizable fashion the callings that, being open to gentlemen, then required educational certification, and that even today carries some stigmatizing authority, though perhaps more so in English departments than elsewhere, I suppose—would somehow turn them toward a world in which, it could be said, "To observe keenly, to reason soundly, and to imagine vividly" are essential operations. What Eliot was proposing was that the Harvard degree become something more than a certificate of status or of readiness for study for one of the learned and gentlemanly professions. In the future the degree was rather to be a certificate of merit, of demonstrated potentiality for participation, at significant levels, in the affairs of the nation.

Eliot seems to have been aware of a kind of *trahison de l'élite,* or at least of a question

whether culture were not selfish; whether men of refined tastes and manners could really love Liberty, and be ready to endure hardness for her sake; whether, in short, gentlemen could in this century prove as loyal to noble ideas, as in other times they had been to kings.

And he was assuring his audience—who no doubt did express

the noble quintessence of the New England character,—that character which has made us a free and enlightened people,—that character which, please God, shall yet do a great work in the world for the lifting up of humanity—

he was assuring his audience that, in transforming a playground into Memorial Hall, Harvard was not merely commemorating past services and sacrifices of her sons from the former regime, but was also promising that, in Eliot's time, the College would be transformed to meet the new "wants of the American community" and "to serve the nation by training men to intellectual honesty and independence of mind." [62]

Of Eliot's Inaugural Address Theodore Lyman wrote, "Such a volley was never fired before in these old walls, and yet there was nothing 'radical' about it. They [the audience, but perhaps especially the Governing Boards] were one and all content with this address—most were even enthusiastic!" And well "they" might have been, for of course what they could hear in Eliot's "views of what a University should be [really, should do]" was the comforting news that the curriculum of the old New England college could and would be secularized, developed so as to be able to serve the expanding needs of the economy. "A university cannot be managed like a railroad or a cotton mill," Eliot announced in one passage of the Inaugural, perhaps for the pleasure of the Faculties. But later on he also announced, perhaps more to the liking of the rest of his audience, "The principle of divided and subordinate responsibilities, which rules in government bureaus, in manufactures, and all great companies, which makes a modern army a possibility, must be applied to the University." [63]

It is as if Eliot intended to impose Adam Smith or even Bentham on, say, Cicero; or to call in the former to redress the balance in not merely the course offering, but also in the entire governance and purpose of the University. Eliot chose his Inaugural Address to announce to the world of Harvard that the College was no longer to be a finishing school for the sons of the families whose heads were sitting before him (many of them also on the Governing Boards) or a preparatory school for the still relatively local, perhaps even family-tied professions of law, ministry, and teaching. He pledged that the College would instead become a training school where those same sons would acquire not only whatever knowledge and skills State Street and Beacon Hill demanded, but also—and far more important—the discipline and sense of responsibility that would make, or help, them to find satisfaction in the callings in which their

62. *Ibid.*, pp. 24, 26, 29.
63. *Ibid.*, p. 27.

rank, to say nothing of their inheritance, required them to function.

For us, though, whose interest is in composition and the study of the mother tongue, and who are perhaps more familiar with the children of Eliot's "poor scholars and preachers of duty," or even children of the working class, than we are with children from "refined homes," who bring with them "good breeding, gentle tastes, and a manly delicacy," for us it is rather a second pledge of Eliot's that must catch our attention. That second pledge was that Harvard was to be a selection mechanism, a recruiting ground for new men for the apparatuses of state and industry, some few of whom might even come to walk the corridors of power themselves.[64]

64. Stuart Hughes' review of his grandfather's "Autobiographical Notes" (*The New York Review*, XXI [30 May 1974], 30–33), is instructive on "new men." See especially his comment (pp. 31 and 32) about Charles Evans Hughes's antecedents and his uncertainty "as to where he belonged."

CHAPTER SIX

Freshman Composition and Administered Thought

Freshman English is our sore subject. Or at least it was until sorer subjects came along: enrollments began to decline, budgets to shrink, and Ph.D. candidates to go jobless. And even these troubles are in part epiphenomena of our troubles with freshman English. English departments were built on freshman English,[1] and their position in the university's curriculum and budget still reflects how many freshman English courses are taught. So in the sixties, when departments condensed their composition courses to a semester or a quarter, or were forced by the abolition of requirements to make freshman English voluntary, the effect reverberated through department budgets and other enterprises, from graduate programs to the sophomore survey. The decrease in number of freshman English courses coincided with the decline in college enrollments, a falling demand for high school teachers of English, and an economic recession, so that the devastation of our professional territory cannot be called pure suicide. But our inability to make sense of freshman English for ourselves and our colleagues has made hard times harder.

This inability is nothing new. In the preceding chapter Wallace Douglas showed how the composition course arose, at a moment

1. W. R. Parker, "Where Do English Departments Come From?," *College English*, vol. 28 (February, 1967), pp. 339–51.

when the modern university was being grafted onto the old aristocratic college. Eliot and Wendell were conscious to different degrees of the social need being met at Harvard, but there is little doubt that the proliferation of freshman English around the country, as the most inevitable part of the whole college curriculum, owed to the university's newly assigned task of training American professional and managerial elites. From the start, the course had a double focus: select those who display the verbal signs of a governing class; and teach them some of the verbal skills necessary for governance. But this focus was blurred in later years and in most universities by other ideals, less crass but more mystifying. Freshman English was to introduce students to literary culture, to fight the corruption of thought and language, or simply to "teach students to think" or introduce them to scholarly ideas about language or teach them principles of rhetoric.

Surrounded by mixed ideologies, and laden with other tasks in addition to the basic two, freshman English grew to confuse those who taught it. Anyone reading this is likely to have an idea how many critiques of the course and how many plans for its improvement are published each year, and what a chaos of views they represent. Furthermore, most readers will recall how generally similar were the critiques and plans of ten years ago, the repetitiveness encouraging in some quarters a shrug: *plus ça change.* . . . And a general dissatisfaction goes back much farther still, so that Leonard Greenbaum could trace a sixty-year history of proposals to abolish or drastically change the freshman course in English.[2]

In spite of the caution that should be engendered by this history, I offer here my own critique of the course—more precisely, of writing texts used in it, and of the assumptions they make about writing in college. I do so partly because an analysis of the institutions that make up our field, and that mediate literature and literacy in American colleges, would be ludicrously incomplete if silent on the subject of freshman English; partly because I think (and will later

2. "The Tradition of Complaint," *College English*, vol. 31 (November, 1969), pp. 174–87.

argue) that the way we present composition to students has something important to do with how America does politics and makes decisions; and partly because I myself have been critiquing and planning (and editing critiques and plans for *College English*) for 20 years and think now that much of that cogitation suffered from the lack of the context that I have belatedly understood and am trying to present in this book.

In 1965, as a consultant to Harcourt, Brace and Jovanovich, I wrote this memo:

What Is Wrong with Present Rhetoric Texts and the Courses They Are Written for?

The rhetorics concern themselves with writing; so do the freshman courses. Naturally enough, for a piece of writing is the only visible product of the freshman course, and we easily assume that the condition of the product is the test of the course. Also, our colleagues in other departments want students who write decently (whatever is meant by that), the outside world now and again affirms its impatience with the verbal incompetence of our graduates, and we ourselves set a high value on good prose. Nonetheless, the emphasis is unproductive and, somehow, dispiriting.

For one thing, the student will probably not do much writing—not expository writing, anyhow—after he finishes college. The writing of letters is a far more slapdash and occasional business than it was before the telephone and the automobile appeared; few keep a journal now. Much of the writing done by a businessman, an engineer, a government employee, or, indeed, a schoolteacher amounts to little more than memos or outlines—something, in any event, quite different from that carefully wrought theme, which embraces a beginning, a middle, and an end, develops its paragraphs by definition, classification, and such, and pays tribute to concrete language, tone, and simile. Aside from writers themselves, it is hard to think of occupational groups whose time is much given to formal writing: lawyers and ministers are the only two that come to mind.

And even if writing were more useful than it is, utility of this sort seems an odd justification for a freshman English course. The physics, history, and German departments would scarcely attempt to justify the presence of their introductory courses in the curriculum by an appeal to the practical value of physics, history, and German in the course of a day's work. This kind of argument applies more decorously to courses in shorthand or mechanical drawing. I am addressing myself, in other words, to the freshman English course in a liberal arts curriculum, not to business English or the like.

But my uneasiness with the notion that the freshman course is about writing follows at least as much from what happens in the course as from what such a notion implies about the purpose of the course and of the curriculum. Let me be, for the moment, even more simple minded than usual: what, then, is writing? It is the activity of moving a pen or pencil across a page in such a way as to produce an orthographic representation of sentences. No one means that, needless to say, when he speaks of a course in writing. But to me it seems that conceiving freshman English as a course in writing concentrates attention on those stages of the activity most nearly adjacent to pen-moving: thinking up transitions, choosing a sentence structure, ordering the contents of the paragraph, finding the word with the right connotation, framing an argument clearly, unmixing a metaphor, and so on. In short, "effective student writing," "decent writing," "good writing," or "effective writing" [3] (to mention the stated aims of four rhetorics that may stand for almost all the rest) is writing that gets content onto the page in a lucid, orderly, and felicitous form. The authors know that writing and thinking interlock in perplexing ways, and they have some earnest things to say about writing as a "way of training the mind in logical thought" (B & W) and as "the art of making up one's mind" (Guth), but really the textbooks are about tidying up and transcribing thought, not thinking.

Now that emphasis is no scandal. In fact, it is the emphasis most of us inevitably adopt when, in the press of academic business, we correct papers or give students advice on how to write them. But it leads to a relatively sterile conception of rhetoric, one that can only encourage in freshman courses the same barrenness that blights the textbooks. Consider the categories. There are forms of discourse—exposition, argument, narration, description, and sometimes others. Each has its methods of development—time, space, definition, reasoning, illustration, comparison, analysis, use of detail, and so on. Moreover, the writer must calculate his style, figurative language, and diction to suit his purpose. And he must see that his sentences are clear, that his paragraphs are coherent, that his entire theme is structured and unified. It is as if the student begins with a subject, amasses a quantity of stuff or a random array of particles—the content of his paper—then arranges what he has by using the prescribed methods, each where appropriate, and finally selects the right language to "express" his

---

3. Hans P. Guth, *A Short New Rhetoric*, p. v (called "Guth" in text); Jim W. Corder and Lyle H. Kendall, Jr., *A College Rhetoric* (C & K) p. 4; Cleanth Brooks and Robert Penn Warren, *Modern Rhetoric, Shorter Edition* (B & W) p. iii; and William T. Moynihan, Donald W. Lee, and Herbert Weil, Jr., *Reading, Writing and Rewriting, A Rhetoric Reader* (M, L, & W), p. v.

thoughts. We do not know much about how thought works, but surely it is not the sort of thing that can be put through paces in this manner, jumped over hurdles, poured into molds, or whatever the right metaphor is. And can a student ever do a piece of "decent writing" (or for that matter, finish any piece of writing at all) by segmenting the process consciously into word choice, sentence analysis, etc., or by running through rhetorical contingencies as a computer scans the items in its memory at each step? The authors of the rhetorics cannot believe this, yet such a view is what their schemes imply.

The treatment of writing within the categories is scarcely more promising than the line-up of categories (two of the rhetorics—B & W and M, L, & W—are greatly superior to the other two, but all labor under the same stale conception of the field). Let us consider what the authors say under three headings: choosing a subject, classification, and tone.

The phrase "choosing (or selecting or finding) a subject" locates the problem: the student has to write something, and, out of a storehouse of subjects, he will presumably pick one, rather than *making* one or making something *of* one that he already has. He must fit a theme to a subject. All four rhetorics tell him that his ready-made subject should be of the right scope for his paper, not "too broad or too narrow" (M, L, & W) and, especially, not too broad. He should find a subject on which he "can say all that has to be said about it in the number of words" he has to write, yet "ample enough to provide matter . . . for the allotted words (B & W)." "All that has to be said"? Is there a set of ideas (atoms of content) attached to each subject, so that choice of subject determines the scope of the paper (and vice versa)? Apparently so, for "no one could write a paper on a vast subject like 'Education in America' " (Guth), and the student must therefore limit himself to "one major point that can be fully explained, illustrated, and supported in the space available" (Guth). Writing is *filling up* a subject of pre-established dimensions.

Not much can come of such a rigid conception of a subject, as is evident in such language as "all that has to be said" and "fully explained." "Fully" by whose standards? The instructions for limiting a subject do not offer much help: restrict it according to your interest, according to area, kind, point of view, etc. Thus, C & K suggest that a narrative paper should cover "only a few minutes" and a descriptive one "no more than one or two walls of a room, the central figure of a painting, or a person's shoes." "George Washington" is too large a subject; "George Washington as a Colonial Planter" is not. "Education in America" should be trimmed down to something like "Science education for gifted students at Washington High," "Health" to "Acids and Alkalis." The rhetorics take no account of the fact that "Science education for gifted students at Washington High" may be, not just a narrowing of "Education in America," but an entirely different subject. They assume that the student has no compelling interest in his initial subject but wants, primarily, to write a theme. They imagine a situation in which a subject collides with a writing requirement, not with a mind. Thus, they make no allowance for the essentially creative process of exploring a topic under the impetus of a genuine intellectual need, according to the topic's own structure.[4]

Classification fares little better, conceived as a problem in writing. The rhetorics introduce it under the rubrics of "paragraph development" (C & K), "patterns of organization" (Guth), "methods of exposition" (B & W), and "developing the ideas" (M, L, & W). Only the last holds much promise, and that promise comes to little because the authors' discussion is so brief. For the most part, classification becomes a way to "sort out miscellaneous material into several major categories" (Guth) or "find a class [for a topic] that will help to develop the topic in the way you want it to go" (C & K). That is, a way to get on with the shuffling and transcribing of already attained ideas—a kind of outlining. Two of the rhetorics recognize that classification is "a way of thinking" (B & W) and "a fundamental function of mind" (M, L, & W), but, from their treatments of the subject, no student will learn more about thinking than that he should arrange his ideas in cohesive groups, and that he may classify the same material in different ways, depending upon the criterion he uses. He will not learn, notably, *how* to learn by classifying, for this conception of his task excludes learning. The world is enveloped in a ghostly paradigm of categories, and the student's job is to find the right ones, to wit, those that are "appropriate to the purpose of the paper" (Guth) and thus will help him achieve "the effect he wants to create" (C & K). Hard questions get easy answers when the problem of writing takes priority over the process of thinking.

The concept of tone lies behind the most suggestive insights of modern criticism and competes for a large piece of the territory occupied by traditional rhetoric. Perhaps, therefore, we ask too much if we expect a freshman rhetoric to penetrate very far into the subject. Even so, the books are disappointing, and in a predictable way. They say that tone should "express" or "reflect" the writer's attitude; he may "vary" or "control" it to suit his purpose. There is nothing about how he should decide what his attitude is, or how he should modulate and refine it—again, the emphasis on writing dictates the terms of the analysis and permits the authors to vault from predetermined content to the process of recording.[5] Moreover, the

4. Here a partial exception must be made of M, L, & W, which contains a good discussion of the way a subject is altered and deepened by shifts in perspective.
5. These strictures do not apply to B & W, which acknowledges the complexity of the subject in a long and satisfying discussion, considers the moral issues involved in tone, treats tone as a modification of meaning, and so on.

discussions of method concentrate on the relatively trivial matter of formal and informal writing and, within that province, limit attention mainly to choice of words. A student reading these rhetorics would not be far wrong to conclude that tone is a matter of judiciously avoiding slanginess.

It would be both uncharitable and misleading to suppose that the rhetorics adequately represent the views of their authors about literature, philosophical or historical prose, good journalism, or any reputable writing whatever. On the contrary, I think, the failure is in their inability to translate what English instructors know and practice, in the other part of their professional lives, into good sense about freshman English. I am ready to blame the failure, in large part, upon a timid conception of the freshman course and an uncreative view of writing.

To me, the description in this memo still seems accurate (for most textbooks published since and almost all that were in print in 1965). The analysis seems right as far as it goes, but partial and much too idealist (where did our "conception" of the course *come* from? How did it answer to our needs?). And the final explanation seems just wrong.

How did I propose to make the course less timid and view writing more creatively? In another memo, I explained that I thought we should fix our teaching efforts on the performance—"behind" the composing itself—of finding something to say, modifying it, deepening it. Without much originality I called this "invention," and went on to say that it draws upon

a great many capacities: those for noticing, responding, seeing consequences, making associations, imagining, being fair, seeing objections, trying models and hypotheses, interpreting, getting at assumptions, testing against moral principles, structuring, remembering, analyzing, seeing X as Y, etc. A ripening of these capacities is much of what we mean by education, for a student in whom they are well developed has great mobility in any intellectual situation. We value his theme in part because we like a skilled performance, but mainly because we see behind the performance his powers of invention, his mobility, his control over experience, his ability to extend and qualify his initial observations. Out of whatever he is given he makes more. He stands in an active relationship to circumstances and events.

The student whose invention is weak, by contrast, cannot write a good theme no matter how orderly his methods of composition. The external world is inert before him and, consequently, so is whatever discourse he reads. He has a small repertory of moves to make when confronted by an obstacle to understanding—indeed, he is unlikely to notice that there is a difficulty, or to be able to isolate it if he does smell trouble.

Well, those were beliefs drawn pretty directly from the ideology of the liberal arts, and compared with the stultifying premises of the textbooks, they still look all right to me.

Yet subsequent experience gives reason to doubt that the diagnosis was deep enough, for the remedy has been at least half-heartedly applied, and the illness persists. "Invention" and its newly coined cognate, "pre-writing," are now commonplace in the talk of English teachers, and many textbooks have concentrated on what students can do before actually writing. Taking another tack, Ken Macrorie (*Telling Writing*), Peter Elbow (*Writing Without Teachers*), Robert Zoellner[6] and others have treated writing itself as a generative and creative process; some have written textbooks; and techniques like free writing have challenged the old idea of writing as packaging. Another large group of textbooks (e.g., Kuester and Friedrich, *It's Mine and I'll Write It That Way*) have made it pedagogically respectable to treat the freshman student as an individual whose experience has validity and whose writing should express that experience rather than the ghostly paradigms that I found so deadening in 1965. And most college English teachers must by now have on their shelves a dozen or more texts that tried to meet the call for "relevance" (to which my memo in a way gave anticipatory voice). Both publishing houses and professors are quick to exploit new doctrines and new slogans, so that each new model of textbook is exemplified by trashy as well as honorable instances. But no one can claim that the discontents I and many others spoke of in the mid and late sixties have been suppressed by the industry.

Nor have courses themselves been frozen in archaic molds or teachers denied the right to experiment and change. Here I must be subjective, but my impression is that most colleges revised their

6. "Talk-Write: A Behavioral Pedagogy for Composition," *College English*, vol. 30 (January, 1969), pp. 267–320.

freshman courses once or more in the late sixties, toward what teachers saw as freedom and relevance, and that this happened most intensely at universities, where the teaching assistants who staffed the courses were themselves the politically awakened and relevance-minded undergraduates of 1960–1965. Courses have been built around engagement in current social conflicts, around media and youth culture, around exploration of self, around encounter techniques. But if in all this change there has emerged a clear line of *progress,* I've missed it. What do we teachers of English, taken as a professional group, "know" about how to teach writing that we didn't know in 1965? I have seen no wide agreement develop, comparable to the general agreement of a few years ago that *something* needed changing. On the contrary, another subjective impression is that many teachers have given up their optimistic experiments of the late sixties and early seventies, and returned to more traditional—and humble—goals. Certainly there are a lot of post-1970 textbooks that could as easily have been written in 1960; more about that in a moment.

If I'm right—if many teachers and departments had bright hopes for making their work more committed, and if those hopes have gradually changed to a corporate cynicism toward composition, has this happened because the hopes were unwarranted or because the changes made in freshman English were not the right changes? Both, doubtless. But I now assign much more weight than I did to the first possibility. I think that we hoped to accomplish more by a change of curriculum or a change of heart than was reasonable to expect, given the way our profession is organized, the way we earn our living, and the institutional setting of our work. I should have taken more seriously the suggestion, in my 1965 memo, that the texts "assume that the student has no compelling interest in his initial subject, but wants primarily to write a theme." Surely they were *right* to assume that. And my analysis of this assumption, in the later memo, now strikes me as deficient, because I thought the assumption character-ized only "the student whose invention is weak."

I went on:

This student, whose name is legion, has little impulse to make his thoughts public . . . . Composition is for him a matter of time-serving, doing what the instructor requires, submitting to a mild, necessary indignity. Writing a paper is an episode quite apart from the business of living . . . . He writes badly because he has no interest in writing because he has nothing to say.

Stirring words, Ohmann. It apparently did not occur to me that even the student who *had* things to say was in plain fact serving time, "doing what the instructor requires," and submitting—if not to an indignity, then at least to a discipline. I urged that we help students by helping them generate ideas, and I seemed to feel that in so doing we would change their basic situation. But of course the student with powers of invention is still a student—a student who can do "what the instructor requires," and do it more to the instructor's liking than can the slower or the more rebellious student.

Well, school is school, and to challenge that fact is to leave the problem of teaching composition behind. On the other hand, to *ignore* that fact is to idealize the writing situation in freshman composition. And, in my own argument, that meant proposing to help students discover more to say, without asking why they would want to say it, or to whom, or what project they might be advancing as they developed one or another idea on an assigned theme. I lamented that writing in college was "an episode quite apart from the business of living," without considering how, for students, school itself was part of the business of living, or how achievements there—including composition class—were related to rewards in and out of school. Of course I knew that writing well was a large step toward success in college and thought (with less conviction) that it would help students afterward. But I never asked myself whether the *way* it would help them afterward might in part depend on the very conventions of textbooks and of freshman composition I was deploring. Perhaps I was asking students to be free, critical, and creative in a situation where society was asking them to be of service, docile, and limited. If so, then the gulf between what writing teachers like me wanted and what we got couldn't be blamed entirely on an inability to teach freshman composition well. The course might actually *be* working well, though not to further those of its aims we particularly endorsed or were even aware of.

So now I want to look more deeply at the structure of our professional thought about writing. I want to see how it reflects those elements of the student's and teacher's situation that are usually taken for granted, either as irrelevant to pedagogy or as inevitable and thus undiscussable. And I want to consider, in this chapter and the next, how the basic structure of freshman composition might relate to the way our society carries on "the business of living" in the world outside college.

As in 1965, I take as my source textbooks for use in freshman composition courses. The procedure is open to an obvious challenge: the books are not identical with courses—they need not be a record either of what happens in classrooms or of a student's experience in learning to write college themes. But advantages overbalance this drawback. The books are accessible; classrooms are not. The books are a constant in composition courses; class practice varies more than do the texts. The books I have selected are used by a large number of students (surely over 100,000 per year); I could not get at any aspect of the experience of so many students without questioning hundreds of teachers and thousands of students. And, by however clumsy a process, the books have been selected as the reigning wisdom of our profession on the subject of writing or as the critiques of that wisdom most likely to become next year's reigning wisdom—selected by whatever makes potential authors prominent among their teaching colleagues, selected by publishers trying to predict the needs of the market, and selected by teachers through classroom adoptions, to the extent that two of the books have reached fifth editions and one book a fourth. I conclude that they do tell us what many English teachers think writing is and that they show us a good deal about how teachers present the subject to their students.

I chose the books, following the most sophisticated sampling procedures available, by taking from my shelf of recent texts (most were sent to *College English* for review) the first fifteen that my hand fell on, which present in an expository way some instruction in writing. One of the books contained an acknowledgment to me, so I dropped it from the sample, as one on which I might be even less than normally objective. So I am working here with fourteen books.[7] Most of them are rhetorics; the others combine rhetoric with a handbook (usage, mechanics, etc.) or with readings selected to illustrate rhetorical points. Apart from the common subject, they vary widely. Some are heavy on logic, some on self-discovery, some on construction of the essay. Some deal narrowly with the time-honored freshman "theme," and some teach writing of all forms and magnitudes. Some scorn mechanics, others are mainly guides to editing one's prose for correctness. Some are traditional, some irreverent. Some take account of our cultural history during the past ten years, others do not. Finally, like my 1965 sample, they vary hugely in quality, ranging from dull or puerile to vigorous and original. Most of them seem to me better than average. But my purpose here is not to sort out heroes and villains or to identify and rate the different approaches to teaching composition. Rather, I wish to see what the books, good and bad, have in common. I want to consider how assumptions that remain constant through dramatic changes in method and style may bear on the continuing "problem" of freshman English—and to what extent our work in that subject is governed by social needs and cultural assumptions that could not easily be changed by the English 101 staff.

Aims

What do the authors of the texts propose to do, to or for their student readers? To ask this question is to start with the obvious, but it may

7. Key to authors in following discussion: Clarence A. Andrews, *Writing: Growth through Structure* (Glencoe Press, 1972) *(1)*; Lyle M. Crist, *Man Expressed; The Realm of Writing* (Glencoe Press, 1971) *(2)*; Peter Elbow, *Writing Without Teachers* (Oxford University Press, 1973) *(3)*; Donald Hall, *Writing Well* (Little, Brown, 1973) *(4)*; John Herum and D. W. Cummings, *Writing: Plans, Drafts, and Revisions* (Random House, 1971) *(5)*; Billie Andrew Inman and Ruth Gardner, *Aspects of Composition* (Harcourt, Brace & World, 1970) *(6)*; Peter D. Lindblom, *Writing the Theme: A Practical Guide* (Winthrop, 1973) *(7)*; Lee J. Martin, revised by Harry P. Kroiter, *The Five-Hundred Word Theme* (Prentice-Hall, 1974) *(8)*; James M. McCrimmon, *Writing with a Purpose*, 5th ed. (Houghton-Mifflin, 1974) *(9)*; Robert Miles, *First Principles of the Essay* (Harper & Row, 1971) *(10)*; Robert Hamilton Moore, *Effective Writing*, 4th ed. (Holt, Rinehart and Winston, 1971) *(11)*; Nell Ann Pickett and Ann Laster, *Handbook for Student Writing* (Canfield Press, 1972) *(12)*; Harry Shaw, *Writing and Rewriting*, 5th ed. (Harper & Row, 1973) *(13)*; William F. Smith and Raymond D. Liedlich, *From Thought to Theme*, 3rd ed. (Harcourt, Brace Jovanovich, 1971) *(14)*.

help fix our bearings. Basically, there are three kinds of answer, none surprising.

Some of the books just offer to improve the student's writing:

to increase the individual student's ability to write as effectively as his own intellectual capacities will permit (11, p. 3)

to present basic rules that will enable the student to write clear, persuasive essays (10, p. xiii)

to turn [your] rare successes into regular occurrences and to help you succeed in all your writing efforts (7, p. 1)

And so on. These authors state their aims quite universally. They do not specify or imagine what the writing is for or under what circumstances it might be done. They think of writing as a generalized competence, one which could be applied in a variety of situations, both in and out of college. As one author says, the processes of writing are "valuable not only in composition classes but in other outreachings of the mind" (13, p. v).

A second group of authors does say what the writing specifically is for:

This book offers the freshman composition student the basic knowledge to write a short theme of the type most often required in beginning composition classes (8, p. vii)

to provide a usable reference for the student writer (12, p. iii)

to guide the student from thought to theme (14, p. v)

The writing they propose to teach is *theme* writing, in order to move students through the freshman course with credit or honor. They sell a specialized product. But they do not doubt its wider usefulness. Nor do they ally writing with any particular social end or with any group of users. "The" student—intended audience of all but one of the books—is defined only by studenthood, not by any other attributes. He is classless, sexless though generically male, timeless. The authors assume that writing is a socially neutral skill, to be applied in and after college for the general welfare.

Only a few of the authors, when they state their aims, imagine a more distant use for writing. And, with few exceptions, even they speak of that use in terms of the individual student, abstracted from society. Mainly, they offer him greater powers of thought or expression or self-discovery than he would otherwise attain. "By learning to write well, we learn methods of self-discovery and techniques of self-examination. Understanding the self allows us to move outside the self . . . . Writing well can be a basis for all thinking" (4, p. 5). The most optimistic author says that "all writing, whatever specific function it has, involves a significant element of creative effort which leads to an expression—in some degree—of the human spirit" (2, p. v). Not surprisingly, he goes on to suggest that the ability to write "is a part of the salvation of man in these troubled days" (p. vi) and sees his book as committed to "the common cause of a more meaningful human experience" (p. vii). Well, maybe so. But the salvation of man is perhaps an unrealistically broad aim for a composition text.

A middle ground exists between passing English 101 and saving mankind: the students' uses of their literacy for social or personal ends in society. Few of the texts address such questions. When they do, they often use formulations like this: "Having communication skills at your command will help you gain confidence in your own ability to function as an individual—a person who can carry his own weight in any social or business situation" (8, p. 4). Aided by composition, you can get on in the world. These authors supplement this individual motive, however, with a social one: writing and thinking logically is "most important to you . . . as a citizen of our democracy," because the "cautious approach to ideas" involved in good writing is "necessary for the survival of democracy as we know it" and "fundamental to the growth of our country" (pp. 4–5). These authors make relatively explicit what almost all assume: composition helps students get ahead in society and also helps preserve society itself in its American form. The authors see their craft functioning within the status quo. They see the users of that craft as pursuing mainly individual goals against an unchanging social backdrop. And they see students (future people, one could say) as undifferentiated, except by personality and personal goals. In short, the textbooks operate without a stated analysis of literacy in technological society and without a politics. That's predictable; as I said, gathering statements of aims in freshman texts yields few surprises. But I think that these commonplace assumptions about individuals and society explain a lot about how we conceive writing and how we teach it.

The Student's Situation

For one thing, they help explain why—in my words of 1965—"the student has no compelling interest in his initial subject, but wants primarily to write a theme," and why composition is indeed for many students "a matter of time-serving." For in abstracting "the student" away from society and history, and in treating composition as an activity apart from politics, the textbooks very narrowly fix the student's imagined circumstances and the possibilities for action there. In this they are realistic. As one writer (14) puts it "In your college work you will frequently be asked to write compositions of several hundred words" (p. 165). That is a given. The instructor requires some writing. And the writing he or she exacts from the student is defined by the form and length of the finished product. Students are to write *the theme* or *the essay* or *the composition*. And that product is "several hundred words" long, or five-hundred words long (8), or "about two pages long" (7). If the authors imagine more varied tasks, they still tend to define each by the genre of the product: "the common kinds of writing one confronts in school—term papers, theses, and so forth" (5, p. 5). The authors who talk like this are in a way fairer to their audience than those who attribute grander meanings to the act of writing. Students write bespoke themes.

Some authors do, of course, go beyond formal causes—*the theme*—in discussing the purpose of writing. One extremely popular book is called *Writing with a Purpose*. It defines "purpose" as *"the controlling decisions a writer makes when he determines what he wants to do and how he wants to do it"* (9, p. 8). Purpose, in other words, is something that emerges from the matrix of the theme assignment, rather than something the student brings from life to English 101. He discovers or determines purpose within the confines of a situation whose rationale is not of his choosing. The most durable of all these books (first copyrighted in 1937) urges that "There should be an objective for your paper other than the completion of a required assignment, for there can be no such thing as good *purposeless* writing" (13, p. 15), yet the author goes on to speak of determining one's purpose after the stimulus of being required to write. For the student to "decide" what he wants to communicate, and to whom, may seem a fairly empty freedom in this context. Similarly, another author (11) enjoins the student in the strongest terms against time-serving: "NEVER write about a topic that you do not believe is worth discussing; NEVER say anything as you write that you do not honestly believe" (p. 5); but soon after this call to integrity comes the familiar, very specific advice on "finding" a topic and "discovering" a thesis (pp. 12–13), which takes for granted the alienating situation. First the assignment, then the purpose.

Some authors do define the student's situation more broadly, seeing writing as inquiry and inquiry as a preface to action—voting, petitioning, speaking before the City Council, etc.—that is, "becoming a participating citizen" (6, p. 1). And one author rather fully characterizes the social setting of English 101, describing the division of labor in technological society, the dependence on knowledge, the way decisions often get made through a network of committees, reports, consultancies, and public relations, and the consequent power that goes with handling words and ideas (1, pp. 197–210). These writers add a dimension to the student's situation: he is preparing for a later social role and for the exercise of some power, though the conditions of his apprenticeship dictate that he be powerless now. And though these writers see the student as moving *toward* a place in society (free citizen; mover and shaker), they do not locate him in society *now*. They see him as newborn, unformed, without social origins and without needs that would spring from his origins. He has no history. Hence the writing he does and the skills he acquires are detached from those parts of himself not encompassed by his new identity as a *student*. With all good will, the authors of the textbooks cannot generate much engagement out of so abstract a student and so ahistorical a situation.

One more thing: the student is almost invariably conceived of as an individual. He acts not only outside of time and history, but *alone*—framing ideas, discovering and expressing himself, trying to persuade others, but never working *with* others to make a theme that advances a common purpose. There is one exception (3). The author here begins by saying that "many people are now trying to become less helpless, both personally and politically," that "control over words" helps, and that to gain this control "requires working hard and finding others to work with you" (p. vii). Unsurprisingly, this is the book called *Writing Without Teachers*, whose author wants an audience, especially, of "young people and adults not in school."

Finding Something to Say

Thinking of the student—a voting citizen, recall—as having none but a personal past, and as intellectually newborn in English 101, entails the strange approach to beginning a composition that struck me in 1965 and which persists today in most of the books. If English 101 is outside history and the student without qualities, then, at its inception, writing must involve locating the self on some system of coordinates. A journey has to start somewhere, and the student seems to be nowhere. Hence the characteristic way that the textbooks talk of "finding," "selecting," "discovering," or "choosing" a topic, and on making it the right size. [My favorite example this time is from (8):

Consider this thesis statement:
The United States is the best of all countries.
Proving this thesis would be easy if you were planning to write several volumes, but you cannot do it in a short paper (P. 33)

Perhaps there are students who could not do it in a multivolume tract, either.]

I want to look more closely at the assumptions on which this way of thinking is based. First, the student has a past but no history. In living eighteen years or more she has accumulated experiences, but not patterned them and not derived from them any central impetus to her present life. The experiences do not connect with one another or with what the student does next. Without bearings or momentum, and told to write a theme, how will she possibly make the first move? I think it is because the authors see the problem this way that they are in such accord about "uncovering ideas" (13).

To wit, the self is the main reservoir of possible topics.

When you can select your own subject, choose one from your own experience . . . . Like many students, you may underrate the value of your experiences, but a personal experience that taught you something about life frequently makes an interesting theme topic (14, p. 166)

Any individual knows most about himself; such subjects, therefore, as personal experiences, feelings, attitudes, and beliefs offer good possibilities (12, p. 74)

Take the first step in becoming a writer . . . : Find out things about yourself that, perhaps, you have never realized before (13, p. 7)

Topics come from your own life (4, p. 180)

One's experiences do not flow or burst into a topic, given their own energy; they are inertly there, waiting to be mined. The other point I want to make about this approach is the way it individuates the student, dividing her experience from that of other people and asking her to find what is most personal in it. She is to cultivate uniqueness.

But since the personal past is inchoate, it will not readily yield up anything as shapely as a topic. The authors must, then, supply the student with a map for exploration, a scanning procedure, or at least a shove into the territory. The least directed shove comes from the author (3) who asks his readers to do a bit of free writing, then "look to see what words or passages seemed important—attracted energy or strength. Here is your cue what to write" (p. 9). Similar advice comes from another author (4): "When we need to get an idea, we must let our inward eyes move freely over our experiences recent and past. A million topics wait for us" (p. 181).

But most of the authors guide us more in the search of inner space, and several propose elaborate schemes. One asks the student to consider ten questions like these:

1. What are my *social* beliefs? (Do I really like people? What kinds of people? What qualities do my friends have? Do I like men better than women or women better than men? Do I like children—as a general rule, occasionally, never? *Why* do I hold these attitudes?)
2. What are my *religious* beliefs? (Do I believe in God? If so, am I a transcendentalist, a Baptist, a Roman Catholic, or do I simply believe in some sort of Supreme Mind? If not, am I agnostic or atheistic? *Why* do I hold these beliefs?) (13, p. 7)

And so on through political and moral beliefs, what I want and expect to be five years from now, what I consider the world's major problem, what would be the greatest imaginable happiness for me, whether I am an observant person, and how I became the way I am. According to the author, it is impossible to think about these ten questions "without having dozens of ideas occur to you," some of which "will be topics about which you could write with some interest and possibly some pleasure" (p. 7).

Another textbook encourages the student—"You *do* have material for writing good papers . . . . You have had a variety of experiences . . ." and then offers a list of 46 subjects (advertising, aggression, ambitions, animals, boys, buildings, cars, etc.) on each of which "you could easily write a five-hundred-word paper." (Compare "show and tell," in the first grade.) Having "selected" a subject from this list or from "a quick mental tour" of what the student has learned in school, she should divide it up systematically: "all sports" into amateur and professional; amateur into college, high school, and other; high school into football, baseball, and so on. Then "select [again] one division you know enough about," "rack your brain" for specific topics in this division ("The Value of High School Football to the Player"), then "select [again] the one you best understand, and you are under way" (8, pp. 28–30).

Another book provides an even more detailed map.

Take out a blank sheet of paper. On the left-hand side, in a column down the margin, copy this list:

Politics	Transportation
War	Social Studies
Education	Housing
Sports	Animals
Jobs	Love
Entertainment	

Somewhere in this list, or any similar list, some flicker of interest will appear. A little bell, a small light, some signal will tell you when you've found a general subject area for your assignment.

From the word that rings the bell, the student should draw a line to the center of the page and write the word again, then begin to subdivide graphically—for example, from "education" to "college education" to pre-law education. Finally, the student can limit the topic further by using words that specify

by number:	*the first*	*three examples*
by quality:	*the best*	*the most difficult*
by time:	*in 1949*	*in the 20th century*
by place:	*in Florida*	*in my neighborhood*
by possession:	*my*	*Mr. Smith's* (7, pp. 2–6)

All these procedures are intended to be—and probably are—quite practical. Students do get paralyzed when told "write something." What I mean to emphasize in describing these propaedeutics is the lack of organic connection between the student's warehouse of experiences and ideas and her choices of action at the present moment. She is to rummage through the closets of her mind as if they were filled with other people's possessions, until she discovers (*selects*) one suitable for the present occasion. And the condescending tone of the above quotations is ample witness to the alienation produced by these assumptions. Alienation: separation from one's self. Alienation: estrangement from the fruits of one's work. Alienation: powerlessness.

After finding, and narrowing down, a topic, the student must frame a central thesis about it. Many of the recommended methods for doing so are as mechanical as the procedures for finding a topic. One book with a highly pragmatic flavor tells the student to make a thesis *statement:*

(1) select a single, limited subject (subject area), and (2) say something specific *about* the subject (predicate area).

A compound sentence is rejected because it has two subjects. The "predicate area" of the thesis statement presents the writer's "point of view." It must be limited, argumentative, meaningful, and exact. With the help of a diagram the student is shown how to select a predicate, and therewith a point of view (registration day was *confusing*, as opposed to *tiring, pleasant*, etc.) (8, pp. 32–7). Though seldom executed quite so ruthlessly, this approach is common: the problem of saying something is reduced to that of having a thesis and that, in turn, to the problem of forming a pivotal *sentence* with certain features.

Fully to appreciate how these books handle the topic of invention, notice one other oddity in standard operating procedure: every book that systematically addresses the question of acquiring something to say tells the student first to find a topic and then derive the thesis.[8] So natural is this order to a situation in which people write at other people's bidding, that its oddity only appears when you widen the context. But do so, and the priority vanishes. People have concerns, needs, impulses to celebrate or condemn, to compact with others or to draw battle lines against them, to explain, appeal, exhort, justify, criticize. Such concerns, needs, and impulses are what lead people to write (and to speak), when they are not writing to measure. And such concerns are much more like theses than like topics. Unalienated writing *begins* in the feeling and belief that rise out of one's life and tries to concentrate them—perhaps by "narrowing the topic," among many other ways. Textbook writing begins in the nowhere of the assignment, moves into the unbordered regions of the student's accumulated experiences, settles on one region—the topic—and *then* looks around for feelings and beliefs to affix to that topic, with supporting details to be added afterward.

Now of course the sequence of topic first, thesis second, was not

8. The books that tell students to begin with free writing or free association—notably (3) and (4)—may, in fact, make a different assumption: namely, that the student has in mind impulses to action, urgencies, proto-arguments, as well as topics, and that free writing can release both topic and thesis at once.

devised by textbook writers to pain students and keep freshman composition forever in business. Given limited enough purposes, they are right to make this assumption, and any other would be mystifying.[9] But though the assumption has pragmatic warrant, it nonetheless contributes to the disheartening triviality of much writing in college. The sample topics developed in the textbooks are a giveaway:

The Benefits of Sports to Factory Workers Employed in a Four-Day Work Week (7, p. 6)

The Treatment of Football Players by the Teachers (8, p. 30)

The Value of Intramural Sports (14, p. 170)

How to Find Out about Summer Jobs (13, p. 17)

Placing a Value on Coins (12, p. 75)

The Vocabulary of Registration (11, p. 12)

And the sample theses:

The vocabulary of registration makes an already confusing process almost incomprehensible (11, p. 12)

Living in a city has four main advantages over living in a smaller town (12, p. 76)

Those who plan ahead and apply early can get a summer job (13, p. 16)

A checking account provides a convenient and safe method of payment (14, p. 184)

Many students on our campus care more about grades than about learning (10, p. 23)

Varsity football should be discontinued at Consolidated High (8, p. 21)

My college education should provide me with preparation for a meaningful occupation, general knowledge and background for conducting my life, and the ability to get along with other people (7, p. 45)

These propositions smack of the seventh grade. But they are offered for college students, and their triviality is the natural outcome of "finding a subject" and then finding something to say about it.

9. Compare the various sayings of (2) about writing—for example, "it's the stuff of which men communicate to each other and testify to each other's heart and soul" (p. 1); how well would this commendable idea help a student get his bearings in most composition courses?

Arguing

When the student, without a history and without a place in society, does stake out a location—a topic and a thesis—where does he go from there? This depends partly on what pattern he chooses—description, narration, exposition, argument, etc. Of these, I want to focus on the last, since argument is the most deeply embedded in an imagined social matrix. By argument some idea of how people influence one another, relate thought and action, derive convictions and change society is implied.

In keeping with their ahistorical bent, the freshman English textbooks place argument in a highly idealized setting. They see rational persuasion as almost the sole means by which people change people. Persuasion, in turn, is a largely formal matter of shoring up a proposition with the right kinds of support. And, of course, this means that the authors lift the dynamic of argument out of the lives of arguer and audience. Generally, they envision no prior alignment of people and forces in society that cannot be overcome by a well-conducted argument; and, if they do, they put it under the rubric of "closed minds," regrettably beyond the reach of argument.[10] In short, they work from a crippled theory of where ideas come from and how they take hold. What they say about argument is not exactly *wrong*, and much of it is useful as far as it goes; but it leaves out so much that its applicability in non-academic society must be limited indeed. A number of the authors would surely endorse the view of the author (4) who writes that "Most of the time, we persuade by being reasonable—and also by seeming so" (p. 198). But who are "we," and what are the direct object and complement of "persuade"? My best chance of persuading an enemy might be to combine intimidation with an appeal to his self-interest. Carrot and stick. Persuading an ally whose consciousness is close to mine may require even less reasonableness—allusions, hints, and reminders may do it. But if I, my audience, and the issue at stake are all

10. Author (9) advises the student to ignore those who agree with him already or who are unpersuadable, and to address those in the middle—"perhaps a majority"—who can be won over by a sound argument (p. 335). Rhetorical triage?

unspecified, then argument will be a bloodless set of formalities: "sometimes we write arguments, in which we try to persuade the reader of a thesis" (p. 196). The reader may be "the opposition" (p. 201), but he has no concrete relation to the arguer; they are outside the social nexus. Thus, "We should seek to imagine all possible rebuttals to our position, and answer them" (p. 201)—as if rebuttals were just a row of logical possibilities that could be picked off like ducks in a shooting gallery. Back in reality, some rebuttals are answered with irony, some with innuendo, some with invective; some are ignored; some are begged; and some (even) are met with point-by-point rejoinders. It depends on what openings the particular situation affords, who is in on the argument, and what is at stake.

But, out of history, the imagined writer and reader of these texts are prophylactically sealed in an environment of disinterestedness. The author with the fullest (and in some ways best) treatment of persuasion advises, "When you have decided clearly what you yourself believe, you need to think as carefully about why others disagree" (11, p. 320). Fine. But soon he is rephrasing, "you must . . . examine carefully the case against you. Why have your opponents adopted the other side, particularly on the major issues?" *Case*, *opponents*, *issues*: he is thinking of it as a *debate* (and calls it that).[11] Now a debate, of the most restricted academic kind, is precisely an argument abstracted from history and from the lives of the participants. You can argue either side of the "case." And there are no consequences. I don't contend that this author (11) thinks of all argument this way, but the model is significantly apparent. And it presents a predictably naive view of how minds are changed: "writing the argument consists in leading the presumably hostile reader through the same processes of thought that you have yourself gone through" (p. 320). But so many paths of thought are closed off by interest. A particular "thesis" is knit into the whole belief structure of its holder—into his "consciousness." Imagine Cesar Chavez leading the brothers Gallo through the "processes of thought" by which he arrived at his position.

11. Author (8) says that the "thesis statement must be the trumpet call that sounds the challenge—you on one side and your reader on the other" (p. 34). It's like choosing sides for a game of capture the flag.

This author (11) defines argument as a kind of writing "in which evidence and reasoning are presented persuasively in order to convince a possibly hostile reader that certain opinions are preferable to others" (p. 273). The language is telling. An "opinion" sounds like something you can easily put on or off, something well removed from your circumstances and needs. Hence, you can choose from an array of opinions those that are "preferable," by some objective measure. I think of two laymen matching their opinions about the existence of life on Mars.

Most of the texts use similar terms when they define and discuss argument:

After proposing . . . a statement, the writer must take measures to make it convincing . . . . He must defend it with evidence (10, p. 13)

To write a persuasive paper, you must first identify the central idea or proposition your paper will develop. Then select specific materials to support your argument . . . (12, p. 26—this from authors who have just said that such a paper tries to "influence the reader to act")

You are trying to explain to the reader that your point is a sound one. Your paper will have no other purpose than to support the validity of this main point, which you will argue by presenting all the logical reasons and sound evidence you can muster (8, p. 34)

In attempting to prove, illustrate, or explain a particular thesis, many points will appear as possible supports. You should carefully evaluate all the points in relation to your purpose, and select only the strongest and most important . . . (7, p. 79)

The argument consists of a "statement," "idea," "proposition," "point," or "thesis," plus evidence and reasons.

These latter resemble theme topics, in the view of the authors: they lie in various storehouses of the mind and can be brought out when needed. Thus phrases like "select specific materials," "select only the strongest" points, and "all the logical reasons . . . you can muster," in the quotations above. An argument is an *artifact* built of "materials."

When you have gathered a series of valid arguments, you must organize them (4, p. 203) the main divisions in the support [of a thesis statement] are usually reasons (6, p. 327)

argumentation is a process of reasoning in which a coherent series of facts and judgments is arranged to establish a conclusion (14, p. 119)

rational arrangement of material (11, p. 317)

These structural metaphors run through the whole treatment of the subject, confirming my belief that the authors have idealized argument, leaving out process, society, and most of the material world. Here, in the textbook world, ideas come from nowhere, interact in arguments, and, if arranged correctly, change people's minds. I don't deny that rational argument plays a role in changing minds; obviously it does. But to understand how it does, and within what limits, one must surely consider how the ideas people have relate to the ideas they *need* to have, not because of logic but because of their material and social circumstances. Argument divorced from power, money, social conflict, class, and consciousness is pseudo-argument.

But perhaps pseudo-argument is good training for entry into a society with a pseudo-politics (Sheldon Wolin's epithet). Where basic decisions—building the society around automobiles and oil, destroying Vietnam—are mainly made and confirmed through a network of bureaucracies and other complex organizations, by processes almost imperceptible to the "citizen" and certainly inaccessible to him through official politics; where both political parties share a vast ideological common ground; where the media constantly show people that everyone's interest, more or less, lies in increasing consumption of ever more numerous products; where class conflict has at least until just the other day, been unmentionable; and where the ordinary technician or manager or professional or white collar worker (i.e., the college student of yesterday) has little role in making social choices except to facilitate and sometimes narrowly modify basic policies that are mainly taken for granted: such a society, if its dominant groups could specify what kind of education the privileged half of youth would receive, would want argumentation taught in pretty much the way these books present it.

The study of abstractly rational persuasion (a) plays down materially rooted conflict of interest, (b) supports the ideology of the open society with decisions democratically and rationally made by citizens all of whose arguments have an equal chance of success, and (c) trains students to be skillful at putting into a standard and "objective" form arguments in which they have no great personal stake—arguments, in fact, that someone else may have required them to construct. Perhaps each stable society achieves the kind of argumentation that is most helpful in preserving its status quo.

Let me be clear about my own argument. I do not, of course, hold that the Rockefellers and du Ponts or the Kissingers and (Gerald) Fords are managing English 101, or even that they would do it to their best advantage if they were. I am holding, rather concretely, that an educational system is responsive to the personnel needs of the economic system; and, less concretely, that the educational system will support the tacit ideas of the dominant groups in the society.[12] Thus, if I say that the sections on argument in most of these books could be titled "Argument for Organization Men," I do not mean that this is the result of anyone's explicit design, but only that the parts of a society fit well together—except in times like the late sixties when conflict came out in the open and when educational systems suddenly appeared oppressive to their clients and dysfunctional to the leaders of society.

So I would now amend my 1965 critique of freshman composition. Though I still see in many of the texts a deadening narrowness of conception, I no longer think that we could collectively make our writing about writing, and our teaching of it, larger in spirit by internal reform, such as emphasizing invention and creativity. Such improvements would still have us teaching a kind of composition adrift from social process, and from the social identities of both students and teachers.

12. I cannot *prove* my thesis—which is to be sure a far from novel one. But I am trying to provide, in this chapter and in the whole book, enough instances drawn from one corner of the educational system so that my thesis will be convincing to those (reasonable) readers whose understanding of the world is not totally at odds with mine.

And suppose we did somehow manage to bring these identities into the English 101 classroom and the freshman theme. That would mean a very different sort of teaching from what we and our employers are used to. It would mean having students develop their writing skills in the process of discovering their political needs, and as an aid in achieving those needs. It would mean encouraging students to form alliances with one another based on real life interest, and letting the skills of writing grow through collective work. And of course some of these alliances would come into conflict, since students are of different classes, races, sexes, ages.[13] In short, it would mean bringing politics—everyone's politics—into composition, rather than just the politics of the establishment, which are now implicit in the course and made to look like no-politics. And if we did this we would quickly lose our apparent usefulness to those with the most at stake in the system, and in the process lose our own small but secure place in it. In short, I no longer see freshman composition as *perversely* confining. Its thinness is socially useful. I would not look to change freshman English a whole lot without changing American society, too.

Organization (and the Organization Man)

In the books' discussions of "finding a topic" and of argument I found two common tendencies: to divorce writing from society, need, and conflict and to break it down into a series of routines. These strategies are pedagogically handy. They also accord well with the kind of thinking and talking and writing demanded in the large institutions where most mind-workers earn their livings—with what I will discuss in a later chapter as *planning*. Much of what the books say about writing should be seen in this context. Their teaching on the organization of a paper is, along with their teaching on argument, a particularly clear instance.

Here structural metaphors and the idea of the theme as artifact

13. I am thinking of the plan for teaching outlined in Brent Harold's "Beyond Student Centered Teaching: The Dialectical Materialist Form of a Literature Course," *College English*, vol. 34 (November, 1972), 200–14.

are, of course, inescapable and not so significant. What I would like to emphasize instead is the problem-solving approach to the organization of a piece of writing. A *problem* (of which more in Chapter Seven) is a chunk of reality distanced from the self and made objective. There it can be manipulated, and a solution found. To cast something as a problem is to remove conflict from it: we have a common interest in solutions to problems.

The books treat organization this way. "Every paper raises its own problems, and one of the choices the writer must make is to select one overall organizational pattern from among several that might work almost equally well" (11, p. 80). The writer needs a heuristic to make his way through raw materials that are at the outset disorderly.

As you gather material and clarify your purpose, you will begin to discover the plan by which your paper can best be organized . . . . Most materials naturally fall into one pattern of organization rather than another (9, p. 46)

No one can write an effective paper without a plan for it . . . . One useful means of planning a paper is a formal outline (13, p. 287)

The student is to project his materials onto one plan or another, or find and exploit the plan that is concealed within his materials.

Either way, the books suggest that abstract plans do exist and that the student can choose from among a finite number of them. As one author (11) says, above, "one of the choices the writer must make is to select one overall organizational pattern"; and he goes on to "consider the major patterns that are available to the writer." So does another (9); after saying that most "materials" fit easily into one "pattern of organization," he describes "the patterns most commonly used: illustration, comparison and contrast, analogy, classification, process, and cause and effect." Other authors (12) tell the student first to "select" details, then decide which "method of development" to use in presenting them: "There are several common methods of development to choose from, such as example or illustration, comparison and contrast, cause and effect, and definition" (p. 80). The authors of one book (14) tell the student that to achieve coherence he must "first arrange your materials" in order:

"The kind of order you use will depend on your purpose" (p. 85). They proceed with a different, but equally familiar, set of ready-made patterns—narrative, descriptive, and expository.

Even when the list of models is eccentric, the underlying idea usually remains the same. Thus, one author (8) offers only one procrustean model: an introductory paragraph of 50 to 75 words with a thesis sentence at the end, followed by three developmental paragraphs of 150 to 200 words each, and a concluding statement. Its theory of organization is quite similar, however: "Assuming you have discovered that you have something to say, you cannot begin to write it down effectively until you have a fairly specific idea of the product you are supposed to create" (pp. 7–8). The "product" is of external origins. And another author (1) divides "basic patterns" into two kinds, the "organic, which derives from the subject, and the classical, which derives from the application of an external form to the subject." His list of external patterns runs to sixteen, including some of the standard ones, but also the *"in media res"* pattern, the "disclaimer," the "elimination pattern" (eliminate possible solutions till only one is left), the "interview pattern," etc. (pp. 144–7). But he, like the others, speaks of a "choice" of patterns. This language of choosing or selecting or applying patterns portrays the student as surveying a batch of "materials" that he has gathered, and then fitting them into a pre-existent form. This procedure (a useful one, undeniably) not only distances the composition from the student, it also domesticates it within social forms.

Some of the heuristics emphasize process, rather than pattern. Most elaborately, one pair of authors (5) has the student begin with a helter-skelter "zero-draft," perhaps three times as long as the finished paper will be. Then he is to "search the draft for passages that seem to be sufficiently long and unified," use scissors to cut them out, store them in a binder, then sort these promising passages into batches that cluster around subtopics, consolidate topics, shuffle the clusters into various tentative orders, then write the *first* draft, incorporating material discarded earlier where appropriate (pp. 97–102). Actually, there are many more steps than these. The authors are trying to give the student a foolproof recipe. A machine could be programmed to follow it. Curiously, the most iconoclastic of the texts (3) recommends a similar procedure, though not nearly so regimented: start with free writing, let "centers of gravity" emerge, then edit.

Editing means figuring out what you really mean to say, getting it clear in your head, getting it unified, getting it into an organized structure, and then getting it into the best words and throwing away the rest. (p. 38)

But the author does distinguish sharply between the early stages of the process—"growing"—and the editing stage: "Editing is almost invariably manipulative, intrusive, artificial, and compromising" (p. 38)—a necessary evil. He recognizes clearly the external pressures that govern process at this point and the end of the spontaneity and discovery he so values. For this author, though, the necessary distancing and objectifying are only an intermediate stage: the writers he addresses will not package their product in a size and shape made standard by the organization of technological society, they will put their writing before the teacherless writing group, where it enters again into process—social process this time.

The Reader

For one author (3), writing is "a transaction with other people" (p. 76). The readers are real, if somewhat arbitrarily assembled. Furthermore, they are not just an audience. They comment, respond, point to what in the writing makes them feel a certain way. At least at this stage of writing, they are collaborators. And another (3) imagines people present at other stages, too: "If you are stuck writing or trying to figure something out, there is nothing better than finding one person, or more, to talk to" (p. 49). These improvised audiences are neither in a position of power over the writer (teacher, boss), nor in submission, at a distance, to the writer's authority and expertise. They are equals, and the writing is strongly affected by them.

None of the other books places the writer in such a concrete social situation. Their abstraction of writing from history, society, and politics encourages an abstract view of the reader. And the conception of writing as problem solving tends to reduce the reader to part of the problem. For whatever reasons, the reader—like "the" student writer—shapes up as classless, sexless, and fairly bloodless.

For one thing, the student is not to see himself as already having a relationship with his readers; readers are selected or imagined or invented, *arbitrarily,* along with subjects, theses, and patterns. "When we come to write we must decide who and what our audience is" (1, p. 15). Decide? What kind of writing have "we" undertaken to do, that we have not conceived an audience as integral to it? The anomaly is sharpest in one book (7), which takes students through the selection of a topic and the framing of a thesis, and *then* says, "At this point in your planning, you need to consider two further aspects: audience and purpose." It is necessary to "identify" the audience, because its background will affect the content and organization of the composition (p. 47). The student who follows this plan is asked to proceed a long way in developing his ideas before envisioning the social situation in which he is to give them utterance.

With the reader such a relatively minor element in the writing situation, it is not surprising that some of the books go no farther than, for example, advising students to keep a consistent point of view because "A reader is likely to become confused if you change from the past to the present tense, from a singular to a plural noun, from an objective, matter-of-fact tone to a subjective one, or from the active to the passive voice of the verb" (14, p. 107) or that some of the advice sounds a little like public relations wisdom: "try to project a definite, positive image of yourself and your character . . . . Praise your opposition (with restraint). . . . Give up part of your argument, admit that your position is weak (only in a minor way)" (8, p. 76). Neither is it surprising that most of the books see the reader as primarily a mind to persuade, or to inject with certain new information:

If the intended reader knows very little about a subject, you must try to present the material as simply as possible . . . . But if he knows the subject in detail, you can use terminologies and complex references. . . . If the intended reader is unknown, you must include all details needed for *clear* development (12, p. 102)

Of course all the authors know, and some say, that writing does many things beside transmit information and opinion. But in counseling the student about the reader, they seem magnetized by the constative fallacy (J. L. Austin's term). I think this happens because they don't imagine the writer and reader as *already* related to each other, socially and dynamically.

Nowhere does this seem plainer than where the authors characterize imagined audiences, to give students an idea of how to adjust rhetoric to readership. Audiences are painted in homely terms: "You use words with your best friend that you do not use with your grandmother," and similarly in writing, "If we write a letter to the college newspaper, we choose the words from a pool different from the one we use when we write a thank-you letter to an aunt" (4, p. 38). Or chattily: one book lists ten likely audiences running from "your parents and other relatives" to "people who work for government agencies," dwelling on employers:

Here is a very complex situation, especially in a large organization. Large organizations tend to be multi-layered. . . . The president probably was a high school dropout. In any case he is also the hardest one to write for. . . . The stupid ones appear only in Hollywood films (1, p. 16).

This book categorizes readers by education, willingness to read, social level, general interests, and so on: its breakdown is more sophisticated than that of any other text in my pile. Yet the audience is still divorced from the writer, and all the analysis culminates in a final injunction to determine not only the "general level" of the audience, but their "individual differences": "You can't please everyone and you shouldn't try to. There is a mean in every case which you should strive for—and let the extreme idiosyncrasies fall by the way" (p. 18). And most of the books fall a good way short of the social awareness displayed by this one. They class readers as engineers and artists, hostile and friendly, specialized and general, mainly for the purpose of finding the most appropriate tone or level of diction or ration of detail. Writer and reader engage—to repeat—outside time, history, and real circumstances.

Style

Among these textbooks, there are some that willingly adopt the models of organizational and administrative writing, and others that do not. My preceding selections have, I hope, shown that even the resisters adopt more than they wish of the administrative cast of mind. In discussing style, however, they have a chance to declare their allegiance—perhaps because the great world cares less about style than do English teachers.

Those who accept the idea of writing as problem solving may use almost the same language I am using: "What matters most is that you see style as conscious choice and realize that there are many solutions to each problem in communication" (8, p. 190). (Though this writer hedges his bets, by going on to say that "your style is *you*.") The textbook authors talk about style as a collection of "devices" to "reinforce the meanings of . . . words (11, p. 191) or as "choices" that are a "product of purpose" and help implement it (9, p. 169) or as something to be "polished" for clarity at the end of the writing process (10, p. 160). They urge the student to form his style consciously and according to pragmatic needs—for efficiency.

The resisters, in a more romantic tradition, invite the student to see style as expression. We "construct the world of our own prose style" (4, p. 25). Less organically, style is *"what you as an individual contribute to the expression of what you have in mind to say and write"* (13, p. 37), or "the flair with which the message is written" (2, p. 39). Both groups agree on one romantic tenet, though: style comes from the unique individual psyche:

Every writer must acquire his own style . . . . Your style reflects your personality . . . (13, p. 44)

Style relates to personality . . . always personal (2, pp. 39–40)

the need for originality . . . farm your daydreams for original verbal images that express feeling (4, pp. 76–7)

The writers split, then, into those who make style an overriding expression of personality and those who subordinate it to immediate practical needs. Writing for the self or writing for the task at hand. Here, as often in bourgeois thought, self-fulfillment and doing one's job appear to be at odds. The textbooks—with one notable exception (1)—say nothing about the social context of style or about the politics of style. They do not open up the possibilities, so richly developed in American discourse recently, of style rising out of race, class, or group.

Usage

But of course freshman English does teach the style, broadly defined, of the managerial and professional classes. Style of thinking, style of work, style of planning and organizing, style of language. For most of a hundred years, the purpose was fairly explicit. Composition was to train students to speak and write as gentlemen, and it did so by affirming the prestigious language habits of society and discouraging or shaming other habits by ruthlessly applying a few rules of usage and shibboleths of grammar.

English teachers as a group have become more sophisticated about language in the last twenty years, and you will not find in many textbooks the idea that one usage or dialect is absolutely correct. In giving up this myth, however, our profession has been left scrambling to find another—one that will justify our practice, now as before, of teaching language in a way that preserves class lines. That means that a number of textbooks that do not mention class or power when they discuss argument or organization or style do mention class and power, however indirectly and with however much embarrassment, when they discuss usage and dialect. Needless to say, this necessity can be disconcerting for teachers in community colleges, whose class position is most marginal. The authors of (12), for example, short-circuit the question by beginning,

Rightly or wrongly, people judge a person's education and intelligence on the basis of his vocabulary, spelling, and word choice. Both in school and out, using words inappropriately puts you at a disadvantage. (p. 124)

Having introduced class bias as an undiscussable fact of language and life, they then hide the issue behind a mystifying idea of "most people": "you write 'I have known him a week,' rather than 'I have knowed him a week,' because 'I have known him a week' is more acceptable to most people" (p. 151). By what count? And which people?

The three books in my collection that have attained fourth or fifth editions, and presumably reached the largest number of students by virtue of their appeal to the largest number of teachers, all strike positions on usage, two of them in extended discussions. And each of them at least mentions the social and economic issues. One author (9), who comments on grammar and dialect in a scholarly, descriptive way, is the most reticent of the three on the social implications of using one or another brand of English; he ties his definition of "standard" to education:

standard English is the usage of educated speakers and writers of English. The schools, which are committed to helping young people to educate themselves, generally stress this dialect. (p. 135)

In shifting the issue to the schools, this author (9) effectively neutralizes it, since schools are supposed to be good for everyone, an avenue toward equality. But here and there he sounds a different note: "following the conventions of language may help [the student] communicate better and so make him a more powerful person" (p. 352). One might ask, "communicate better" to whom?

The other two are more explicit. In his foreword, one author (13) concludes by saying,

an attitude of "anything goes" can be, and repeatedly is, costly to students in business and social affairs. The late Will Rogers was genuinely humorous when he remarked: "A lot of people who don't say ain't, *ain't* eatin'." And yet, in certain clearly defined circumstances, using *ain't,* misspelling a word, employing an unidiomatic expression, or saying *went* when *gone* is indicated can cost a job, advancement, a social opportunity, or even a potential friend. English composition has many values, one of which is practicality. (p. vii)

The author repeats the Rogers quip 83 pages later, to introduce the section on usage, but without commenting on its genuine humor. He goes on, "The use of 'good English' will not guarantee success in any area of your life; but whatever goals you set, ignorance of standard practices in speech and writing will make those goals more difficult to attain." This and the caution about "ain't" seem to me among the most important (and unpleasant) truths revealed to students in all fourteen textbooks.

One author (11), like another (9), is a bit more oblique: "having entered college, you are preparing yourself for admission to the educated minority, and you need to know the minority dialect used by educated people." But the educated minority and its dialect have other roles in society than to be vessels of knowledge and culture: educated English is "the dialect in which the nation's major work is done" (p. 453), whereas "vulgar English" is "language in well-worn overalls . . . not used by those who have learned the standard forms" (p. 252). The metaphor of the overalls, in neat opposition to the phrase "major work," tells us the lay of the land better than the talk of a "minority dialect" of educated people.

English teachers, like their books, do teach students that a speaker or writer runs a constant risk of betraying through his language some shameful inferiority. A recent article shows that both high school and college English teachers proclaim standards of usage they themselves, along with many of the most famous writers of English and American history, often violate. The author, Mary Vaiana Taylor, goes on to suggest that

English teachers establish and protect absolute standards for linguistic performance because in so doing they are establishing and protecting their own prestige, and they feel it is necessary to establish and protect it because they are themselves linguistically insecure.[14]

Others have shown that these insecurities are greatest among the middle and lower middle class and among women—the groups to which most schoolteachers of English belong. So the anxiety and the sense of linguistic hierarchy they teach to students are deeply

14. "The Folklore of Usage," *College English*, vol. 35 (April, 1974), p. 761.

involved with class and status and are felt by English teachers themselves.

The textbooks did not invent standard English, much less the class structure and racial structure of American society. That most of them endorse it is no scandal. Most do not do so consciously; their endorsement is an inescapable consequence of the anxieties I have just mentioned and of setting out to teach composition as a means to advancement in the world outside. Some kinds of language and thought work better than others toward this end. Textbooks and English teachers try to teach those skills. In the process most teachers tell students (and themselves) that these skills are the *best* uses of language and mind—not the skills of a particular class in a particular productive system. This is mystification, and I have tried in this chapter to show how it works, by suppressing the social and potentially political content of English.[15]

But I don't want to hold English teachers specifically to blame for this failure of vision. Certainly, economists and political scientists have more to answer for. And the whole university has tacitly and understandably adopted and acted upon an ideology that aligns professors' interests with those of governing groups outside the university.

15. Somewhere in this chapter I need to say that I, too, have written a "rhetoric" for freshman composition courses, in collaboration with Harold C. Martin and James H. Wheatley: *The Logic and Rhetoric of Exposition*, 3rd. ed. (New York: Holt, Rinehart, & Winston, 1969). I want neither to claim exemption for it from the criticism offered here nor to indulge in breast-beating. It's a scholarly book, as composition texts go (and—there may be a connection—a very limited commercial success). It doesn't talk about students and composition courses at all, but about "the" inexperienced writer, and mainly it offers theoretical perspectives on writing. This makes it susceptible to two of my central charges here: my fellow authors and I did not differentiate one student from another, and we did not offer an analysis of our readers' places in historical process. And certainly our treatment of argument (I wrote it) commits the sin of abstraction from circumstances. On the other side, even from my present standpoint the book does not seem to trivialize the process of writing or make it an alienated, manipulative skill. There is a good deal in the book about writing as action and interaction, about the way writing implies and partly constructs a social "world," and even about "the politics of writing."

I also want to note, here, that, since writing this chapter, I have reread William E. Coles, Jr.'s "Freshman Composition: The Circle of Unbelief" in *College English*, vol. 31 (November, 1969, pp. 134–42), and found there an analysis in some ways close to this one. I am happy to acknowledge a forgotten, but apparently significant, influence.

Also: How would we have to write our composition manuals to escape this kind of criticism? Each book would have to define its audience in quite unaccustomed terms: working class black students, upper middle-class white students heading for the professions, etc. Each book would have a clear social aim, with a twofold job of raising social and rhetorical awareness (theory) and teaching composition as social and political practice, seeing the English classroom and the university as arenas of struggle. As things stand now, few colleges and few commercial publishers could accommodate such a conception.

CHAPTER SEVEN

Writing, Out
in the World

Imagine, now, an extremely long Chapter 6½, missing from this volume. In it I present empirical research on how freshman English affects the student, especially in the more elite universities. I trace, not so much improvement of skills, as inculcation in styles of problem solving and in preferred modes of thought—showing how young people bound for high places in society learn what a successful (an *admired*) piece of writing is and how to make one. Then I work out from that elaborate demonstration in two ways. First, I show how the values of freshman English, both professed and unconscious, filter "down" into secondary and elementary schools. Here, I emphasize the attitudes toward language and its uses that future schoolteachers acquire from their own university teachers and textbooks and the ways schoolteachers apply those attitudes in rather different surroundings. And, second, I show quite precisely how freshman English itself responds to the needs of powerful groups in the larger society. I show what kinds of intellectual training are most wanted by corporations and government among their managerial recruits and also what self-disciplines and what tacit beliefs about society and social process. And I show how these needs are communicated, very inefficiently to be sure, through the internal structure of the academic community and how they leave an unseen but deep imprint on the teaching of writing. Then I am ready for a final step:

to detail educational profiles of a select group of contemporary leaders, such as influential theorists, government policy-makers, chairmen of boards. And I am able to show, fairly concretely, how they learned the kinds of writing and thinking in which they have so distinguished themselves.

In this imagined chapter I *prove* what in actuality I can but state: that there are complex causal relationships among the university teaching of composition, social class, and the management of our society. Since Chapter 6½ would take ten or fifteen years to write, I leave it unwritten. Without it, Chapters Six and Seven are to each other as two end links of a chain that is mostly under water: you know the other links are there, but not how many or of exactly what size and shape.

Specifically, I have in Chapter Six offered an analysis of the goals freshman English sets for young people some of whom will become the leading theorists and decision-makers of the year 2000 unless the world order changes by then. Now, in Chapter Seven, I offer three sample analyses of writing and thinking done by people in such positions of leadership in roughly the years 1965 to 1970. I hope to show that the writing of the powerful and influential shares some characteristics with the required writing of their college-age sons and daughters; that these characteristics are fairly important to the style of thinking and planning that guides the most powerful country in the world; and that this style has some systematically dangerous features when it operates not in the classroom but on the stage of history.

I arrange these studies in order, from most abstract to most pragmatic. The first is about writing by "futurists," the planners and think-tank forecasters and technological prophets who try to make forecasting of the future scientific and, thus, useful to governments and corporations. The second is about liberal writers on U.S. foreign policy, who write theory but in a context of developing events they try to explain. And the third is about writing done in a very immediate context of action: the memoranda included in *The Pentagon Papers*.

Talking About the Future

There is an ancient female hypocrite in *The Way of the World* whose declared policy is to "let posterity shift for itself, she'll breed no more." The slogan's modern form turns up regularly in futurist writings: "What has posterity done for us lately?" This is supposed to indicate the extreme of irresponsibility. Those of us who live now do owe posterity something, it is held: at a minimum we should save a bit of oxygen and water for them, and better, we should select a tolerable future, which for them will be the present. Since we can't consult them as to their preferences, we have to choose a future—or rather a congeries of possible futures—that meet *our* sense of the good and the beautiful. We will hand them a world they never made, along with the assurance that it is the optimum future of those we were able to conceive and bring into being.

This seems to me a fair though flippant summary of how those writers to whom I refer in this section—the professional futurists, research institute staffs, systems analysts, and the like, not the doomsday futurists or visionaries—see the future. I mention their curious position regarding posterity in order to stress at the outset two critical points: first, that big time futurism is not a disinterested exercise of the imagination, but an adjunct to policy-making (he who pays the piper . . .) and, second, that, in the very nature of things, futurists are people who help arrange the lives of other people. These facts should be kept in mind, for the futurist idiom often loses track of them.

How do the futurists talk? Let's leave out the matter of jargon; some are addicted to it, others write cleanly and in ordinary English. The ideas implied by the ordinary English are what will concern me here. I will simply list some related characteristics, and then comment on them as a group.

(a) Especially when all the stops are out, futurists tend to speak—like many humanists—of Man. One says, "As man's numbers mount, he will make increasing demands on integrated systems of transportation to move himself and his goods." [1] Another: "The

1. Najeeb E. Halaby, "Transportation," in the Foreign Policy Association's volume,

advances that will give man more control over his social destiny
include discoveries in neurology, physiology, genetics, psychology,
and mathematics, as well as in the physics and chemistry that
underlie computer and communication technology." [2] Isn't it misleading to suggest that the homogeneous human race, acting in
concert, will do these things? Ask yourself how decisions actually get
made on transportation systems and the use of sophisticated methods
to control "social destiny." Men and women in general have literally
nothing to say about such matters, but particular men have a good
deal to say—including, not insignificantly, Najeeb Halaby and Ithiel
Pool, the authors of these sentences. Futurists tend to speak of Man,
people, anyone, society, as if the whole lot of us were acting
univocally and cooperatively, as if there were no differences or
conflicts among us. Pool raises the question of "how society will
achieve a balance between its desire for knowledge and its desire for
privacy," yet plainly it's the F.B.I.'s desire for knowledge that
conflicts with *my* desire for privacy and not a division in the
disembodied ethos of society. Speaking of weapons, D. G. Brennan
says that "guidance performance in the year 2018 is almost certain
to be limited more by what people choose to develop than by what is
basically feasible." [3] Which people? Just us folks? The vagueness
falsely implies a democracy in such choices. Or again, "If anyone
wants them, aircraft capable of orbital speeds . . . may be technically feasible well before the end of the century." Clearly Brennan
doesn't mean to say, what he does say, that if you and I want such
aircraft they will appear. The slip is characteristic: futurists write as
if the most powerful group in American and other industrial societies
were identical with *all* people.

(b) Futurist writing also leans heavily on a close cousin of "man,"
the reassuring pronoun "we." We will do this, we must not do that,
we can do the other. The difficulty may be superficial in a claim like
"we can . . . influence the motion of air, changes in temperature,

---

Toward the Year 2018 (New York: Cowles Education Corporation, 1968), p. 40.
Hereafter abbreviated *2018*.
2. Ithiel de Sola Pool, "Behavioral Technology," *2018*, p. 88.
3. D. G. Brennan, "Weaponry," *2018*, p. 12.

and the phase transformations of water,"[3a] and so control the weather, for no reader could expect to be offered in time a cheap backyard appliance for this purpose. Yet the "we" is often casually deceptive, doubtless even to the writer: "Technology . . . will provide us with increasingly cheap communication that knows no limitations of distance."[4] And "computers will permit us to simulate exceedingly complex systems. . . ." Is he talking about "us" English teachers? Simulation of this kind is not likely to be the ditto machine of tomorrow. It's expensive. Again, in the hortatory conditional mode: "Unless we master the art of maintaining a stable world while preserving the maximum amount of freedom . . ."[5] bad things will happen. But which of us will in fact be party to the framing of this *pax futurae*? Not all, and equally.

Particularly when futurists get to brainstorming and recommending, odd things happen to "we" and "us." Toffler says "we might consider creating a great international institute, a world futures data bank," and later, "Let us convene in each nation, on each city, in each neighborhood, democratic constituent assemblies charged with social stocktaking. . . ."[6] It is hard to imagine who Toffler thinks can do these magical acts. In these phrases I hear a man abstracted away from his real situation in society, from a true perception of power and of audience. In this he is very like the writers of the composition textbooks and their imagined students. The danger is that we ordinary readers will allow ourselves to be gathered into the futurists' phony "we." This rhetorical device implies an audience who conceivably *could* perform the social manipulations and miracles Toffler envisions and that's not you or I, as things run now.

(c) Another way futurists avoid saying who will do what and to whom is by simply omitting the human agent, where that information is quite pertinent. The passive helps in this, of course, as when

3a. Thomas F. Malone, "Weather," *2018*, pp. 63–64.

4. J. R. Pierce, Communication," *2018*, p. 59.

5. Dennis Gabor, *Innovations: Scientific, Technological, and Social* (New York: Oxford University Press, 1970), p. 45.

6. Alvin Toffler, "The Strategy of Social Futurism," in Toffler, ed., *The Futurists* (New York: Random House, 1972), p. 123. Reprinted from Toffler's *Future Shock* (New York: Random House, 1970).

Herman Kahn speaks of "what is to be avoided or facilitated" [7] in
the future, or when Toffler says that "scientific futurist institutes
must be spotted . . . throughout the entire governmental structure
in the techno-societies . . . ," [8] or "futurists should be attached to
every political party."

These writers get the same effect, roughly, with what I might call
the impersonal-preemptive use of the word "necessary": "the kind of
decision that may be necessary" (by what inexorable logic?); "It is
necessary to mobilize a force of thinkers, such as the Encyclopedists
were in the eighteenth century, to provide visions thirty or more
years ahead"; [9] or "the problem of the future consists in defining
one's priorities and making the necessary commitments." [10] The
word "necessary" is a relational term—necessary to somebody, given
certain values and intentions. Use of the word, freed from the other
terms of the relationship, implies that your necessity is my necessity
is General Motors' necessity. This is generally not true.

Similarly, deletion of the subject from infinitive phrases or
participles can imply that everyone shares in a plan or action, when
the slightest reflection refutes the idea. Here's a good example, from
Toffler: "the best way to deal with angry or recalcitrant minorities is
to open the system further, bringing them into it as full partners,
permitting them to participate in social goal-setting, rather than
attempting to ostracize or isolate them." [11] This sounds like a truism.
But who in fact is capable of "dealing" with these minorities,
bringing them into the system, other than those who run the system?
(For instance, the engineers of black capitalism or affirmative
action.) The rhetoric hides a contradiction—that "minorities" both
will and will not share equally in making the future. They will be
"full partners," yet "dealt with." The confusion is especially
poignant in Toffler, for he is aware of the elitist bias in technocratic

7. Herman Kahn, *The Year 2000; A Framework for Speculation on the Next Thirty-Three
Years* (New York: Macmillan, 1967), p. 6.
8. Toffler, "The Strategy of Social Futurism," p. 115.
9. Gabor, *Innovations*.
10. Daniel Bell, "The Year 2000—The Trajectory of an Idea," in Bell, ed., *Toward the
Year 2000; Work in Progress* (Boston: Houghton Mifflin Co., 1968), p. 8.
11. "The Strategy of Social Futurism," p. 122.

planning and, with the conscious part of his mind, he makes a bid to rescue futurism from elites. Yet the managerial habit of shaping reality through intellect is too strong to shake, and it is that habit that supports the role of our technocratic elites.

Another way of obscuring the agent: by making abstract nouns, or concrete nouns referring to hardware, the subjects of verbs referring to acts that could in fact only be performed by people. Commonplaces of futurism are promises like "infrared laser radar using holographic techniques will provide three-dimensional spatial information. . . ." [12] Brennan cannot believe that lasar radar acts independently of its masters, but that's what the sentence says, and the habit of mind is contagious. My last example combines misplaced concreteness with misplaced abstraction: "These authors are concerned principally with . . . opportunities that tools open up. It remains for diplomacy and for social policy generally to determine whether wisdom will infuse the use of those tools." [13] Here agency has receded entirely behind an army of artificial constructs—no danger if only confusion and dullness were at stake, but something of a menace if the language encourages the common belief that somebody out there—some committee of experts—will take care of everything.

(d) I won't give examples, but endemic in futurist writing is the use of relational terms—like "necessary," which I've already mentioned—as if they were absolutes. Perhaps the two most common are "problem" and "knowledge." Problems are problems *for* somebody— in nature there are no problems. To conceive of a particular situation as a problem is to build in a bias: those who formulate the problem do so with an eye toward a solution that favors them. In fact, something about you may even *be* my problem, and, if I speak of *the* problem, I suppress your interest in the case. So with the problem of the underdeveloped nations, the problem of crime in the streets, the problem of minorities, and other well-worn pieces of furniture in the living rooms of bureaucratic minds. "The" problem of crime is

12. *2018*, p. 10.
13. Emmanuel G. Mesthene, "Introduction," *2018*, p. ix.

two very different problems for unemployed black youths and for suburbanites. Similarly, knowledge pure and simple sounds like a universal blessing, but plainly behind the idea of knowledge is the relation, someone knows something. If knowledge is power, it is power for those who have it or can hire it for their ends, not for everyone, equally. Some inequality is probably inherent in knowledge; to blur the inequality through language makes it more dangerous. Unqualified use of relational terms is a means by which many futurists, like the writers of the freshman texts, equate all people, ignoring great differences of position in historical change.

(e) I'll end my survey with two examples of futurist talk, somewhat more concentrated than the foregoing, which seem to me to conceal and confuse action—the process of bringing on the future—until it virtually disappears. First:

The age of cyberculture must be built by the entire corpus of human knowledge and human achievement—by an interaction of the arts, the sciences, and the philosophies.[14]

In a world where a corpus builds an age, where the arts and sciences and philosophies "interact" without any visible human beings, I'm in trouble, and suspect that someone may take advantage of my cognitive blackout. My second:

We'll have to ask ourselves whether . . . the ethos of competition and growth should not be replaced by an ethos of responsibility. . . .[15]

Very likely. But who are "we" that ask ourselves this? And in what arena of action might anyone do something remotely like replacing one system of values with another? When ethos succeeds ethos, does that not generally happen through conflict, and to the *dis*advantage of some? Both these writers are manipulating abstract concepts far above any grounding in historical process or the present moment.

14. Alice Mary Hilton, "The Bases of Cyberculture," in Hilton, ed., *The Evolving Society* (New York: The Institute for Cybercultural Research, 1966), p. 19.
15. Erich Jantsch, as interviewed by G. R. Urban, in Toffler, ed., *The Futurists*, p. 214. Reprinted from *Can We Survive Our Future*, ed. G. R. Urban and M. Glenry (New York: St. Martin's Press, 1972).

(f) There is, then, in futurist writings an often severe tension between language that implies equality of all and proposed actions that imply continued rule by a few. The style is philosophical and generally humanist, but the ideas tend to be those suitable to the powerful. Take the root idea of futures, plural. Olaf Helmer, a leading theorist, urges us to drop our notion of the future as "unforeseeable but unique and hence inevitable," and to think instead of a "whole spectrum of possible futures," whose *probabilities* we may in some measure control.[16] The aim, it seems to me, is for the futurist to think of intervening not just in his own future, or even our mutual future, but in futures, whole states of the world. *The* future, I move into, prepare for, struggle to affect. *Futures,* I select among, or try to, if I am a futurist. The attitude is one of dominance, of making other people's choices.

Nor should that be a surprise. Futurism, I said at the outset, is an aid to planning, the activity by which our industrial states reduce uncertainties and maintain the control they have over change. Governments and industries are the main agents of planning; they set its direction and its goals. The research and development budget for our military establishment alone is in the neighborhood of seven billion dollars annually. Facts like this make somewhat quaint the suggestion of futurists that "we" are all in it together, and that the sophisticated techniques of forecasting are on "our" side.

As Herman Kahn points out, good futurism must be interdisciplinary, a coordination of the expertise of many, in order "to address realistic policy issues in the form in which they are likely to arise." [17] Precisely: the form in which they are likely to arise for those making decisions on policy. Futurism is too expensive and difficult an activity, now, at least, to be bought by any but corporations and governments, and it will therefore surely serve the interests of the powerful as they see those interests. To the extent that futurists perfect their craft, it is likely to mean increased control of the future by those who control the present—that's a modest forecast of my

16. Olaf Helmer, "Prospects of Technological Progress," *The Futurists*, p. 154.
17. *The Year 2000,* p. 4.

own. And to the extent that the language of futurism masks this truth it is dangerous to all of us "plannees."

Bertrand de Jouvenal, one of the most thoughtful philosophers of the future, pointed out that

An assertion about the future is a perfectly ordinary occurrence. In the bus, I overhear a stranger saying: "I will be in Saint-Tropez in August." He "sees himself" in Saint-Tropez, although he is now in Paris . . . . But the future is available allowing him to assert something that is not now the case . . . .[18]

There is an interesting difference between "I will be in Saint-Tropez in August" and a futurist's forecast. The speech act of the man on the bus is in fact more than an assertion, it is something close to a promise. He *commits* himself to doing his best to bring about that bit of his own future that will have him in Saint-Tropez in August. The futurist offers his forecasts with personal disengagement from their consequences. He is a man trying to dominate the future with thought, projecting on it his technology-assisted vision. But he has another relation to the future, inevitably: living his way into it, participating in its formation, exerting the influence he has moment by moment. It would be unfair to remember *only* this side of the futurist's acts of forecasting. But often his language asks us to remember only the other side, to exempt the futurist's work itself from politics.

I argued in the last chapter that a covert pseudo-politics runs through the freshman English textbooks and their authors' ideas about writing. In the world of these books, social choices are made by rational debate, in which all have equal voice; choice is determined by cooperative action of the participants. Power is played down. So are the relations between ideas and material circumstances. And "the" writer plies his craft quite objectively, working in the interest of truth and the general welfare, so that economic and social affiliations do not influence him. Futurist writers seem to subscribe to these assumptions. They offer an array of futures, weighing the

18. "On the Nature of the Future," in *The Futurists*, p. 282. Reprinted from *The Art of Conjecture* (New York: Basic Books, 1967).

choices among them with little reference to *who* will actually choose, and by what means. And most of these writers have managed to lose sight of their own place in historical and political process, so that their language sets action and conflict at a distance, as does the ideal language of freshman composition.

How to Argue in Liberal

Futurists like those quoted in the last section seek and get audiences partly *because* they claim to be unaffected by immediate historical pressures. Rhetorically, they are on a peak, overseeing a broad stretch of time and all of human affairs. Of course some are expert in transportation, some in genetics, some in weaponry, but, since forecasting means projecting whole futures, the forecaster cannot rest upon a narrow competence in one department of historical change. Perhaps the necessity of adopting a galactic perspective explains some of the distancing and blurring of person in the rhetoric.

I turn now to men who are listened to, partly because they do stand in or close to one stream of historical process. They are foreign policy experts. Many but not all have been directly involved in making policy, as well as writing about it. They also tend to survey a briefer span of time, especially future time, than the time spans of the futurists. In their essays, they look back on recent policies and acts, and forward to future ones, trying to mediate between thought and action. These writers interpret the present and recent past and seek an orientation for the future. But they do not directly advise policy-makers: the authors write to whoever will read them and seek to influence through intellect rather than to gain power. They assume a situation rather like the imagined situations of the freshman textbooks, in which every party to a debate tries to marshal the best evidence and the best reasons, and so make his opinion prevail.

This holds particularly true for one part of my sample: the articles in the January, 1970 issue of *Foreign Affairs*, a semi-official journal (sponsored by the Council on Foreign Affairs) of American foreign policy debates. These articles are scholarly and restrained, part of a quiet and deliberate discussion. The rest of my sample comes from a *viva voce* debate, a conference in June, 1968 at the Adlai Stevenson Institute of International Affairs, whose proceedings were published as a book, *No More Vietnams?* [19] Here the personal feelings of the writers and speakers are nearer the surface. But a number of argumentative strategies are salient in both samplings of liberal, foreign policy rhetoric, and I propose now to record and discuss some of them.

It's a Problem

The policy theorists seem to build their discourse on a model of *problem formulation*. Its deep structure looks like this:

(1) A vexing situation described, as a set of dilemmas, difficulties, unwanted consequences of policy, etc.
(2) Isolation of the problem(s)
(3) Discussion of the problem's complexity
(4) An intellectual set toward the problem, with general implications for policy

But the form varies, and I want to draw attention less to structure (more about that in the next section) than to what I see as, by all odds, the main intellectual strategy of these arguments and to some of its consequences.

The energy of the essays flows into stating the problem; there is usually a strong sense of accomplishment, of having arrived at the center of things, when the writer reaches this point. The pressure here is to conceptualize every conflict, every difficulty, every dissatisfaction, every messy situation, everything *bad* as a problem. In my test issue of *Foreign Affairs* (hereafter FA), these are a random assortment of the things labeled problems: the fact that the people to whom the United States sells arms often use them for purposes the

19. *No More Vietnams? The War and the Future of American Foreign Policy*, ed. Richard M. Pfeffer (New York: Harper & Row, 1968). Abbreviated NMV in text.

United States didn't intend; North Vietnamese intervention in South Vietnam; the collapse of the Dominican government; reduction of the sufferings of a nation; the fact that giving military assistance may get the United States involved in recipients' conflicts; the difficulty of stopping the "brain drain," while respecting the free movement of people. These problems embrace a great variety of phenomena; perhaps all they have in common is reference to actual or possible events that are disquieting to American officials.

These situations are broad but at least concrete. Very abstract things also shape up as problems:

The central problem of American policy—of any policy—is the relevance of its end to specific cases (Stanley Hoffman, NMV).

the long-term problem in Vietnam is how far, where, and when America should commit itself in the future to involvement in securing international peace and stability (Ithiel de Sola Pool, NMV, p. 203)

The problem now is how to adapt to introversion without succumbing to isolation (Samuel P. Huntington, NMV, p. 218)

Problems are stated in the most general terms possible. This move toward abstraction—"ends," "cases," "involvement," "stability," "introversion," "isolation," and so on—achieves wide application at the expense, often, of losing touch with real acts and people. Notice that in each of these three quotations the "problem," stripped of conceptual language, amounts to how and when the United States shall send troops and arms into other countries. The act of problem formulation often leaves far behind that part of the concrete world from which it departs. As a strategy, it reduces the world to data, the raw material of theory.

Most characteristically, it turns *conflict*—of ideas, of interests, of armies—into a purely intellectual difficulty. And it minimizes conflict another way, already familiar from the last section: by implying that "the" problem is everyone's common problem, within the universe of discourse, and that "we" all have a common interest in a solution. Though in the *No More Vietnams?* debate, Hoffman is on the opposite side from Pool and Huntington, all three accept as a matter of intellectual style both the problem strategy and the

[handwritten margin note: You are adopting the New Critical doctrine of the mastery of style]

accompanying wish that skillful framing of the problem may command agreement of all. (In fact, of course, all three write from a rhetorical position very close to that of the U.S. government. More on this theme later on.)

The Problem Is Complex

The strategy of problem-formulation camps conflict. But conflicts do exist, and The Problem must reflect them. It does so by appearing to these authors as *complex*. They dwell a good deal on what Pool calls "the complexity of reality." "Simple generalizations . . . are hazardous" (Thomas G. Sanders, FA, p. 298) could well be the slogan of liberal problem formulators. Henry Kissinger says that "The problem of defining a national interest under present circumstances is most elusively complex" (NMV, p. 12). (It was, of course, taken as a problem in definition, from a managerial standpoint—yet Kissinger wrote this in the midst of a deep conflict over national interest, whose parties saw it as much simpler, and not purely intellectual.) Geoffrey Kemp in his article on "Dilemmas of the Arms Traffic," begins by saying that America's supplying other countries with arms "gives rise to a series of policy problems which, though often simple to identify, are not easy to resolve" and hedges his way through these problems assisted by formulas like "There is no simple answer," to conclude that "there are no easy policy conclusions and no substitute for treating each request for arms on its own merits . . ." (FA, pp. 274–84). Some authors go farther. Graham Allison, Ernest May, and Adam Yarmolinsky, in "Limits to Intervention," say "It is essential to recognize not only that no simple doctrines are readily to be discovered but that the questions themselves are not easy to understand" (FA, p. 246). Needless to say, this skeptical posture often has pragmatic use. Simple views are sometimes simplistic. But not always, and liberal skepticism tends to foreclose the possibility of direct routes to truth or right conduct. As Galbraith wrote, "Modern liberalism carefully emphasizes tact rather than clarity of speech." [20]

20. John Kenneth Galbraith, *The New Industrial State* (Boston: Houghton Mifflin, 1967), p. 22.

It also tries to accommodate all objections, evidence, arguments, perspectives, in an exquisite, gradual adjustment toward the never-attainable whole truth. Reading many of the articles is like negotiating a labyrinth. Thus, one section of Kemp's article on selling arms begins, "It is often argued that the United States should simply refuse to supply to certain, if not most, countries." He counterposes the argument that if the United States refuses to sell, the Soviet Union, France, or China will step forward. Then two examples (Egypt and Indonesia). But even granting this, Kemp continues, "should the United States be concerned?" Soviet policy was advanced by sales to Egypt, but not by sales to Indonesia. Furthermore (and here he turns to the example of Peru), if the United States tries to resist supplying an ally, other countries may sell it arms that are not even militarily useful. "But once military rationality is introduced into the discussion, another set of problems needs to be weighed." If the United States efficiently adjusts sales to the military needs of the buyer, the buyer may use the arms efficiently against U.S. interests. So "what would happen if the United States drastically reduced its program of military aid and sales in Latin America in the belief that the present policies work against long-term United States interests?" Again, other suppliers would be ready with offers, and just as much would be spent on defense (FA, pp. 280–82). And so on. Costs and benefits are weighed. Contingencies multiply. Scenarios are worked out. ("If . . . , the repercussions in Canberra and New Delhi, as well as Djakarta, Bangkok and Kuala Lumpur, might be very serious.") The "delicate equilibrium" of world politics demands this hypothetical dance—the only kind of rhetoric that incorporates and does justice to available knowledge.

We Can Never Know Enough

There are other consequences of squeezing reality into problems, which then necessarily look complex. To gain intellectual mastery over the portion of world and time which is conceived as a problem, one must know a great deal and structure what one knows by sophisticated models. Thus, in reckoning why U.S. policy failed in Vietnam, thinker after thinker stresses intellectual shortcomings. Kissinger laments that Americans "conduct their foreign policies with a lack of historical knowledge" and thinks that "many of our difficulties in Vietnam have turned out to be conceptual failures" (NMV, pp. 13 and 11). (This might strike the Vietnamese as a bit of academic imperialism, on top of the other kind.) Again, Hoffman and Pool, dove and hawk though they be, find common ground here. Hoffman says "There is no substitute for area expertise, historical knowledge" (p. 196), and Pool admires "his powerful plea for local knowledge instead of platitudes" (p. 204), but faults him for not wanting that knowledge in the form of hard data. Not every liberal writer shares Pool's chauvinistic faith in "the vital importance of applied social science for making the actions of our government in foreign areas more rational and humane than they have been" (p. 205), but no one seems to doubt that knowledge is what qualifies people to make and criticize policy. Pool stigmatizes even Fulbright as an anti-intellectual, just as Robert Scalapino had earlier denounced the Vietnam teach-ins as displays of anti-intellectualism, staged by "performers" few of whom had ever been to Vietnam. If extensive and sophisticated knowledge is the sine qua non, then of course policy-making must be left to experts, with the rest of us being let in on the "debate" from time to time through the media. Liberal rhetoric is discourse among experts.

The Golden Mean

Needless to say, this kind of negotiation with reality seldom arrives at dashing conclusions. When so many possibilities are taken into account, there is a tendency to strike a moderate course—moderate within the range of thinkable alternatives, though not necessarily for the eventual recipients of policy. A set of tacit premises governs the outcome of liberal arguments. (a) Since reality is complex, simple ideas are inadequate. Participants in the Vietnam symposium worry a lot about an "overgeneralized" reaction to the war (i.e., no more Vietnams). (b) Extreme positions are irresponsible, dangerous.

Condemnation of Goldwater and the John Birch society was the popular reflex of this view in the early sixties, as was condemnation of the new left by the time the experts met to reconsider Vietnam. (c) The truth can be reached only gradually, incrementally. (d) Above all, action should be grounded in full deliberation (by experts) and, hence, cautious. (That is to say, of course, that departures from whatever we are *now* doing should be made cautiously—present policy may be anything but moderate.)

This means that many arguments end with pulled punches. Here, by way of example, are some summings up from the *Foreign Affairs* articles. On the conflict between Congress and the President in foreign policy: "the Executive and the Legislative Branches must respect each other's rights and sensibilities"; "We in the Congress" (the author is Jacob Javits) "must avoid throwing the gauntlet down before the Executive. But we must also have in return greater respect by the President . . ." (p. 234). On "Limits to Intervention": "The time is ripe for . . . reëvaluation." The Administration should cut back "general purpose forces" to the Eisenhower level. But not too far—it is not true that "one can always squeeze another $X billion out of the defense budget" (p. 261). On the upcoming SALT talks: "We should not expect too much." The talks will probably abate the arms race, but meanwhile "we cannot neglect the business of putting our arms-procurement processes in order" (pp. 271–73). On selling weapons, I have already quoted Kemp's conclusion that "there are no easy policy conclusions" and that we should treat each request individually. On American policy toward Greece: "we must carefully distinguish between military policy . . . and political policy . . . ." Send arms for Greece's defense; don't alienate the Junta and perhaps drive it toward Moscow (!); but "continue stressing disapproval of the regime" and "urge moderation" (pp. 310–11). On Cuba: the U.S. boycott has "made more difficult the export of revolution" and, hence, had its value; but it also perpetuates in Cuba a "siege mentality," making it easier for Castro to mobilize the people and solve economic problems (p. 321). (This is presumably bad.) On the brain drain: "In short, we can afford to be relatively relaxed about migration but not to be complacent about its causes"

(p. 372). The authors, whatever their style or politics, instinctively gravitate toward the on-the-one-hand-on-the-other-hand form. It is almost obligatory, at the end of a liberal argument, to present one's conclusions as a via media. The truth, or the best conduct, is imaginatively positioned between two alternatives, alternatives less good *because* more extreme.

And, of course, the style of moderation in these arguments supports the tendency of liberal problem formulation to play down conflict of interest. The authors try to absorb all points of view, and amalgamate them into a great consensus that excludes only the remote and almost mythical Enemy and a rout of domestic anti-intellectuals and extremists. Consensus is the aim of these modest conclusions, as it is of seeing troubles as problems, of keeping the discussion technical and value-free, and of working toward objective knowledge as the way out for us all.

Liberal argument achieves this harmony by a considerable abstraction of immediate circumstances. Most of the authors I have been discussing had direct or indirect roles in making the policies they discuss (contrast the objectivity of a scientific paper—the scientist has no personal involvement in the phenomena he describes). Yet it is rare to find one of them describing his personal involvement, what he has at stake, who he takes to be on his side and who on the other side—much less his social class, family connections, income, race, or sex. The preponderance of liberal argument is conducted by people who resemble one another a good deal in these last-named characteristics. This same abstraction of circumstances can be found, of course, in what the freshman textbooks say about argument, as it is implicit in the way they place the student writer outside history and apart from such categories as wealth, power, and class. Yet I think that both the advice of the texts and the practice of the theorists and policy-makers are best suited—not only to a technological society that sets great emphasis on expertise, knowledge, and planning—but to those members of such a society with most power and privilege. For this is a rhetoric that masks power and privilege, and any asymmetrical relationships of the writer to his fellow human beings, just as it either masks conflict or suggests that conflict derives from misunderstandings rather than from (say) the resentment of the powerless and their wish to share more equality.

Noam Chomsky says, aptly, in his discussion of Vietnam policy-making:

It is possible to give some useful advice to an aspiring political analyst who wants his work received as thoughtful and penetrating—advice which surely applies to any society, not merely to ours. This analyst should first of all determine as closely as possible the actual workings of power in his society. Having isolated certain primary elements and a number of peripheral and insignificant ones, he should then proceed to dismiss the primary factors as unimportant, the province of extremists and ideologues. He should rather concentrate on the minor and peripheral elements in decision making. Better still, he should describe these in terms that appear to be quite general and independent of the social structure that he is discussing. . . . He can then be fairly confident that he will escape the criticism that his efforts at explanation are "simplistic" (the truth is often surprisingly simple). He will, in short, benefit from a natural tendency on the part of the privileged in any society to suppress—for themselves as well as others—knowledge and understanding of the nature of their privilege and its manifestations.[21]

The tendency of the liberal rhetoric I have been scrutinizing is precisely to set aside large and simple truths, or moral positions, in favor of technical and peripheral ones.

The Memorandum as Act

The theorists of *Foreign Affairs* and *No More Vietnams?*, however close they are or have been to the making of decisions, are outside the war councils as they write. Theirs is a rhetoric of theory. Continuing my movement from theory to practice, I want to look now at the language used by powerful men who make decisions of consequence. *The Pentagon Papers*[22] opens a window on men doing precisely that. Some of the prose in these volumes is of course interpretive and narrative and written long after the fact. And some of the documents

21. *For Reasons of State* (New York: Pantheon Books, 1973), p. 65.
22. *The Pentagon Papers; The Defense Department History of United States Decision Making on Vietnam,* The Senator Gravel Edition (Boston: Beacon Press, 1971), in four volumes.

themselves are speeches and other public relations efforts. Set these aside. What remain are hundreds of memoranda, each a link in the chain of acts that was (and is) American policy in Vietnam. Memoranda are orders, requests, advisements, recommendations, pleas, reports made to superiors, and so on. The writers of memoranda sit in the stream of events and try to direct it. They employ power directly. Hence, these memos nicely complement the less engaged writings described in the last section.

By meetings, memoranda, and allied forms, the members of an organization try to grasp the import of past events and to exercise a measure of control over future events. By meetings and memoranda they form policies and execute them, with the aim of assuring their own survival in a future harboring as few surprises as possible. Meetings and memoranda are main instruments of planning, prime media of discourse in a complicated technological society.

I venture to guess that memoranda have greater importance, relative to meetings, in large organizations where many departments must coordinate their work. There, certainly, a memo is often something quite different from the hasty recording of a thought or act which is implied by the word. It is the attempt of an official (or a group) to marshal the data within a purview, to frame a cogent argument, to give an opinion weight in council—and, of course, to show the writer and his department off to advantage. A good memo lasts a while, gets wide readership, and becomes a kind of fixed point for future discussions and future memos.

The picture I get from *The Pentagon Papers* is that during the crisis years of Vietnam our policy-makers lived in an atmosphere of memoranda. Memos had a tangibility and immediacy for them greater than the Vietnamese people or countryside. The state of American policy at any given moment could be measured by the memos people were reading and writing and debating. Thus, the Pentagon historian traces the shift of policy away from Westmoreland's sanguine wish to send ever more ground troops to Vietnam, through dozens of interrelated memos in the late spring of 1967—from Westmoreland to himself; from the Joint Chiefs of Staff; from Alain Enthoven (a systems analysis); a long series of drafts from John

McNaughton, like Enthoven an assistant to McNamara and an opponent of the heavy military line at this time; from Walt Rostow and so on, until the "floating" of one of McNaughton's drafts on May 19. Then another Joint Chiefs of Staff memo, criticizing the "make-do" position of McNaughton, and recommending that his deaft not be forwarded to Johnson. Then detailed responses from William Bundy and Nicholas Katzenbach. Katzenbach's memo surveyed disagreements in previous memos on the subject—between Vance and the CIA, between General Wheeler and Vance, between the State Department's intelligence group and the CIA, between the Defense Department and the CIA, etc. Then on June 12 McNaughton submitted still another draft memorandum for the President, "in which he incorporated the views of State, CIA and the JCS [Joint Chiefs of Staff]." And of course the memos discussed and quoted in *The Pentagon Papers* are only the most important inter-agency ones, each doubtless resting atop a heap of internal staff memos in each agency. These men who were determining the course of millions of lives did so largely through the instrument of writing. For them writing was their work, their mode of action, their exercise of power. Writing can hardly be more consequential than are these memos.

Yet it is well to begin with what Undersecretaries and Special Assistants have in *common* with English 101 students: an assignment. The warmakers do not even have the occasional freedom enjoyed by freshman of "selecting" their topic. The topic is assigned, if not by a superior, by the situation itself. Furthermore, it is always fundamentally the same: What shall we do next? In short, these men for whom writing was the exercise of power share something else with the powerless students imagined by writers of freshman texts: for them too, the topic comes first, then the thesis. They must devise a thesis for the purpose, rather than giving verbal form to some urgency of their lives. Though they write toward the making of violent history, in the writing predicament itself they are extremely confined, with even less freedom than the ordinary composition student. The boundedness of their task probably explains the brain-rotting sameness of the memos that constitute this documentary history. But it has greater consequences than to make a boring book.

Notably, the form of the "assignment"—What shall we do next?—tacitly assumes the additional phrase, "to achieve U.S. aims in Southeast Asia," which rules out questioning, or even discussion, of those aims. Though the memorandists work in the inmost circles of government, they write as technicians searching for the marginally best course of action within a rigidly prescribed policy. As many commentators have said, *The Pentagon Papers* are remarkable for containing virtually no discussion of American global strategy, its practicality, its morality, or the interests it serves. The memorandists are our statesmen and strategists, yet here are found no statesman-like analyses of world politics and of our country's historical role. And what is unquestioned naturally remains unaltered. Noam Chomsky said,

The most striking feature of the historical record, as presented in the Pentagon study, is its remarkable continuity. Perhaps the most significant example has to do with the political premises of the four administrations covered in the record (and we may now add a fifth). Never has there been the slightest deviation from the principle that a non-communist regime must be imposed, regardless of popular sentiment.[23]

And Leslie Gelb, chief compiler of the Pentagon study, wrote that "no systematic or serious examination of Vietnam's importance to the United States was ever undertaken within the government." [24] That was not part of the assignment.

When the goals of policy do appear in these memoranda, it is usually in a ritualistic and perfunctory list, before the real business of writing. In November of 1964, before the bombing of North Vietnam, McNaughton begins a memo on that and other "options":

1. *U. S. aims*:
   (a) To protect US reputation as a counter-subversion guarantor
   (b) To avoid domino effect especially in Southeast Asia
   (c) To keep South Vietnamese territory from Red hands

23. *For Reasons of State*, p. 28. Chomsky's very rich analysis of *The Pentagon Papers* is called "The Backroom Boys," and this essay of mine is in part a footnote to his account of how the Vietnam strategists reasoned in their backrooms.
24. "Vietnam: The System Worked," *Foreign Policy*, vol. I, No. 3 (1971); quoted by Chomsky, p. 50.

(d) To emerge from crisis without unacceptable taint from methods used (III, p. 601)

And in his memo recommending the first large commitment of ground soldiers to Vietnam, McNamara says "our object" is to "create conditions for a favorable outcome" without getting into a war with China or the Soviet Union or losing the support of the American people. He then defines a "favorable outcome" as having "nine fundamental elements," of which these are samples:

(a) VC stop attacks and drastically reduce incidents of terror and sabotage
(d) GVN [Government of Vietnam] stays independent (hopefully pro-US, but possibly genuinely neutral)
(e) Communists remain quiescent in Laos and Thailand
(h) VC/NLF transform from a military to a purely political organization (IV, pp. 619–20)

With goals conceived in such rudimentary and unthinking terms, and dismissed so brusquely, it is small wonder that they remained constant through the total transformation of the war (from a guerrilla conflict to a technological massacre) between 1964 and 1968, or that the more dubious concepts—"protect US reputation," "domino effect," the "independent" government of South Vietnam, the "terrorism" of the NLF, etc.—retained their power to bewitch. And small wonder that the moral issues are filed away under neutral headings like "unacceptable taint." These matters are simply outside the universe of discourse for the memo writers.

Occasionally an official grows uncomfortable with the tightness— or even the morality—of the assignment and, like a rebellious student, questions its premises. So McNaughton writes, in May 1967, after two and a half years of vigorously pursuing the aims mentioned above: "the 'philosophy' of the war should be fought out now so everyone will not be proceeding on their own major premises, and getting us in deeper and deeper," and asks for a redefinition of "success" (IV, pp. 478–9).[25] But there was no such philosophical

25. He also mentions "the amount of suffering being visited on the non-combatants in Vietnam," but only as one cause of the American people's "distress," and hence of the

debate. Even dissenters from the Vietnam policy like George Ball, who eventually left the Government, observed the convention of not raising basic issues; Ball's dove-like July 1965 memo, "A Compromise Solution in South Vietnam," assumes U.S. goals and runs through the usual cost-benefit analysis of alternatives, in recommending that the Government negotiate (IV, pp. 615–19).

Because of the tacit gentleman's agreement not to discuss big questions, and because decisions are made through a gradual evolution of memo positions, a further movement toward the center occurs. Positions on the margins look extreme and tend to get excluded; alternatives become few and only narrowly different. Thus, through the great debate of May 1967 on further escalation, two proposals for troop deployment (go to 700,000; increase only slightly to 525,000) crystallized as the "discussable" ones and three for bombing North Vietnam (increase it to include harbors and the outskirts of Hanoi and Haiphong; cut it back to the area below the 20th parallel; keep it the same). No one suggested, or even mentioned, troop withdrawal, or reduction of the far more devastating bombing of *South* Vietnam; on the other extreme, no one talked of nuclear arms, and only the generals mentioned invading North Vietnam. The assignment not only excludes "philosophy," it excludes all tactics but those most like present tactics. So smart men spend their time imagining and contriving furiously in a small cage, which becomes less and less habitable, but from which no one can conceive a way out, since it is not permitted to speak of opening the door.

With the assignment a given, a memo writer has limited freedom not only in what he can say, but in the form of its saying as well. His writing strategy is pretty well defined by his situation: (1) he is to answer the question, what shall we do next; (2) there is a fixed and rather precise list of goals that any action must move toward; (3) there is the present situation in Vietnam, the United States, and the rest of the world. His task is to relate (1) to (2) and (3). Essentially,

---

war's becoming "unpopular" (p. 478). This way of handling moral questions seems quite consistent with his earlier concept of "unacceptable taint."

all the memoranda in *The Pentagon Papers* are variants on a single form of argument, dictated by the situation. The full paradigm is this:

(1) Statement of aims
(2) Analysis of the present situation, and how far the United States is from achieving its aims
(3) List of possible courses of action
(4) Likely advantages and disadvantages of each, in terms of the stated aims
(5) Recommendation

Of course different rhetorical situations lead to variants. The writer may be responding to another writer's proposal and limit his evaluation to it. He may (especially if he is a general) have been asked only to list or assess a number of alternatives, leaving step (5) to someone higher up. Or, if the dialogue is specific enough, steps (1) and (2) will often be omitted as unnecessary. And, of course, the order may be varied—(3) or (5) may come first, and so on. But these modifications are intellectually and rhetorically insignificant. All thought runs in the pattern sketched above, whether or not the pattern shows through the finished memo in precisely its ideal shape. The most compulsive freshman English texts do not more tightly confine students' themes than the Vietnam "problem" does the writing of the Pentagon memos.

To put the obvious label on the paradigm, it is a model for *problem solving*, in the same way that of the Foreign Affairs articles was *problem formulation*. Any model reduces complexity—exchanges faithfulness to reality for finiteness. If you have to decide something tomorrow or next week, it is helpful, maybe necessary, to sort reality out on a familiar grid. A problem-solving model supplies a grid that connects reality to a desired future by one or more acts. To do that, it must pick out those elements from reality that have the most salient ties to the desired future. This is, of course, an abstraction of elements from the present in a way that reflects one's own needs and interests. It is worth looking at some consequences of this intellectual strategy, honored by freshman rhetorics in theory, and more rigidly by the Pentagon memos in practice—as indeed it is to some degree in each complex and technological society.

As I've said, the aims (step 1 in the model) are rather simply put, and quite unchanging. For that reason, the memorandists' analysis of *present* reality is also simple and stable. From 1964 on a set of categories turns up with considerable regularity in any comprehensive analysis. Aside from the obvious military ones, the set includes "the morale of the South Vietnamese," "Hanoi's will," "American lives," the "domestic political situation," "world opinion," the U.S. balance of payments, the "risk of heightened world tensions," the "likelihood of confrontation with the USSR and China," and the American will to "bear burdens" like those of Vietnam. (It does not include the mass killing of Vietnamese people or destruction of their society.) The fixity of these notions further restricts the scope of the problem solving.

In effect, the ingenuity of the American strategists, kept by the ground rules from exercising itself on steps (1) and (2), is left for steps (3) and (4)—precisely the most technical ones. I can't illustrate except by quoting, and I'll choose McNaughton's memo of November 7, 1964, since I have already quoted its extremely spare statement of aims (its analysis of the present situation is hardly more elaborate). At step (3), it offers three "options": "continue present policies," "fast/full squeeze" (step up the war), and

OPTION C. *Progressive squeeze-and-talk.* Present policies plus an orchestration of (a) communications with Hanoi and (b) a crescendo of additional military moves against infiltration targets, first in Laos and then in the DRV [Democratic Republic of Vietnam], and then against other targets in North Vietnam. The scenario should give the impression of a steady deliberate approach. It would be designed to give the US the option at any point to proceed or not, to escalate or not, and to quicken the pace or not. These decisions would be made from time to time in view of all relevant factors (III, p. 602)

Then follows a page-long, more detailed outline of Option C—military actions, broken down into "present" plus three subsequent "phases," and into a total of eleven steps, such as "T28 strikes against infiltration-associated targets in Laos" and "34A Marops and Airops" (legitimated? including "black bomber"?); political actions ("Taylor 'noisily' to Washington"); terms for negotiation (III, p. 603); and "information actions" (propaganda). Though this is a simpler-than-average instance of step (3), and though it was to be elaborated later, it shows where McNaughton's brain was working hardest. Step (3) takes up over half the memo. Yet, needless to say, there is nothing particularly novel or intellectually adventuresome here.

Step (4) affords a like opportunity for technical refinement, but because it calls for matching the options of step (3) to the categories of reality posited by step (2), it offers even less room for originality. The mechanical quality of the thinking shows most clearly in some of the military memos. An October, 1967 memorandum from the Joint Chiefs of Staff summarizes for the President ten possible actions to "increase pressure" on North Vietnam, listing with each act advantages and risks. For example,

2. *Mine NVN deep water ports*
    .   .   .
    Advantages
        Reduce import of war-supporting materials
    Risks/Impact
        Soviet Union may cancel existing negotiations with the U.S. and initiate propaganda campaign

        Possible Soviet action to increase tensions in other parts of the world but major confrontations would be unlikely

        CPR [China] would strengthen defensive posture and may increase military aid to NVN; unlikely to initiate offensive air or surface actions
9. *Expand Operations in Cambodia*
    .   .   .
    Advantages
        Disrupt sanctuaries
        Reduce supplies to NVA/VC
        Improve intelligence
        Discourage use of Cambodia as sanctuary for NVA/VC forces
        Provide self-defense of U.S. forces

Risks/Impact
　　Cambodia would protest expansion of operation to Cambodian soil
　　and might seek to defend its territory
　　Adverse political reaction (IV, pp. 534–6)

For now, I want to stress the impact that this kind of model has on
thought and action: it routinizes war.

　　Notice, too, that most "advantages" are narrowly military, while
the risks speak to other categories of reality such as "world opinion,"
"domestic political situation," and "confrontation" with China or
the USSR. This points to one of the persistent assumptions of the
whole war: that military advances are always good, within limits set
by political reaction. If the generals had not been checked by the
latter, there is little doubt that our Government would have used
whatever force was necessary to win a military victory. Of course it is
the job of generals to win, and political impact be damned. The
more surprising and dismaying revelation of *The Pentagon Papers* is
how much the *civilians* running America came to share this
perspective. Perhaps the neatly symmetrical form of step (4), and the
mechanical quality of the whole paradigm, helped dull their senses
and make the unspeakable a daily routine.

　　An all-pervasive metaphor accompanies the argumentative strategy of step (4): that of cost and benefit. Pairing up advantages and
risks without judging which way the balance tipped might satisfy the
generals in some circumstances, but it could not satisfy the technicians in the White House, State Department, and Defense Department, who after all had to emerge from the analysis with decisions.
They must solve the problems, even if it means subtracting cabbages
from kings. Thus, McGeorge Bundy in February, 1965, advocating a
course of "sustained reprisal" against North Vietnam for "offenses"
in the south: "While we believe that the risks of such a policy are
acceptable, we emphasize that its costs are real." These costs include
"significant U.S. air losses," "an extensive and costly effort against
the whole air defense system of North Vietnam," high U.S.
casualties, and arousal of American "feelings." "Yet measured
against the costs of defeat in Vietnam, this program seems cheap.
And even if it fails to turn the tide—as it may—the value of the effort
seems to us to exceed its cost."

To appreciate what kind of thinking this is, consider what these costs are in fact "measured against." First, against the benefits expected from the "program," "improvement" of the situation in South Vietnam. This breaks down into three main items: "a sharp immediate increase in optimism in the South," which might lead to a more effective government there; "a substantial depressing effect upon the morale of Viet Cong cadres"; and "damping down" the "charge that we did not do all that we could have done." Second, as Bundy indicates, the costs of the "program" must be measured against the costs of *not* undertaking it and of "defeat in Vietnam." Earlier in the memorandum these, too, are expressed in quantitative terms:

> The *stakes* in Vietnam are extremely *high*. The American *investment* is very *large* . . . . The *international prestige* of the United States, and a *substantial part* of our *influence*, are directly *at risk* in Vietnam. [my italics]

Toward the end of the memo Bundy says that the chances for success (all three benefits listed above) are "somewhere between 25% and 75%," but even if the policy fails and we get only benefit three (damping down the charge of inactivity), the policy will be "worth it."

Please bear with me while I put this in the schematic form that Bundy's reasoning implies.

A. If we don't follow the policy, and meet defeat, the tally is:

Plus	*Minus*
No more air losses	Loss of our investment:
No costly bombing of NV	international prestige
American feelings not aroused	influence (extent?)
No more casualties	

The minuses outweigh the pluses.

B. If we do follow the policy, and it succeeds:

Plus	*Minus*
Optimism in South (extent?)	Air losses
VC morale down (extent?)	Costly bombing of NV

Damp charge of inactivity   American feelings aroused
Avoid minuses listed under A   more casualties
The pluses outweigh the minuses.

C. If we follow the policy, and it fails:
    Plus   *Minus*
    Damp charge of inactivity   Air losses
    Avoid (partly?) the minuses of A   Costly bombing of NV
                                             American feelings aroused
                                             more casualties
    The pluses still add up to more, though not by so much.

I won't carry this analysis to the ultimate absurdity of guessing
what numerical values Bundy set on each of these costs and benefits;
enough to say that unless there is *some* quantification, in a common
system of weighting, the whole show of "measuring" collapses and
we're back with less objective ways of arguing. Yet how *can* we
translate so much VC morale into so much American prestige into so
many deaths of American fliers into so many dollars spent on
bombing, etc., etc., etc.? (Not to mention effects totally omitted from
the system, such as deaths of Vietnamese.) Patently, this way of
thinking is quite empty, a reckoning divorced from substance, a
headful of cotton candy. Yet the model calls for it, the intellectual
training of these men supports it, and the metaphors clothe it in
spurious objectivity. And so, of course, this policy and many others
like it were put into effect, with results for which the argument seems
peculiarly inappropriate.

Critics of the war often remarked that this way of thinking
reckoned costs only relative to American aims and not costs to South
Vietnam. More precisely, those results of an act that count as costs
are those that trouble the memo writer's consciousness or threaten
his well-being. Add to that the technical quality of the decision-mak-
ing (the Pentagon analyst speaks once of an "option" being
"analyzed across a matrix of many factors"—IV, p. 438) and its
abstractness, and some odd judgments emerge. William Bundy can
argue against asking for 200,000 more men to Vietnam, because that

would mean calling up the Reserves and *that* would cause a "truly major debate in Congress," which, in turn, "could only encourage Hanoi." Alain Enthoven cites as another reason for opposing this overrunning of Vietnam with troops, that it would increase "piaster spending" and add to inflation in South Vietnam. And the Pentagon analyst himself concludes 250 pages on the bombing of North Vietnam by saying that "its most significant contribution" may turn out to be that *stopping* it led to negotiations.

What arguments like these have in common is a lunatic incommensurability. Even now, reading these strange documents, I want to shout, "You destroyed the South Vietnamese people, and talked of piaster spending. You held off from still greater killing only because open debate in America about doing so might encourage the North Vietnamese." The main point to make, in this context, is that since the suffering of the Vietnamese didn't impinge on the consciousness of the policy-makers as a cost, it had virtually no existence for them—at least not in these memoranda. In 1962 and 1963 and 1964, one does read a good deal about the various governments of South Vietnam, their stability, and their cooperativeness, because those factors were material to American "success." But by 1967–1968, when power in South Vietnam was nakedly American power, there is much less to be heard in the memoranda about Ky and Thieu, much less about the people of South Vietnam, who had been made a nation of refugees by American policy.

And, in general, the problem-solving mode of writing, because of the severe technical restrictions it lays on argument, makes people into elements of the problem, to be manipulated conceptually as well as physically. It abstracts them in strange and repellent ways, of which the systems analysis reported by Enthoven is perhaps only the most extreme: his study analyzes enemy deaths as a function (a) of the number of U.S. troops in Vietnam and (b) of the aggressiveness of the North Vietnamese and the NLF, concluding that the latter is more important and that granting the generals the full troop increase they requested would only increase deaths from 2121 to 2460 in an ordinary week. We can be grateful, I admit, that this argument finally "worked." But that no other way of contemplating

Vietnamese deaths had slowed the war is a depressing comment on what the technician's mind is capable of, and on the technical premises underlying this mode of composition.

One more example: for a long time, around 1964 and 1965, the South Vietnamese people figured in these memos mainly in the form of that abstraction, their *morale*, and how it might respond to one or another course of American action, particularly that of bombing North Vietnam. Remember, McGeorge Bundy spoke of an "increase in optimism" if the United States should bomb the North more, and of a "depressing effect on the morale of VC cadres." But he went on to say that the effect over a longer time was uncertain, and that perhaps "like other stimulants, the value of this one would decline over time," so that the United States should quickly prod the South Vietnamese to more effective fighting while they were still high on our bombing of the North (III, p. 314)[26] McNamara adopted the same conception in evaluating the bombing "program," once it had been tried for a few months. Morale was "raised" by the bombing at first. But now that the "bombing programs" have become "commonplace," morale is "not discernably better" than before. "In a sense, South Vietnam is now 'addicted' to the program: a permanent abandonment of the program would have a distinct depressing effect on morale in South Vietnam" (IV, p. 387). To our planners, morale was like a patient's bodily functions, responding one way or another to medication. And of course what they perceived as morale was mainly the cooperativeness of Vietnamese officials toward American policies and the willingness of Vietnamese soldiers to fight. A wider perspective on the issues might have led the memorandists to consider the morale of the other Vietnamese, those whose lives and society were being totally disrupted by another "bombing program," far more brutal than the bombing of the North, and barely mentioned in these volumes—doubtless because its victims were not among what Bundy called "articulate groups" and so could not register on the cost meter of the American planners.

26. Similarly, according to Bundy, American military response to the Gulf of Tonkin incident was for the Vietnamese "a short-run stimulant and a long-term depressant" (pp. 314–15).

What definitely does register is how the U.S. Government will appear in other *significant* people's eyes, and how those people will respond. It is not unusual to find a particular course of action weighed for its probable impact on Hanoi, on the South Vietnamese government, on Congress, on the American people, on China, on the USSR, on America's SEATO allies, on friendly countries elsewhere, and on "world opinion." As Hannah Arendt wrote, "image making" lay at the root of American policy. Our "credibility," our "prestige," the domino theory, and a host of strategic concepts rest on what people think of what we do. McGeorge Bundy's memo on retaliatory bombing, which I have quoted several times, ends with nine "action recommendations," seven of which are public relations steps, manipulating in advance the responses of others to our move. Hawks and doves alike make appearance the acid test. Long after South Vietnamese morale was no longer a consideration in determining the level of American bombing in the north—in March of 1968—Paul Warnke, the strongest opponent of bombing in the upper layers of the administration, wrote that increased bombing (1) would not "break the will of the North Vietnamese leaders," (2) "would further alienate domestic and foreign sentiment," (3) could, if by accident we hit U.S. prisoner of war camps, "alarm their wives and parents into vocal opposition," so that "reprisals could be taken against them and the idea of war crimes trials would find considerable acceptance in countries outside the Communist bloc" (IV, pp. 251–2). This last argument may seem enigmatic, but it is at least in keeping with the tradition of cost-benefit thinking, which was obligatory, in the cause of war or of peace.

One of the worst outcomes envisioned in these arguments is that an adopted strategy, if it goes awry, will make the U.S. strategists look bad.

Our air actions in the South should be carried on at a maximum effective rate. This could include substantial use of B-52's against VC havens, recognizing that we look silly and arouse criticism if these do not show significant results. (William Bundy, June, 1965; IV, p. 612)

. . . a temporary and illusory "victory" which, if it unraveled, would make

our whole effort look ridiculous, undermine the gains in confidence that
have been achieved in Southeast Asia and elsewhere, and have the most
disastrous effects on our own American resolve to bear burdens in Asia and
indeed throughout the world. (William Bundy, June, 1967; IV, p. 503)

"Silly" and "ridiculous" are not the adjectives that would come to
most people's minds, any more than for the bombing of Dresden or
Nagasaki, but perhaps they are as appropriate as any to the feeling
one gets, reading the Pentagon memoranda, of a vast war game, an
intricate technical exercise, conducted by the varsity team, very far
from real human pain. The rules of the *writing* game did not, of
course, cause Vietnam. But they made it easier to think and do the
unthinkable, because of the way they interposed mechanical analysis
between the men of power and human and moral issues.

Such thinking has something to do with the division of our labor
into small parts, so that the whole design is hard to see. The generals
are the clearest example, in this dismal collection. But the Harvard-
and Yale-trained statesmen seem willingly to have assumed the
narrowness of thinking that goes with a technical problem. To find a
less confined style of thought and writing, one almost has to go back
to the very beginning of *The Pentagon Papers*, to a memo from
Roosevelt to Hull in January, 1944:

Indo-China should not go back to France but . . . should be administered
by an international trusteeship. France has had the country—thirty million
inhabitants for nearly one hundred years, and the people are worse off than
they were at the beginning . . . . The people of Indo-China are entitled to
something better than that (I, p. 10)

Policy, people, and morality nearly in a single breath. Roosevelt
would never have made it as an undersecretary in our more
advanced age.

Or as the ideal student of English 101. For, to return to the
beginning of this discussion, English 101 has helped, willy nilly, to
teach the rhetoric of the bureaucrats and technicians. Its architects
would doubtless prefer Roosevelts to Rostows, but the constraints
upon English from the rest of the university and especially from

outside it are strong. Though the writers of the textbooks and the planners of courses may be generalists and humanists by intent, they can hardly ignore what passes for intellectual currency in that part of the world where vital decisions are made or what kind of composition succeeds in the terms of that part of the world. Problem formulation and problem solving, distancing of people, abstraction away from historical circumstance, disappearance of the writer as a being with social attributes, and denial of politics: these are threads that run through both the textbooks for English 101 and the examples of successful writing I have considered. Perhaps the similarity goes some way toward explaining the usefulness of our subject, English, to America.

IV

The Professional
Ethos

In Section II I looked at some of the institutions that house—and the ideas that permeate—the teaching and study of literature in America. And with Wallace Douglas, I considered in Section III the other side of our subject: literacy, writing, the pragmatic use of language. I have argued that, as we organize our time and energies around these two sides, we have struck an uneasy and mainly unconscious compromise between what we want the cultural role of language and literature to be and what society wants from us and from these subjects. It is time now to be more exact about these relations, and to connect them in turn to some mundane facts of life and work in this society.

University and college English departments are the best place to analyze this nexus. From the teacher's viewpoint, departments are the main fact of his or her working life. A department gives her her apprenticeship as a graduate student and teaching fellow. A department awards her the M.A. or Ph.D. degree, the latter being necessary for full membership in the profession. In doing so, it strongly urges upon her its values and ideas. Several departments consider her credentials and interview her for full-time jobs; one of them hires her. It gives her her first work assignment, along with implicit or explicit standards for success and failure. It and other agencies of employment are mainly responsible for reappointing, promoting, or firing her. Within the department, she takes part in making educational policy and applying professional values in meetings. Her material well-being and her self-esteem, then, depend rather heavily on departments. I believe that most teachers feel themselves to be mainly "situated" in a department.

On the other side, university departments are the most important agencies in deciding the kind of literary culture society gets, and in responding to the needs society (parents, boards of education, trustees, regents, employers, etc.) makes known for culture and for the skills of literacy. That is because English and English Education departments train those who teach these subjects in school, inculcating in the process beliefs about what literature is, what good writing is, and how these subjects should be taught. In many parts of the country, these same departments also greatly influence the development of state and local curricula and certification requirements. And, of course, members of university departments write and edit most of the textbooks school children read as they learn what society thinks literature and composition to be. This cultural effort may not produce best-sellers in the conventional sense, but it surely is responsible for more man-, woman-, and child-hours spent with books than are all the trade publishers.

Why are there departments? Where did they come from? How do they meet this conjunction of needs? Oddly, neither sociologists nor historians of education seem to have thought much about these questions. The next two chapters are my shot at an answer, as, more broadly, are Chapters Ten and Eleven. So my focus gradually widens now, to the American academy and its functions. The issues this book has posed so far cannot be resolved without this wider perspective.

CHAPTER EIGHT

What English Departments Do

Shaw said that all professions are conspiracies against the laity. So it is in our profession, the teaching of English in college, and English departments are the conspirators' cell groups. The argument of this chapter and the next will support Shaw's aphorism, but will have to sacrifice its neatness: for, in academic fields—and perhaps in all professions—the conspirators think of themselves as working overtime to serve the laity. It seems to be characteristic of professions that they conceive their own advantage to be in the public interest. No professional would put it so crudely as Charles Wilson did when he said, "What's good for General Motors is good for the country," but the sentiment behind academic ideology is the same. I'll try to account for much that is familiar yet puzzling about departments by seeing them as instruments of our professional aspirations, engaged simultaneously in service to and conspiracy against the laity.

Not everyone will agree with me that the ways of departments are peculiar, that there is anything to explain about departments in general. So I will start with three perfectly typical instances of how departments bend our thought and practice away from what a naive observer would expect and, perhaps, away from what most people who teach English want. The first is a listing in the Association of Departments of English publication, *Vacancies in College and University Departments of English for Fall 1971*:

MISSOURI SOUTHERN COLLEGE, Joplin, Missouri 64801. Rank open, PhD or ABD, Renaissance, salary open. College and Public School experience desired. 12–15 hours per semester: Freshman Composition, World and English literature. Possible summer work, 20% annual salary. Missouri retirement, health and medical insurance. College is a new and growing four-year institution, department of 22. Harold Cooper, Chm., Arts and Sciences Division.

The job offered in this ad was doubtless the bridge between studenthood and an independent career for some young person; it is a signpost along the way in the most critical rite of passage of a working life. And at just that point it asks the graduate student to present himself or herself, not just as a college teacher, nor even just as an English teacher, but as a renaissance scholar. Naturally the student's graduate training has strongly supported this self-definition.

Yet to me, it is not at all obvious whose interest the arrangement serves, though everyone takes that arrangement for granted. Most students choose graduate work in our field because they like literature and writing and think that they would like to teach them to college students. I know few whose design was to be scholars, and almost no one who intended to be something as specific as a renaissance scholar. It is even less likely that the people of Missouri or the students of Missouri Southern College feel a need to have this field covered at Joplin. As for the planners of this "new and growing college," the English literary renaissance can hardly have figured in their vision, but evidently departments did, and this ad is one entailment of building a college around departments. Does the department itself need a renaissance specialist? It is not even clear that the winner of this position was to teach a renaissance course, nor, unless the department is unusual, does it act as a community of scholars whose intramural discourse requires all fields to be represented. Most likely the familiar calculus of departmental balance and coverage is behind this ad: in the minds of its 22 members, the new department at Missouri Southern College must look like other departments. This exigency is independent of anybody's need for a job teaching a particular field, yet it governs the definition of the teacher, and the way our institutions shape our work. Why?

The second instance: in an article called "Building an English Department in a new University," [1] Homer C. Combs describes his task at Florida Technical University in Orlando, founded 1968. "The job is full of challenge, completely absorbing, but one that consumes quantities of time in the process of making initial choices and decisions." This "challenge," as he sees it, is to attract colleagues who want to be "part of a new, vital effort," and he recommends that "cautious young men and women, trustful of tradition," not interest themselves in jobs at Florida Tech.

The structural choices that Combs, in fact, made were principally these: (1) to hire young assistant professors with Ph.D.'s, rather than established scholars, in the expectation that "by the time the university is ready for established professors to teach graduate courses, some of the present group should have progressed to the same ranks, with their own claim to scholarly fame"; (2) to devise a freshman course that involves students in both reading and writing; (3) to "offer both a literary emphasis and a writing emphasis in the English major." Each choice is embedded in a network of decisions that were *not* choices, that were not even consciously made, so far as we can tell, by the planners of Florida Technical University, or by Professor Combs: to arrange the curriculum in courses, to have a freshman English program, to organize undergraduate study of language and literature around a "major" in English, to one day offer graduate work, to build a teaching force that includes scholars with established reputations. What necessity forbids making these things a matter of choice, in this situation? The decision, apparently, to provide the University with an English department. And doubtless that, too, was a decision that was never consciously considered. I hold that the departmental assumption does most of our educational planning for us, ensuring that new universities will be rather like old ones for both students and faculty.

My first two instances indicate the effect that thinking in terms of departments has in the hiring of new faculty members and the

1. *ADE Bulletin* (*Bulletin of the Association of Departments of English*), 21, pp. 29–31. This is the May issue 1969; all my references are to issues of the late sixties and early seventies, and I shall omit dates from now on.

founding of universities. My third instance suggests that the habit of mind is as compelling among teachers and at institutions that are solidly established. I quote from the synoptic minutes of a meeting of the Executive Committee of a major midwestern English department:[2]

[The chairman] expressed his distress at the ranking of the . . . English Department in the ACE Report. He believes it represents a sad decline. The corollary is that we must scrutinize scholarly production with continuing vigor and perhaps try to achieve at least a limited infusion of distinguished senior staff . . . In the discussion which followed, it was suggested that the whole Department might be involved more fully in attracting luminaries. [X] felt that we shouldn't misinterpret the rankings, since there is a time lag involved and we have had many retirements at the same time. He believes that in fact the amount and quality of publication is increasing. [Y] . . . believes we must generate things inside the University to bring attention to our activities. [Z], following up this idea suggested we might have conferences, attracting prominent speakers. . . . [The chairman] then suggested that he [Z] and [W] might serve as a subcommittee to receive suggestions of this kind.

Ordinary and perhaps justified concern, yet astonishing in its way. This English department has been one of the most prominent in the country since before 1900. It draws good graduate students and places them well (though the present job crisis has doubtless had an impact). A job there is a plum. There are a dozen department

2. A rambling note about sources, with one curious turn. In preparing to write this chapter, I wrote to friends and acquaintances at about 25 colleges and universities, asking if they could send samplings of departmental memos, minutes, internal newsletters, and the like. Many obliged, and I owe them thanks, which I will not repeat individually, for documents that I shall quote from time to time here. In my letter I said I would feel free to quote from materials sent, and asked that my correspondents not send anything confidential or sensitive. Perhaps the midwestern chairman who sent me the minutes here excerpted did not notice that caution. Be that it as it may, when it happened that I delivered part of this chapter as a talk at his university, he expressed dismay at the violation of decorum I had committed in naming his institution and some of his colleagues. In deference to his wishes and those of another member of that department whom I consulted, I have omitted proper names and identifying clues from this excerpt. My purpose is not to embarrass friends and colleagues, and, indeed, it will be apparent that my analysis is critical, not of the department involved, but of the professionally created anxieties that made the department react as it did—and that made the chairman ask for secrecy, later. This aftermath makes the example even more illustrative of my thesis.

members or more whose reputations I know, though they are not in my "field." This is a healthy department by marketplace standards. More to the point, the concerned department members do not suggest that their effectiveness in teaching or research has diminished or that they feel any local need for more "luminaries" among their number. Apparently the department's work is going forward well. The "sad decline" has occurred, not in the department or its undertakings, but in highly subjective perceptions of the department's reputation by those polled in the Cartter Report, most of whom can know little or nothing directly of the department's quality. As one member plausibly suggested, the trouble might even be that the names of some well-known faculty already in the department do not everywhere free associate with the name of the university. Yet this largely or entirely mythical decline stirred the department to action. A committee is formed; senior appointments are being sought. The department is mobilized as if its honesty had been impugned, or its budget halved, or as if it were a restaurant demoted by the *Guide Michelin*. The Cartter Report has robbed no member of the department, nor will any member's work be improved by the addition of distinguished faculty, yet such is the power of competitive, departmental thinking that the Chairman and Executive Committee feel in some way diminished by their new rating.

Such thinking tugs hard on most of what faculty do in their work, shaping the plots we call careers, providing myths of prestige, determining the forms we teach by. It is significant that the Cartter Report, the principal comparative index of institutional quality among universities, takes departments as the units for rating: they are at the center of our self-image, and of the value we set on our professional selves. In many ways departments and the departmental ideal have power that extends beyond, and is greater than, that of the colleges and universities to which departments are formally subordinate. And as Jencks and Riesman note, "large numbers of Ph.D.'s now regard themselves almost as independent professionals like doctors or lawyers, responsible primarily to themselves and their colleagues rather than their employers, and committed to the advancement of knowledge rather than of any particular institution." [3] This shift in the locus of power from the administrators and trustees of universities to faculty members and departments is at the heart of the "academic revolution" Jencks and Riesman describe.

The influence of departments extends outward beyond elite universities, or even new four-year institutions like Florida Technical University or Missouri Southern College. Junior colleges, with their very different purposes and without the juniors, seniors, and graduate students who justify specialized offerings in universities, have organized automatically and almost universally in this way. Junior colleges have changed some of our forms: for example, fewer than one-half the English teachers in junior colleges are in "English departments." But they *are* in departments, by whatever name. High school education, too, is formed in our image. As Wallace Douglas well argues (*ADE Bulletin* 20, p. 13), "there has always been a very close connection between the needs of the colleges and the education offered in the high schools . . . the high school began as 'the special protege' of the university, and . . . high school people have always looked that way for sanction of their aims, methods, and programs." It is a cliché by now that *Silas Marner* was taught in thousands of high school English classes in the 1960's because Harvard, in a surge of modernity, required Silas Marner of candidates for admission in the 1880's. Such cultural standards are handed down to the schools, and so diffused through the entire society, basically, by university departments of English.

When Thomas Wilcox did his survey of undergraduate programs in English, now published as *The Anatomy of College English*,[4] There

---

3. Christopher Jencks and David Riesman, *The Academic Revolution* (Garden City, N.Y.: Doubleday, 1968), p. 14.
4. San Francisco, Jossey-Bass, 1973. I refer to this version when possible. But Wilcox kindly supplied me with his manuscript of the book before publication, and, in a few instances, I use statistics omitted from the published book. The unpublished version was a HEW report, "A Comprehensive Survey of Undergraduate Programs in English in the United States," May 14, 1970. Even then, of course, some of the statistics and conclusions were out of date; they are more so now. But for convenience I refer to Wilcox's findings in the present tense—hoping that our present may be allowed to encompass eight years.

were 21,000 full-time teachers of English in four-year institutions. English was the largest department at two-thirds of these colleges and universities. How were and are they constituted, these curious institutions in which we work? I shall present three characteristics pertinent to my theme.

First, a department is a *hierarchical* group, arrayed in the usual ranks at 98% of the institutions (Wilcox, pp. 4–5). Below the bottom rank are teaching assistants and other part-timers. Above all ranks, in a sense, is the chairman. He is elected by his colleagues at only 7.5% of institutions (Wilcox, p. 40); generally, his authority comes from outside the department. His formal power over colleagues is great, especially in the critical matters of promotion and tenure: in 43% of departments, the chairman alone recommends advancement; in another 22%, the chairman and his advisory committee do (Wilcox, p. 22). Elsewhere, the senior members promote or fire the junior. In virtually no department is promotion decided by a vote of all members.

Yet surely, this is a strange hierarchy. Orders do not move down along its conduits, as in a military line of command or even a corporation. The assistant professor does not report to an associate professor or give daily assignments to the instructors below him. On the contrary, most departments try to avoid a strong sense of subordination within the regular ranks and even suppress the order of hierarchy in daily tasks. Titles are rarely used on office doors or in the departmental office. Colleagues call one another by first names. The more self-confident the department, the more value it is likely to set on independence and full collegial status for members in the lower ranks. New or less confident institutions may stand on the ceremony of "Dr." or "Professor," whereas more ivied universities make a point of "Mr." Rank is not power, so much as it is a background condition largely ignored in the daily work of the department.

But if rank is not power, it *is* status. Thus the great exception to the egalitarianism of departments is the matter of personnel decisions, before which junior members quietly leave the room. In promotion, reappointment, severance, and the award of tenure a

department readjusts its internal relations of status, awarding or
denying rank according to its estimate of the professional achievement of the faculty member and the status of the department itself.
(In the call for letters from outside referees, and in the questions "Is
this the best person we can get in Milton?" and "Would you give
him tenure at your university?" is an implied measuring of the home
department against others, and against the best position it can aspire
to in national rankings.) Hence the exquisite care departments invest
in these decisions—probably more at most places than in decisions
about the curriculum itself. This is to say that departments are the
determiners of professional success, the arbiters of *careers*.[5] A professional career differs from a non-professional working life precisely in
that the professional moves upward in distinction, but not from a
state of subordination to one of command. He is in theory
independent from the moment he passes through his final initiation
rite. In a university, this independence holds up 99% of the time, but
vanishes when the faculty member is up for promotion. It is a
complex fate to be a junior member of a department.

Power, as opposed to status, does, of course, exist in departments,
and power not distributed among equals resides mainly in the
chairman and his executive aides. The chairman may assign
teaching loads and specific courses, adjust salaries, hire new faculty,

5. Departmental newsletters are revealing; they chronicle the extramural doings of
faculty as much as internal affairs. The newsletter of the University of Massachusetts
(Amherst) department, December, 1970, includes much amiable chat, but also two
single-spaced typed pages of the recent publications of members. The Michigan
newsletter for Spring, 1969, discounts its boasts with mild irony, but boasts
nonetheless: "John Styan has become a force in the drama, literary and theatrical, on
both sides of the Atlantic, with four books already out and one emerging."
"Restoration and Eighteenth Century is kept alive by Allison. . . ." "Our most
distinguished missionary to the fallen world beyond Ann Arbor recently has been
Robert Super, who read three lectures at Northwestern. . . ." Louis T. Milic,
chairman at Cleveland State, writes that "Prestige literally is an illusion," but
resignedly agrees that "A new university must build a reputation." And the newsletter
(*The Unicorn*, March, 1972) in which his reflections appear includes the usual career
notes—"William Cherubini was a discussant of one of the papers at the Midwest
MLA meeting. . . ." "Harold Dailey delivered a paper on . . . before the first
general session of the Annual Conference of the Research Society for Victorian
Periodicals at the University of Illinois, Urbana." Etc. As I read them, these
periodicals mainly reassure department members and graduates that their home place
is an honorable one to be affiliated with.

determine how money is spent on departmental programs and activities. Whether he acts autocratically or democratically in these affairs he always has more impact on their resolution than his colleagues. And the ideology of chairmanship in contemporary universities stresses the distinctness of his role. Wilcox notes that the job of running the shop is increasingly delegated to a chairman conceived as administrator, and that, at many universities, the chairman needn't be a scholar-teacher, *primus inter pares* (pp. 42–3). The pages of the *ADE Bulletin* are full of injunctions by deans and other administrators that, as Bruce Harkness puts it, "The day of the happy amateur is over" (*ADE Bulletin* 19, p. 13), that the chairman needs to be a sophisticated manager, that he should have a professional administrative assistant, that he can exercise great influence over programs if he learns how to identify the sources of power in a quasi-democratic setting.

Robert B. Heilman's account of how it feels is a typical one:

the chairman needs a usable attitude to the working of the post and of his working in it. Let him avoid clichés about accepting challenges and conducting dialogues. Let him not think of himself basically as a servitor. . . . He should not, at the other extreme, think of himself as essentially a big policy man . . . . As a matter of fact, a good deal of policy is made by the very handling of routine and detail—by the selection of committees, the working out of teaching schedules, the management of those lesser parts of the budget where there is little room for choice . . . Let [the chairman] be prepared for drudgery, and at the same time find, in the machinery amid which he inevitably lives, the devices by which gradually to move affairs in a better direction. "The Ghost on the Ramparts" (*ADE Bulletin* 19, p. 4).[6]

This person's role is quite different from that of the free professionals he works with, and as several *ADE* writers suggest, he must have his administrative power if they are to have their freedom.

We can reasonably see the chairman as interpreter between the bureaucratic world of contingency, which is the university at large, and the sheltered world in which individual teachers aspire to dwell.

6. This essay, along with other reflections on the profession, is reprinted in a book by Heilman also titled *The Ghost on the Ramparts* (Athens, Georgia: University of Georgia Press, 1973).

"The departmental executive officer . . . finds himself caught between this new world of hard-driving management and the old world of administration by personal conversation. The administration insists that he and his department conform to established management routine; his colleagues stridently scoff at such routines and do the best they can to undermine them" (John Gerber, Chairman, Iowa, *ADE Bulletin* 15, p. 4). Precisely: the chairman's power comes from the multiversity in which departments find themselves, and it is necessary because decisions have to pass back and forth between a managerial and a professional setting. Robert Rogers notes that the chairman has become a maker of important decisions as universities have become more complex, and power has been decentralized, and shifted partly to the faculty. He also suggests that "The best departments . . . nearly all have five- or ten-year plans of development . . . in which existing strengths are inventoried, goals are set forth, and specific requirements for systematic, orderly growth are detailed (*ADE Bulletin* 15, p. 17). Planning is the characteristic activity of the technostructure, Galbraith argues. Universities need to plan ahead, in the new industrial state, much as do corporations or governments. So the department chairman is at the farthest outpost of "progress." He is the remotest arm of the central administration, and professors consent to his having managerial power, in exchange for protecting their own very different way of life. The distribution of power in departments, in short, is such as to nurture faculty members' ideas of themselves as professionals.

The second point I would like to make about departments concerns the extraordinary place that recruiting holds among their activities. Gerber says that staffing "may be our greatest satisfaction in the job" of chairing (*ADE Bulletin* 15, p. 8), Heilman says that for him "appointments are the most interesting of all tasks" (*ADE Bulletin* 19, p. 9), and Harkness, speaking as a dean, advises that the main job of a chairman is that of recruiting faculty members. "Choosing faculty is the one thing in which a chairman must not fail" (*ADE Bulletin* 19, p. 15). This emphasis seems natural, I think, only because we rarely stop to ponder it. No department head in a government agency or corporation would consider replenishment of the ranks to be his supreme task or the measure of his success. After all, there is work to be done. An academic department's work is teaching, mainly. No doubt good recruiting does lead to good departmental teaching, but that's not the way chairmen and deans talk about it: they speak of the "strength" of the department in the different areas, its "balance," its general "quality." They regard making a new appointment as fitting a piece into a puzzle, which, if properly completed, forms the image of a distinguished department. Recall that the midwestern department chairman, faced with a decline in rating, thought immediately of appointing a senior luminary, for whom no need had been felt in the daily work of the department previously.

Another oddity about recruitment is that universities and colleges let departments do it. The administration and trustees have the formal right to appoint, but the actual power almost always resides in departments. Similarly, 81% of English departments find that their personnel recommendations generally or always carry.[7] If faculty appointments are so critical to the well-being of a university, and if departments have this responsibility, it's worth seeing how they carry it out.

How in fact do departments carry out their extraordinary powers of appointment? Unsurprisingly, Wilcox identifies such practices as these: (1) hiring is generally done by special field, especially in the most influential universities (but remember the vacancy at Missouri Southern College); at 32% of the colleges and universities, the English department looks *only* for specialists, and this figure is 48.6% in departments with graduate programs, 50.6% in large institutions;[8] (2) departments in large universities are much more likely to hire at the top—40% did so between 1964 and 1967;[9] These lustrous appointments are the main indicators of achievement in the profession, which lead to upward mobility and fame; (3) though

7. The unpublished HEW report, p. 34.
8. Wilcox, p. 14, for the first of these figures. The other two were on p. 17 of the HEW report.
9. Wilcox omits this figure from the published book. It is on p. 19 of the HEW report.

teaching ranks first or second among stated criteria for advancement in 86% of the institutions, and scholarship in 35% only,[10] those departments concerned with reputation value scholarship more highly, so that success is defined for everyone by publication and the notice that accompanies it. In brief, the division of rewards in this system lends support to the values that faculty have made pre-eminent in American higher education: specialization, research, visibility among peers, loyalty to the guild rather than to the college or university. The highest emotion and interest fix on the transactions that cement or alter our meritocracy. Too: admission and accreditation are critical acts in any profession. In the control the department exercises over entry and advancement, it shows itself as the main seat of our professionalism.

My third set of anomalies in departmental conduct have to do with curriculum. Since these anomalies are familiar enough, I'll be brief. As universities have given over the selection of faculty to departments, so have they consigned their right to plan the very nature of instruction. There are still some requirements imposed by the whole faculty, to be sure, and in some colleges there are general education courses beyond the control of any department. But by far the largest amount of instruction goes on in courses and programs that are under departmental authority. And departments lead in initiating and abolishing courses. So it is hardly an exaggeration to say that when a student looks at the array of educational possibilities before her, she is looking at the invention of departments. What have English departments done with this considerable freedom?

Freshman English is a fixture, of course, even though its importance has recently been lessened. But its presence in the curriculum does not come from departmental initiative—it is the other way around, in fact, of which more later. Beyond freshman English Wilcox found that the survey of English literature was still the foundation of the department's own program—required of majors in 47% of the colleges and advised in another 42%.[11] And the survey is

10. The HEW report, p. 36.
11. Wilcox, p. 138; but see p. 162 of the original HEW report for the exact figures.

what its name implies, a view in miniature of the literature in our territory. Though it is arranged in chronological order, few would argue that the survey embodies any serious history or goes beyond the boundaries of the department's academic space.

The survey is gateway to the major, and virtually all four-year institutions offer a major in English. Why? It may not be a bad way to organize some students' time, but is it the sole right way, as its universality implies? Only once among the departmental plans, curricular proposals, and critiques of our field I've read have I run into the thought that departments might do better without the major (Kenneth Eble, "A Newer English," *ADE Bulletin* 27, p. 17). Yet as a program—an integrated sequence of educational events—the major is in disorder. Wilcox reports that it is amorphous, without evident principles to justify its substance or sequence (pp. 137–38). Apparently the concept "English major" is a necessary but empty one. We would not feel comfortable without such a program in the catalogue, but what it comprises is up for negotiation at each college. I submit that this happens for two reasons. First, the tacit principle behind our model for it is the Ph.D. curriculum. But that sort of "coverage" is impossible to cram into a liberal arts major, hence the various compromises. Second, since comprehensiveness is out of reach, undergraduate departments realize the professional ideal not through their whole programs but through individual courses, among which the major steers her way. The chief way of organizing our field for undergraduates is still periodization, which preserves the separate units of a Ph.D. experience even though the gestalt is unachievable. A hodgepodge of other academic specialties (drama, Melville and Hawthorne, history of the language) make up the rest of the curriculum. The English department, given its head, plans curriculum by filling the catalogue with courses matching professionally designated special fields.

In this skeptical frame of mind, examine what some of the elite departments say they are doing. From time to time, *New Literary History* prints under the general title "Literary History in the

University," statements about curriculum.[12] These differ a great deal from one another. The emphasis at Yale is interpretation of major works, at Hopkins intellectual trends within the field, at Berkeley the context of literature, and so on. The curriculums, too, are varied. Yet they have a common basis. The range of issues that trouble departments is roughly this:

1. How does literary history fit into our professional life? How can we place it in the curriculum? In scholarship?
2. What shall be the legitimate fields and modes of study? The challenge of new criticism to literary history is the backdrop of this question. Every statement—and I gather every curriculum— tries to strike a balance between an interpretation of individual works and a historical treatment. The attempt at reconciliation serves also to justify the presence in a department of both kinds of courses and to make professional room for different modes of scholarship by the faculty. The statements from Berkeley, Irvine, and Hopkins list books by department members to illustrate variety. All the departments claim to be pluralistic. They hold the umbrella of professional legitimacy over as many fields as possible.
3. How does the faculty work out its diverse interests? At Hopkins, in internal dialectic (in Humanities Seminars, History of Ideas Club, etc.); at Wisconsin, by division of the curriculum into areas of specialization, with which faculty and students can "identify," and so gain some sense of "community."
4. What does the field as a whole "need"? Adams says there is a need for literary theory, which motivates the Irvine program. Jordan says that we "need to recreate the past," as a means of doing justice to literature in the present. In most discussions the field is conceived as an organism with its own metabolism, diseases, needs for aliment and therapy.

12. I refer to the ones about Yale by Martin Price (Winter, 1970), Johns Hopkins by Ronald Paulson (Spring, 1970), Berkeley by John E. Jordan (Spring, 1971), Irvine by Hazard Adams (Fall, 1972), Wisconsin by Charles T. Scott (Spring, 1973), and Stanford by Bliss Carnochan (Winter, 1973). Ralph Cohen, editor of *NLH*, kindly let me see the latter two in advance of publication.

The priority of professional issues like these seems to me to explain a certain thinness in most of the statements. The Wisconsin one is almost wholly preoccupied with the right time and way for graduate students to specialize in a chronological field and the balance between such concentration and coverage of all fields. At Berkeley, the issue is drawn between those department members (who are they?) who want to study works "in isolation," and those (most of the department) who think that "the individual work must . . . be seen in its context, of which literary history is a part." The department at Irvine, with the advantage of starting fresh, takes as its major premises that English shall work closely with Comparative Literature and Creative Writing, and that they will be concerned with theory and its relation to critical practice. Irvine, like the rest, assumes departments (Foreign Languages and Literatures broke up into the usual fields as soon as growth permitted), special fields, courses. Only in the statement from Yale does one get the tension of debate about where truth might abide among the various schools and fields, about the way history and art really are.

Doubtless such a debate is outside the limits of what these chairmen and spokesmen thought themselves invited to prepare. Still, *sub specie eternitatis* their statements seem remarkable because of their limits. The subject is academic program, but students hardly figure in the rationale offered by teachers, except (e.g., with Berkeley and Wisconsin) as a body of opinion and a market—fluctuating—for courses. About students' existential needs and about the relationship of their education to the work they are preparing to do there is surprisingly little. There is virtually nothing about society outside the academy, about how departments conceive *its* needs, about the effect they hope to have on society through their scholarship or their students. Aside from the piety of a few references to great scholars of earlier generations, there is no sense of a past, particularly an institutional past. The departments relate their work to literature and the history of ideas, sprung loose from the more mundane history of American universities—and freshman composition—on which all literary history in this country is parasitic, in a sense to be explored in the next three chapters. And, except for Yale, there is little attempt to found curricular choices in a struggle toward truths about literature and history. It is to be sure *natural* that the chairmen would have conceived their accounts thus; I mean simply to point to the strangeness of what "natural" has come to mean for us and our profession.

One can imagine goals for literary education that are at least worth considering and different from these: to educate students as critics of our verbal culture; to give them an understanding of the fictions (in Kermode's or Frye's sense) we tell one another, which give direction to our politics, our work, and all our acts; to nourish self-understanding and self-realization as literature supposedly can do. The elite graduate departments are not of course deaf to such considerations. But when they lay out their goals and methods in a professional setting they stay on safer ground. And these are the designers of our profession's self-image.

Given this conservatism at the center, it is instructive to note how the undergraduate English offering has responded during the years since Wilcox's survey: years of the most insistent pressure for change from minority groups, from students impatient with purely professional training, from the new groups admitted to our rapidly expanding university system, from disaffected faculty. For there is no doubt that change has occurred. Some has been imposed from outside the department: the MLA found, in response to questionnaires, that by 1971 "over 40% of the four-year colleges and universities had reduced or removed their English and foreign language requirements for graduation" (John H. Fisher, "Facing Up to the Problems of Going Interdisciplinary," *ADE Bulletin* 32, p. 7). But there has been movement toward change from within, too. Sitting at the center of the whirlpool in 1969, John Fisher observed that "The subject of English in this country has been used to inculcate a white, Anglo-Saxon, Protestant ethic," and went on, "My own feeling is that the game is just about played out" ("Movement in English," *ADE Bulletin* 22, p. 41). The perception is not unique amongst us, and it would seem to dictate sharp change.

Fisher's own proposal, in other articles, is that the humanities become interdisciplinary.

A successful interdisciplinary education seems to me the antithesis of the free elective. . . . The key to an effective interdisciplinary education seems to me a "systems" approach. That is, not to think of individual courses or individual fields or departments, but of an interrelated series of courses and independent study activities. ("Facing Up to the Problems of Going Interdisciplinary, p. 7)

And elsewhere:

Probably it is simply too much to ask of English departments that they become departments of the humanities and embrace all things. Nevertheless, if I were a chairman, I would be discussing joint programs with the departments of speech and television, and I would be laying great stress on what the MLA annual meeting treats under the headings of "popular culture" and "literature and society." ("The King's English in a Working Man's World," *ADE Bulletin* 26, p. 20)

Fisher's suggestion is less than revolutionary, but he does ask that departments base their teaching on models other than the strictly professional one and that they resist their proclivity to think solely in terms of courses.

Immediately following this last article by Fisher is one by William David Schaefer (then chairman at UCLA, and now Fisher's successor as Executive Secretary of MLA), called "Good Grief, John; Not That." Schaefer rejects the idea of joining with speech and television, but says that he will recommend to his colleagues "that we continue to be flexible in all aspects of program and planning." He explains:

I will encourage my colleagues to continue to be sensitive to and respond to requests for special courses, offering not merely the old standard in "American Pop Literature," but, under our floating rubric of "Contemporary Themes" and "Literature and Society," courses such as "The Proletarian Novel," "The LeRoi Jones School of Afro-American Writing," "Violence in American Literature," "Tolkien and the Christian Hero," and "Contemporary Themes of Innocence and Experience." Whatever happens to the departmental budget, I will urge my colleagues to delete not a single course from our series of undergraduate seminars—24 each year with a limit of 15 students taught in student-requested subjects such as "William Carlos Williams," "Robert Lowell," or "Nabokov," as well as "The Occult in

Medieval Literature," "The 17th Century English Lyric," and "Elizabethan Platonism"—to mention just a few of those being offered this year. (p. 24)

It should be no surprise that, so far, Schaefer's vision is nearer reality. For it preserves the *course* as the basic unit of curricular thinking, and the device for meeting students' interest in helping determine the content of their education. And it permits going on to say—with Schaefer—but we will *also* "continue to insist that any student who graduates from UCLA having chosen to major in English should complete courses in Milton and in Chaucer, as well as the two-course sequence in Shakespeare"—or whatever the local equivalent is.

An informal survey by John Kinnaird [13] shows that departments have been quick to realize the advantages of Schaefer's solution: they have allowed a proliferation of new studies and approaches, new "relevant" contents and styles—yet without yielding any ground near the professional heart of the curriculum. In all but a few of the 71 institutions he surveyed, Kinnaird found the standard requirements for the English *major* more or less intact. Only nine departments had open majors; and a few traditional courses had been eliminated. Yet the departments had added dozens of new courses: black literature, ethnic literature, film, female studies, science-fiction, psychoanalysis and literature, the literature of adolescence, satanism, the city, and so on. In short, the opportunity for English departments to reconceive their task has been bypassed in favor of a set of conveniences that preserve *both* the professional habits of a lifetime and the popularity of the department's offerings. The force that makes English departments so timid in exercise of their curricular power is, I think, less a WASP ethnocentrism (look at our courses in black literature) than a professional one.

In these three areas, then—internal distribution of power and status,

13. "What's Happening to the English Curriculum: A Survey and Some Reflections," *College English*, vol. 34 (March, 1973), pp. 755–72. There is much evidence that the trends reported by Kinnaird have continued, in Elizabeth Wooten Cowan, ed., *Options for the Teaching of English, The Undergraduate Curriculum* (New York: MLA, 1975). I'm grateful to Ms. Cowan for sending a pre-publication copy.

staff appointments, educational planning—English departments act to enhance the professional self-image of their members. I have tried to show that this kind of professionalism makes departments more conservative than they might be in using the considerable powers they possess. They serve the discipline and its traditions and respond to social change only within that framework. In a pinch, they will preserve what is familiar, while adding the new as necessary, in convenient packages.

Naturally this modus operandi has led to tensions in the last few years, as professional habits have been challenged by financial cutbacks, the job crisis, criticism from students. There are jeremiads and warnings. A dean like Bruce Harkness can tell chairmen that society will "demand to know why our own graduates in English can't read and write better and aren't more liberally and vocationally educated. The truly new thing is that we will have to answer these perennial questions." And, with even more bite:

Students will suddenly realize that the administration has not turned down their petitions from perverse motives but from motives ultimately related to the academic freedom of the faculty. I see a few signs that students are already beginning to realize this and ask for their own academic freedom. (*ADE Bulletin* 19, p. 22)

But the more general attitude persists that when society devalues our services it exhibits a temporary aberration. "If a department is meeting its obligations to the students and to the profession, it will simultaneously be meeting the major part of its obligation to society" (John Gerber, "The Chairman and His Department," *ADE Bulletin* 15, p. 6). What's good for General Motors. . . . To press the identity of one's own interests with those of the larger society is the normal task of ideology, and we teachers of literature have our own ideology.

Behind such justifications of our acts, which appeal to universal welfare, it is often not hard to see the welfare of the English professor. Thus, Jacob Adler writes:

we can demand scholarship [of English teachers] because scholarship needs to be done . . . . Every great author needs reinterpreting for every age.

Every age produces new eminent writers who need interpretation. Our own age has produced, and is producing, new insights from other disciplines which need to be applied to literature. ("The System and Its Consequences," *ADE Bulletin* 18, p. 19)

Do the great authors need reinterpreting, or do *we* professors need to reinterpret them? *Who* needs to apply to literature insights from other disciplines? Adler's rhetoric, common enough, is that of presenting local interests as categorical imperatives. The verb "need" is the equivocator in this excerpt. Its parallel can be found in many such passages. Often needs are abstracted away from the professors, put as immutable givens, or as needs of "the department" or "the college." The Director of the Office for Research Contracts at Harvard asked the Harvard English Department to help him define the needs of such an organization. Doubtless to everyone's amazement, he was then able to identify these needs: additional funds for faculty salaries, additional faculty, additional secretarial assistance, more office space, more funds for graduate students, more funds for visiting professors and sabbaticals, and funds for publications of books—"which although valuable may not have a wide commercial appeal" (Robert E. Gentry, "Planning, Submitting and Administering Grants and Contracts," *ADE Bulletin* 19, pp. 29–30). It is easy to imagine what gains there would be for Harvard and for the general culture were the needs of this indigent department met. As Heilman says well, though with a cynical inflection scarcely to my own taste, "too often . . . loyalty is not even to the profession but simply to the professor himself, and such a loyalist tends to regard improvement in the institution as an automatic by-product of privileges for himself" ("The Ghost on the Ramparts, *ADE Bulletin* 19, p. 6).

A faculty tries to look out for its immediate interests, like every other group. Departments work to advance faculty interests. Our myths of cultural need and the general welfare are the song to this dance. That there should be such myths for teachers or any other group is quite normal, as I have insisted. But in the content of the myths, and in their relationship to what the groups actually do for society, there is room for variation. The professional ideology of English teachers emphasizes transmitting high culture and generating new knowledge. Why should this be so, when surely we spend, as a group, a tiny proportion of our time in scholarship and only a relatively small proportion teaching on the higher slopes of culture? What we do most is teach—and mostly lower level undergraduate courses. Everyone recognizes this. Yet a chairman whose understanding is explicit—"Though much of this *Newsletter* [of the Michigan English Department, Spring 1970] is devoted to a summarizing of scholarly activity, it remains true that the Department functions primarily as a teaching body"—can in the same breath say that "the most signal achievement" of the department during the past two years has been a reduction in teaching load to two courses per semester, for all faculty.

I don't believe that many English teachers are lazy; rather, the tension here is between the kind of work we see ourselves as doing and the kind society is most willing to pay us for. An explanation is required for the fact that English teachers don't claim more credit for the part of our work that society values and less for the part that society hardly knows of and would probably disapprove of if it knew more.

I think that the explanation is not far away. Much of what we do with society's full sanction is work demeaning to professional egos and, in fact, morally dubious. Freshman composition, responsible according to William Riley Parker for the very existence of English departments, is certainly the subject for which most of our colleagues in other departments and (as far as they care) the general public hold us primarily accountable. It occupies 40% of the teaching time of English departments, including their graduate assistants (Wilcox, p. 63). Yet the kind of acculturation practiced in it, with red pencil and *Harbrace Handbook*, is not the kind Matthew Arnold or the professional ideologues have envisioned.

The bulk of our teaching time beyond freshman English goes to the major program: Who takes it? One of Wilcox's most intriguing statistics is that more than two-thirds of the English majors (68.5%) are women (p. 129). It seems likely that the imbalance owes, not to any "effeminacy" of literary culture, but to two basic socioeconomic facts: that the main job for which a major in English specifically prepares one is teaching English in secondary school and that this work—less prestigious and worse paid than most jobs for college graduates—is still mainly relegated to women. High school English teachers perform one stage earlier the acculturation—grammar, usage, verbal decorum—we attempt again in freshman English. From society's point of view this is the main work that we do ("Oh, you teach English? I'd better watch my grammar").

We train young people, and those who train young people, in the skills required by a society most of whose work is done on paper and through talk, not by physical labor. We also discipline the young to do assignments, on time, to follow instructions, to turn out uniform products, to observe the etiquette of verbal communication. And, in so doing, we eliminate the less adapted, the ill-trained, the city youth with bad verbal manners, blacks with the wrong dialect, Latinos with the wrong language, and the rebellious of all shapes and sizes, thus helping to maintain social and economic inequalities. Most of these are unwilled consequences, and, since they also run counter to the egalitarian ideology of the larger culture, it is not surprising that the English department fails to point them out when justifying its pay.

Besides, the relation between these consequences and our work is not even apparent to most. Daniel Berndt of USOE is worth quoting:

members of the academic community have difficulty in understanding the connection between their own elitist values and the racism of the institution within which they operate. Their own humane liberalism is quite irrelevant in the face of an educational world which institutionally discriminates. Our definitions of quality cause more discrimination and waste more human resources every day than all the overt racists could manage in a lifetime of effort. Given the opportunities to teach in, give money to, do research with, or vote power for, we will exercise the options in favor of places that rank high in the production of what are conceived to be quality Ph.D.'s . . . . Entrance into and power within those colleges and universities are preserved by a system of tests and measurements, grade-point averages, and self-regarding criteria of quality which, intentionally or not, discriminate against those who are not trained in institutions attuned to those criteria and staffed by their graduates. (*ADE Bulletin* 20, p. 23)

Alan M. Hollingsworth may be right in supposing "that the snobbishness and implicit biases of college English departments are reinforcing secondary English teachers in their support of a destructive system of ability grouping in the schools" ("Last Chance for English?" ADE *Bulletin* 26, p. 43). He mentions a school that had resolutely remained untracked since 1954, with continuing resistance from just one department—the English department. And he refers to Alfred Yates, ed., *Grouping in Education* (London, 1966) for evidence that, in spite of the damage tracking does, "secondary teachers in general, and English teachers in particular, strongly favor the track system." Without entering this controversy, I do think it clear that in guiding our lives by the professionally validated hierarchies, in competition for places in elite institutions, we college teachers also vote with our feet for a track system. And at least in some of our leaders' public pronouncements it *is* possible to spot attitudes that nourish the English department's work as sorter-out of elites and domesticator of the rest. Part of the background for professional conversation is the familiar hierarchy of institutions. Harvard, always, as the example of undoubted quality: "If an applicant presents a *summa* degree from Harvard, shall we say, it is unlikely that anybody will ask for supporting evidence. If, on the other hand, he presents straight A's from Slippery Rock. . . ." (Bradford A. Booth, *ADE Bulletin* 20, p. 19). More often than Slippery Rock, we're given fictitious examples of the boondocks—"Podunk State," etc. Harvard itself shares the implied values: "There may be a place for such a minimal concept of preparation, a teaching Ph.D., but it is not Harvard." [14] To be sure, these distinctions are often real enough: I mean to comment, simply, on the way that a world of haves and have-nots is taken for granted.

Chairmen also turn up on the side of regularity and social norms, by and large. This appears in much value-free wisdom about crisis management. English departments are "the attractive homes of both reformers and revolutionaries":

14. Harvard English department *Newsletter* (February, 1971), p. 2.

That is why you chairmen will spend so many of your waking hours talking to students about every facet of your job and every one of their grievances and demands . . . you will listen patiently to reckless accusations and unfounded charges. . . . You will be agreeable, I dare say, to putting students on some, perhaps most, of your departmental committees. . . . Grim though the prospect is, you may also be subjected to intense pressure to reveal your salary schedules and recommendations. (Gwin Kolb, "The Crisis in the Profession," *ADE Bulletin* 22, pp. 9–10)

The chairmen are assumed to be neither for nor against the "reformers and revolutionaries," but only for what Kolb calls "the tranquility of your schools." As a former associate provost, chancellor, and whatnot, I know the feeling. Administrative neutrality is three-quarters the executive's natural urge to make it through to martini time.

Departments can sometimes be observed passing on the discipline more directly, as in the Nevada (Reno) handbook for teaching fellows in English (Fall, 1970):

You have been hired because the Department felt you capable of handling your teaching responsibilities. It is, however, no secret that teaching fellows . . . have been under fire from a number of places in recent months. For your own protection, the Director of Freshman English will visit your class at least once a semester. . . .

These rules are minimal rules. . . . You deserve freedom in your classroom to teach effectively. We do urge you to remember, however, that you are not a one-man or one-woman university. . . . If you feel bold enough to put your own job on the line for some cause or issue, take time to remember that you may endanger others as well and temper your actions accordingly.

Full membership in the profession is available to these novices only upon payment of certain dues, as the tone more than the substance of the injunctions communicates.[15] Most subtly, the profession's

---

15. At Texas, the director of freshman English (James Sledd, scarcely a conservative), has to include in a similar handbook the following warning: "The students' religious, moral, and social views must at all times be respected; but on one subject, the use of drugs, respect for their views must never in any circumstances become encouragement to commit a felony," in "Notes on Freshman English" (Fall, 1970), p. 7. The caution is understandable; yet it must rather damp one's enthusiasm for pursuing unorthodox ideas in the classroom.

endorsement of society's values and anxieties shows in the half jocular way chairmen talk to one another about deviants and troublemakers—"the bushy-haired reformer," "the parliamentarian who is forever . . . requiring the chairman to report on the activities of the past month," "the relevantrepreneurs," "the cantankerous, the niggling, the undependable, the disruptive."

If such attitudes work nicely in support of the acculturation we are expected to supervise, however, they are by no means necessary to it. Let me reiterate that I do not accuse our profession of voluntarily turning the crank of society's machine of repression. Some of us are repressively inclined, others are not. The point is that, institutionally, we perform certain services at society's behest to earn a livelihood, but these services are not the parts of our work that accord best with professional dignity or with what we think society *ought* to want from us. Ideology tries to make reality match up with desire. And the ideology we use, whatever our external politics, is the very widespread ethos of professionalism, as adapted to our own field at work.

CHAPTER NINE

Why They Do It

I am arguing that many peculiarities of English departments, and of the way teachers act through them, can best be understood as the result of a clash between the professional claims of the faculty and the externally imposed conditions of our working lives. The department is a faculty member's professional home, the locus of his career.[1] It acts as an extension of his professional superego. In pursuing this idea it will be useful to step back from the details of English department life and see what shape professionalism takes as a more general social phenomenon.

For it is general. Everett C. Hughes, the most illuminating theorist of the professions I've come across, describes the "librarians, insurance salesmen, nurses, public relations people, YMCA secretaries, probation officers, personnel men, vocational guidance directors, city managers, hospital administrators, and even public health physicians," among others, who take his seminars partly to be able to demonstrate that "some occupation—their own—has become or is on the verge of becoming a true profession." [2] Follow Hughes's discussion a bit farther. All these groups are trying to get to the same place, but their starting points differ:

The insurance salesmen try to free themselves of the business label; they are not selling, they are giving people expert and objective diagnosis of their

1. John Fisher says this well, in his analysis of the obstacles to interdisciplinary programs, "Facing Up to the Problems of Going Interdisciplinary," *ADE Bulletin*, 32, p. 8.
2. "Professions," *Daedalus*, vol. 92 (Fall, 1963), p. 658.

risks and advising them as to the best manner of protecting themselves . . . . The librarians seek to make themselves experts on the effects of
reading, on bibliography and reference, rather than merely custodians and
distributors of books . . . . The social workers earlier were at pains to prove
that their work could not be done by amateurs, people who brought to their
work naught but good will. The YMCA secretary wants his occupation
recognized not merely as that of offering young men from the country a
pleasant road to Protestant righteousness in the city, but as a more universal
one of dealing with groups of young people. All that is learned of
adolescence, of behavior in small groups, of the nature and organization of
community life is considered the intellectual base of his work. (p. 659)

And so on. Would-be professionals try to convince the public (a) that
they have something to offer that society vitally needs; (b) that they
offer it in a way that is detached and objective—"having in a
particular case no personal interest such as would influence one's
action or advice" (p. 660); (c) that they "know better than their
clients what ails them or their affairs" (p. 656); (d) that this expertise
cannot be won by apprenticeship alone, rather, "the skills that
characterize a profession flow from and are supported by a fund of
knowledge that has been organized into a . . . *body of theory*";[3] and
(e) that long training in a professional school is necessary to master
that knowledge and those skills.

If the public will grant these premises, then it will have good
reason, in mere self-interest, to allow the professions some rather
special benefits. One is independence from the marketplace. Professionals do not sell to customers, they perform services for clients.
(Even if the professional man draws a salary, he is *not* an "employee"
or an organization man, but a free agent who happens to be "at"
Indiana, not "working for" Indiana. They may charge for these
services "in accord with the standards established by one's colleagues, even if the client receives no satisfaction or benefit" (Jencks
and Riesman, p. 202). (When was the last time an English teacher
had his pay docked because a student wrote no better at the end of
the year than at the beginning?) In fact, the client can't judge

3. Ernest Greenwood, "Aspects of a Profession," in Sigmund Nosow and William H.
Form, eds., *Man, Work, and Society* (New York: Basic Books, 1962), p. 208.

whether he has or has not received fair value; the professional himself is the judge of what's good for his clients, and for society in general, in the area of his competence. As Hughes puts it, the motto of all professions is *credat emptor*. As a corollary of this faith and respect, the client tells the professional "all secrets which bear upon the affairs in hand" (Hughes, p. 657). The relation is a private and confidential one. The classroom, like the doctor's examining room and the confessional, is an inviolable sanctuary. Further, as only professionals can judge what the client needs, they are also sole judges of what constitutes a qualified professional. (Jencks and Riesman define professionalism by the increasing concern for what practitioners think and a declining concern for the laymen's assessment.) They persuade the society to give them control over training, examining, and licensing of new recruits, and to enforce this exclusive right with police power (Greenwood, p. 211). In effect, they have a guaranteed monopoly in their area. Furthermore, as they can direct police power against "quacks" and "charlatans," they are themselves immune from prosecution for mistakes—except, of course, by their professional colleagues.

Hughes says, in another context, "Many of the specific rules of the game of an occupation become comprehensible only when viewed as the almost instinctive attempts of a group of people to cushion themselves against the hazards of their careers." [4] In sum, a profession is in many ways the nearest approximation offered by bourgeois society to title and rank. Small wonder that undertakers prefer to be morticians, and teachers professors.

In addition to the claims that the profession is invaluable to society, and the benefits asked in return, it also maintains some comforting myths mainly for internal use. I'll mention two. One is the idealized relation of professional to client, a relation, as Hughes says, "partly reality, partly stereotype, partly ideal nostalgically attributed to a better past or sought after in a better future." The commonest complaint of professionals is that someone—other workers or the public—interferes with the basic relation. "The teacher

4. *Men and Their Work* (Glencoe, Ill.: The Free Press, 1958), p. 108.

could teach better were it not for parents who fail in their duty or school boards who interfere" (*Men and Their Work*, p. 75). What bothers the professional most is "the differing conceptions of what the work really is or should be, of what mandate has been given by the public, of what it is possible to accomplish and by what means . . ." (p. 76). This description must fit academic people better than almost any other professionals. Our lives are full of resentments against unsympathetic and uncomprehending legislators who think we have a nine-hour work week, against regents and trustees, against interfering alumni, against administrators who drown us in paper work and committees, against refractory buildings-and-grounds men, and, of course, above all against students, who have such difficulty seeing their educational deficiencies aright and cooperating with us in the remedy.

The other central myth is that of the *career*. Greenwood points out that bricklayers and mechanics don't have careers, architects and clergymen do (see "Attributes of a Profession," pp. 215–16). A career implies, not just ascending in seniority, rank, and salary, but moving through recognizable stages, accomplishments, honors. A career is the projection of one's working life onto a value-laden grid—a kind of Uncle Wiggly board—of positions, credits, demerits. Behind this grid, the implied values are those of service to the profession and to "knowledge," not mainly self-interest. When a scholar moves from Associate at Ball State to Professor at Chicago he has, to be sure, improved his salary and work conditions, but the move is also registered by the whole profession, and (say) approved as a meet adjustment of station to merit or lamented as evidence that the Chicago department is on a down slope. As I tried to show in the last chapter, much of what goes on in and around English departments concerns status rather than concrete well-being, or improvement of one's work, and makes sense only in view of the central place that the concept of a career has for us.

And, in general, this conspectus of professionalism seems to explain, at least in part, the anomalies I noted earlier. Departments, ideally, are enclaves within which peer judgment holds sway and guides the delivery of our services to our clients. It is through the departmental curriculum that recruits are guided toward the gateway of the profession, and, in graduate programs, finally earn credentials. Through staffing, department heads further control entry to the guild and determine how swiftly a new recruit negotiates the ladder of success—hence our preoccupation with personnel matters. Departments are thought of as ultimately responsible to the discipline, or to "literature," not to the college or even to the students. Hence the orientation toward the graduate school ideal of the field, and toward the special fields, though these are often distantly related to local need. Department heads try to defend the professional claim that competence in teaching follows only from mastery of our particular body of knowledge. The job that society needs done, we say, cannot be performed by amateurs or journeymen. In fact, the job it needs is not even the job it thinks it needs, for the latter—disciplining young people in spirit and in verbal skills—could be done by schoolmasters (or even by machines?). Almost every aspect of departmental behavior is due partly or entirely to the natural wish to secure professional privilege and status, by convincing society and ourselves that we deserve it.

One of the most poignant crises of recent years, that of overproduction of Ph.D.'s, can be directly attributed, not just to economic forces, but to two professional impulses, whose incompatibility became evident only with hard times. Since the professional school is the heart of professional life and the professional value system, and since graduate departments are our professional schools, we tend to define success as holding a post in a Ph.D.-granting department. Not everyone can fit into the Yale department, but during the fifties and sixties, with the great expansion of universities, faculty at many other universities and state colleges discovered that if they couldn't move to a professional school, they could start a professional school on home ground. This expansiveness could last only as long as prosperity prevented its collision with the other imperative: strictly limit entry to professional ranks, and so preserve the benefits of monopoly. In the post-1968 panic, many faculty in new Ph.D. programs have doubtless felt that their status has declined. But the ramparts of the profession are pretty good security for those already inside. Professors in graduate programs voice consternation, but "excess" graduate students and junior faculty bear the economic privation.[5]

Let me mention one other instructive example. Wilcox found that we have pretty well won that part of our struggle for autonomy that has to do with determining what shall be taught, and according to which pedagogical principles: 94% of departments have this degree of control. But how the competence and classroom performance of *individual* teachers is judged is still very much contested. According to Wilcox's survey, 40% of departments use evaluations from students, in one way or another, and 36% have some system of class visitation. He remarks on the oddity that for the most part the assessment of teaching—our main work—is indirect, and that many teachers object to student rating. But, of course, in the perspective of this chapter, it is not at all odd. The professional knows better than his client what the client needs; student ratings challenge a basic right of the teacher.

Why not, then, judgment by peers, with evidence gathered by visits to class? Richard L. Larson sees a paradox here:

It is among the characteristics of most professions, I think, that members (and their clients) make judgments of the professional performance of fellow-members. Most of us stand ready, in personnel meetings and in published reviews of scholarly contributions, to make judgments about our colleagues' published work. Yet many of us exhibit a curious reluctance to search out ways of evaluating the one activity in which practically all of us engage. ("Evaluation of Teaching for the 1970's: Defining the Problem," *ADE Bulletin* 30, pp. 6–7)

What Larson has missed—aside from the plain error about clients— is the distinction between the professional mission of developing the

5. The other main controversy surrounding the Ph.D. of late is also a by-product of tensions in the struggle for professional status. Those favoring "teaching" degrees like the Doctor of Arts, the ABD, and the M.Phil. point out that the Ph.D. doesn't really train people for the teaching job society needs. These are compromisers, who hope to preserve our position by yielding to social pressure. Defenders of the Ph.D. hope to win a more complete victory in the battle of credentials. They argue that intermediate degrees would lower professional standards—i.e., diminish our control over the definition of our work and of the qualifications for it.

central body of knowledge and the professional service performed for clients. The ethic of detachment, dispassionate pursuit of truth, encourages criticism and judgment of the former. But to as great an extent as can be managed, judgment of service to clients ends with full admission to professional status. The professional is certified— i.e., *defined*—as competent to deal with his clients' needs; he can do this best if his relation to the client remains private and inviolable— even from inquiry by fellow professionals. Thus the defensiveness of college teachers about visitation. When Arthur Eastman proposed it at Carnegie-Mellon he produced little but ruffled feathers among his colleagues; the following response is typical:

Visitation . . . runs counter to the healthy liberalizing trend in American education, and threatens to institute a sterile authoritarianism . . . . The system is envisioned as promoting mutual respect and cooperation among the ranks, but in my opinion it will destroy the good will that exists: it is supposed to provide younger teachers with the helpful experience of their seniors, but I fear that it will produce humiliation and resentment. Young teachers need no reminder of their inferior and precarious status . . . . ("How Visitation Came to Carnegie-Mellon University," *ADE Bulletin* 21, p. 12)

Mutual respect and good will should be granted on admission to colleagueship. Within the profession we should be equals in power, though (recall) by no means in status. So the act of judging is itself an illegitimate exercise of power.

What teachers seem to object to, then, is not one or another means of evaluation so much as the very idea of evaluation. The responses Larson got to his inquiry indicate this:

What a nutty business your friend Larson has involved himself in. To hell with it.

. . . our feeling is that teaching cannot be evaluated very accurately and objectively

. . . any form of evaluation must necessarily be flawed by the very nature of what teaching is

. . . teaching . . . is a way of life, and it seems impossible to separate the effectiveness of one's teaching style from a general effectiveness in generally humane terms

. . . [your project] is doomed to failure (*ADE Bulletin* 30, p. 8)

I'm reminded of Hughes's saying that every profession has "rituals" to protect it against the hazards of a career and that the rituals are particularly elaborate in fields like teaching, "where ends are very ill-defined—and consequently mistakes are equally so" (*Men and Their Work*, p. 96). By and large, departments would prefer not to look too closely at teaching failures. They will probably continue to drag their heels against pressures for more evaluation; this is one way they continue the faculty's struggle for full professional privilege.

In the controversy over evaluation of teaching, you can also hear the deeper rumble of conflict between the professional ideal and society at large. Fittingly, the subject of this conflict has gotten the name, "accountability." To whom and for what are English teachers accountable? A would-be profession tries to secure the right to establish its own answers and regards the intrusion of other claimants as a threat. Most of the crises that drew the anxiety of chairmen over the past few years arose from challenges to professional autonomy: the demand of students for a voice in program and personnel decisions, the collective action of teaching assistants and of faculty acting through unions, the application of "unprofessional" criteria to staffing (e.g., affirmative action plans for hiring minorities and women). Most English faculty support the social goals implied by such demands, yet feel that the demands invade professional privacy.

Out there, beyond students, teaching assistants, and nosey administrators, are regents and legislators, who also may be aroused to intervention. George J. Worth quotes several Kansas legislators:

The legislature questions the way state money is spent, with faculty members not doing much teaching and taking a lot of trips.

I am getting tired of hearing about the needs of the faculty and administration. I want to see more emphasis on the needs of students and hear about the results and benefits of a college education.

There needs to be a measurement of results of a college education. Right now, I think the average parent in Kansas probably thinks if his son or daughter goes to KU the chances are greater that he or she will try drugs, live in a commune or have illicit sexual affairs than if the child didn't go to college. ("Accountability: Evaluation and Tenure," *ADE Bulletin* 32, p. 14)

And John Gerber quotes an Iowa legislator: "We need more Ph.D's in history like we need a hole in the head" ("Public Hostility to the Academy: What Can Chairmen of Departments of English Do," *ADE Bulletin* 32, p. 17). The uneasiness inspired by such remarks can easily be applied to our own field: "we see ourselves as scholars and critics of literature, custodians of the heritage of letters. The rest of the world acts on the assumption that we are people who deal with reading, writing, grammar, and such" (Henry Knepler, "The Mote in the Middle Distance," *ADE Bulletin* 24, p. 36). And an Illinois (Urbana) "Planning Committee Report" of April 1970 rightly derives the conflict from the professional imperatives that we follow:

The general model of the present curriculum is the historical development of the literature . . . . It suggests that literature is primarily a body of knowledge to be studied in terms of historical developments in specialized periods and kinds. While this model may be appropriate for the professional interests of majors and graduate students . . . it surely cannot be regarded as sufficiently broad even to reflect the major critical interests of our time.

Precisely the extent to which "professional interests" coincide with society's interests has again become a question for open debate.

We are feeling tensions now that developed quietly during the fifties and sixties, with the enormous growth in size, prosperity, and importance of universities, and that came noisily to the surface in the political awakening of the late sixties and the economic crunch of the seventies. But these tensions were implicit, I believe, at the very beginning, in the curious circumstances surrounding the early history of English departments.

This story has been well told in William Riley Parker's "Where Do English Departments Come From?" [6] and Wallace Douglas's "Some Questions about the Teaching of Works of Literary Art," [7] as well as in Douglas's chapter in this book. Both Parker and Douglas note the amalgamation of partly contradictory tasks and interests that made up our field. Parker explains how American departments,

6. *College English*, vol. 28 (February, 1967), pp. 339–51.
7. *ADE Bulletin*, No. 25, pp. 31–45.

the scholarly heirs of philology, eagerly acquired the remnants of rhetoric, too, and have since counted on these to secure position in the university. Students "need" to be taught composition, and, rather arbitrarily, scholars in literature are the ones thought professionally competent to teach writing. Douglas follows the equal-and-opposite reaction in this dynamic: given a place in the pantheon of departments, English had to look like a subject. That is, it required the esoteric body of knowledge that is part of the rationale for every profession. That body of knowledge, of course, was provided by literary scholarship. Douglas shows that, given the scholarly rationale of the field, it was natural for faculty to want to *teach* literary scholarship as well as study it and, indeed, that this kind of teaching came to seem the most important, the most central, teaching we do. Hence, the familiar paradox that the part of our job that justifies us to others within and outside the university is the part we hold in lowest regard and delegate to the least prestigious members of the profession.

It takes only a bit more historical context to reveal how congruent is my explanation of how departments behave now with the history that Parker and Douglas tell. They describe the maneuvers of language and literature faculty in laying a claim to professional status, by joining the bread-and-butter work of teaching freshman English to the scholarly work of literary study. Composition supported scholarship, practically speaking, while scholarship enabled those whose trade was teaching composition to present themselves as professionals. What remains to be seen is how the opportunity arose. For needless to say, it didn't happen in isolation.

Everett Hughes, speaking of more recent candidates (than the college teacher) for professional status, says that most of the professions "are practised only in connection with an institution. Their story is thus that of the founding, proliferation or transformation of some category of institutions . . . ." (*Men and Their Work*, p. 133). As long as there have been books there have been libraries, but the profession of librarian arose only with large libraries that circulated books in addition to collecting them. Nursing is an ancient kind of work, but the profession only arose with the modern hospital.

Comparably, the institution that combined the trade of schoolmaster and the gentlemanly avocation of literary scholarship into the profession of "English" was the modern university. American universities passed through a dramatic change in function between 1870 and 1900, their work becoming an essential part of the industrial state's system of production (more about this in Chapter 11). They also changed dramatically in *structure*, to become different institutions. The changes included specialization of students and faculty, more fields of study, the beginning of graduate work and graduate schools, adoption of the research ethos, establishment of a complex administration, division of the university into professional schools and—of course—departments. These changes made it natural for teachers to become professionals. The history of the Indiana University English department[8] shows the process at work.

In 1860, when the Reverend Henry Hibben became the first "Professor of English Literature," Indiana had 99 students and 8 regular faculty members. There were just two courses of instruction a student could pursue, a classical and a scientific; and, though a third—modern languages—was added in 1877, it is fair to say that until the 1880's students pursued rigid and almost uniform programs, which embodied what the faculty thought to be universal attainments of culture. In the late 1870's, Professor George Washington Hoss's description of English studies stressed "writing, analysis of style, and . . . criticism." The latter was to show "the relation of Rhetoric to Logic, Aesthetics, and Psychology" (Davidson, p. 7). And when President Lemuel Moss made a plea for English study in 1878, he said that "To observe clearly, to think accurately, and to speak correctly and forcibly, in English, is the chief goal of all liberal training with us—the outward form of that disciplined mind and spirit which is the one great end of education everywhere" (p. 8). Cultivation of the young was the university's business, and the study of oratory, rhetoric, and literature was part of the orchestration for each student.

8. *The Department of English at Indiana University, Bloomington, 1868–1970*, by Donald J. Gray, Frank Davidson, and others, Bloomington, n.d. [1974]. Professor Gray, who took up this study after Davidson's death, kindly gave me the early part of this history before publication.

In 1884, David Starr Jordan became president of the university. Jordan, later president of Stanford, was one of the eight or ten men most instrumental in reconceiving the American university. Things changed fast under him. Orrin Benner Clark, who had been the Professor in English since 1880, went on leave for 1885–1886, and during the year traveled in Europe as well as earning an M.A. at Harvard. Davidson speculates that Jordan may have suggested the leave and the advanced degree. In any case, it is certain that Jordan pressured his faculty to pursue advanced training and distinction in their fields. To one he offered a professorship in Greek if he would do special studies at Harvard and in Athens; he promised to hold a chair in mathematics for another if he would study in Europe; he made yet another professor of philosophy after his return from the University of Berlin. Jordan also tried to bring distinguished young men to Indiana—notably Woodrow Wilson and Bliss Perry (Davidson, p. 14). Scholarly reputation and advanced degrees became important.

A change in attitude toward the curriculum accompanied these professional demands on the faculty. According to the 1891–1892 catalogue,

During the administration of President D. S. Jordan (1884–91), a radical change was made in the methods of the University. Previous to that time the curriculum was of the ordinary composite structure, made up of those subjects which are the common heritage of all colleges, and the new ones that were demanding recognition. As most of the work was required the inevitable result was that very few subjects could obtain time enough to made [sic] useful in training. Early in this period referred to, this unsatisfactory plan was entirely abandoned by a differentiation of previously existing departments and the introduction of new ones. (quoted by Davidson, p. 11)

Why the old curriculum had suddenly become "unsatisfactory" is a question I shall take up in Chapters Ten and Eleven. But the *new* looks suddenly familiar to our eyes. Instead of three courses, there were eight: Ancient Classics, Modern Classics, English Literature, History and Political Science, Philosophy, Mathematics and Physics,

Biology and Geology, and Chemistry. From this time on, English, though it still had a variable role in what we would call "general education," was a separate field of study. Jordan had invented the English major or gotten Clark to invent it. As Jordan wrote in his autobiography, he relegated the "elementary" subjects that had previously made up the curriculum to the first two years, and

instituted a "major subject" system, by which each junior or third-year student was required to choose a specialty or "major," and to work under the immediate advice of his "major professor" . . . . The natural extension of this emergence of specialized undergraduate study was the introduction of graduate work.[9]

It shouldn't occasion much surprise that the five three-term courses for junior and senior majors included such rubrics as "Anglo-Saxon Prose and Poetry," "leading authors from Chaucer to Hooker," "Dryden to Johnson," "Cowper to Macaulay," "Milton," and "Longfellow and Tennyson." In making his university serious, scholarly, and professional, Jordan had created there the field of English. There were fluctuations, but his pattern prevailed.

The department, in more nearly our modern sense, was a by-product of the change in curriculum. By 1893, Professor Martin W. Sampson led a staff of six; there were academic ranks; there were three groups of English courses, in the "natural groups" of language, composition, and literature, with most of the work elective. Sampson is clear in his mind about the purpose of this enterprise: "We are concerned with the *study* of literature." Not "the method of the professor who preaches the beauty of the poet's utterance," but the method of the one who "makes his student systematically approach the work as a work of art, find out the laws of its existence as such, the mode of its manifestation, the meaning it has, and the significance of that meaning," in short, approach the work "intellectually." [10] As Donald Gray says, Sampson's essay is striking for its attempt to define a distinctly literary study:

9. *The Days of a Man* (New York, 1922), I, p. 235; quoted by Davidson in *The Department of English at Indiana University*, pp. 44–45.
10. William M. Payne, ed., *English in American Universities* (Boston: D. C. Heath, 1895), p. 96.

This concern quite naturally follows from, or accompanies, the notion of a
relatively independent Department of English which itself determines how it
will educate students to know or do something, presumably something
different from the knowledge and talents in which other departments
educate students. (Gray, p. 7)

That is to say, the curriculum has become professionalized. Anyone
can *appreciate* literature; and the best appreciator is doubtless the
person, Ph.D. or no, with the best taste. But to teach the systematic,
intellectual study of literature is a professional calling. Accordingly,
teachers began to talk and act like professionals. Barrett Wendell's
account of English at Harvard stresses that each department
member is "absolutely free" to teach as he likes and that the
department works by the "free and mutually cordial efforts of
teachers differing widely" in style and belief (Payne, p. 48).

Payne's collection of statements from *The Dial* by twenty chairmen
(1895) includes a fair variety, but two recurrent themes suggest the
effort, which parallels Sampson's, to cast out what is not properly
part of the discipline. Both themes show newly enfranchised English
departments trying to reject the parts of their earlier history that fit
ill with the professional image. (a) The chairmen want to distinguish
their work from science ("*parvenu* science, crass, boorish, and
overbearing," as one of their new graduates puts it), their competitor
for students and prestige on one side. They decline to ride on
science's coattails, as philologists equally abstract and technical. This
means declaring independence from their Germanic scholarly par-
entage, but, more importantly, it means claiming a province of their
own within the American academic confederation. (b) Many of the
chairmen would like to shake loose from what Sampson calls "the
bug bear known generally in our colleges as Freshman English" (p.
93) and what Anderson of Stanford refers to as "the drudgery of
correcting Freshman themes" (p. 52). They propose to make writing
competence part of the requirement for admission, either to college
or to the English department's courses. Does this sound familiar?
That the effort failed is indicative of the utility that English
instruction had for the rest of the university and for clients outside:

that it has been repeatedly made is indicative of a profession's natural wish to be as dignified as possible, to gain release from the servile duty of tutoring the young in verbal manners. The chairmen argue that their subject is logically separate from other university subjects and more advanced than school subjects.

At the same time, they hang on to ancient justifications for literary study as *culture*, par excellence. This is the commonest thread of ideology among the 1895 essays. Literature finds its resonance in the better and more refined parts of the self. Through it, students are given "the very words to guide their higher thought" (F. A. March, Lafayette College, p. 77). Their *higher* thought, the very soul. It is at that exalted range that literature affords benefits. Hiram Corson of Cornell, dismissing the purely historical and factual study of literature as unimportant "so far as culture, in its truest sense, is concerned," says that the "true function" of literature is "to quicken the spiritual faculties" (pp. 60–61). Albert S. Cook (Yale) praises literature for uniting *all* the faculties: "To this end no study can be better suited than English, its comprehensiveness, variety, and richness of content rendering it an unsurpassed aliment of the spiritual life" (p. 39). Felix F. Schelling of Penn credits the "peculiar position" of literary study to "its capabilities in developing the taste and artistic discernment" and its "enormous weight against utilitarianism" (p. 133).

It is not hard to hear the voice of Matthew Arnold behind these claims (though oddly enough Thomas Arnold is quoted more often). And, indeed, the authors commonly join the ennobling effect of literature on the self to its supposed effect on the whole society. The one student represented in the collection, Charles W. Hodell, thinks that English literary classics "can be made the instruments of culture for the American youth," as Greek and Latin classics were for English youth (p. 176). Latent here and throughout the *Dial* statements is the idea, traced in detail for England by Raymond Williams in *Culture and Society*, of the social organism as brutalized by industrialism and commercial values and of culture as a separate and arduously maintained remedy. John B. Henneman, who describes literary study in the south, believes that the courses "are at

least doing their share in upbuilding and leavening and spiritualiz-
ing the existing conditions of American life" (p. 166). And Hiram M.
Stanley ties the mission of literature in the colleges to the particular
need of a democracy for culture—"high art in our democratic
civilization is impossible until the general taste be elevated," and this
elevation must come mainly through education (p. 182). The professors were trying to justify their work as generally uplifting for society.

I don't know how much of this message the general public heard
or believed. Probably it competed with another message on another
frequency: English is the sum of verbal attainments needed to make
good in American society. Professor Sanford (Rhetoric, Minnesota)
sounds more realistic to me than most of those quoted above:

where, as in Minnesota, so large a proportion of the population consists of
foreigners who are ambitious and capable, the University must be content to
be a part of this drill [in textbook grammar and rhetoric]. A boy may lead
his class in mathematics and Latin and chemistry, and still be unable to free
his tongue from the Scandinavian accent, or his written work from foreign
idioms . . . the fundamental work of the University must be a struggle for
correctness. . . . (p. 159)

The English department may talk of cultivating the spirit, but it is
also eradicating the stigmata of foreign accent and lower class
speech, freeing ambitious boys to rise in society on their merit. To
some the manners of the liberally educated are as important as the
education. Thus, Albert H. Tolman of Chicago: "Every college
graduate should be able to prove that he is liberally educated by the
grace and skill with which he expresses his thoughts" (p. 91). With
this proof he may earn his place, not just among the cultivated, but
among the leaders of society.

Acquaintance with a common heritage is a second sign of
cultivation. Wallace Douglas points out that the classics had earlier
served this function but could not so easily do so for the new men of
affairs who would come from the middle class. It was necessary

that these "upwardly mobile" young men be given the body of cultural
references and assumptions that study of the Classics had given those in
whose hands control of schooling still rested. Or perhaps in both places

"have placed before them" is better than "be given." For no real gift was involved; the crucial fact about the process was that it sorted out those who could and would internalize the values and behavioral norms that schooling was intended to transmit. So it is today: that is why examinations were and remain so important a part of schooling. (Douglas, p. 36)

English literature was at hand, and convenient, to a bourgeois elite, as the classics had been in more aristocratic times.

The new universities were making themselves essential to American society: as sources of new knowledge that might have practical application in industry, as transmitters of the skills and attitudes that managers would need, as training schools for the professions. English as a discipline did not put itself forward initially as a critical part of this complex, nor was it quick to adapt its ideology to its functions. But the rest of the university valued English, both for its supposed work of teaching students to write and for the high cultural tradition to which English departments laid claim. Besides, students liked studying literature. So English had a piece of solid ground, initially, in the fluid academic institutions of the 1880's and 1890's. But to keep that place, and compete as an equal, English had to become a profession along with disciplines like chemistry and engineering, disciplines whose use to industrial society was so much clearer. In consequence, English departments have played down the less professional side of their work and built around the more professional, with the results I have examined in this chapter.

Of course the concept of professionalism has no more than a mediate explanatory power. It can't be the final answer to the question, why are English departments the way they are? A deeper answer would have to bring together history, sociology, and economics in a way that is beyond my reach, though I will make an attempt to outline such an answer in the next two chapters. I will just enter here my opinion that professionalization holds a key place in bourgeois society. It is partly as Harold C. Martin said, writing about English departments from his perspective as college president:

The necessary specialism of our society has both produced and resulted from specialism in higher education. Directly and not-so-directly, the rewards of society, especially at the lower and the median levels, go to the specialist; and our academic structure, bourgeois to the core, shapes itself to these rewards. (*ADE Bulletin* 15, p. 18)

Specialism—the dividing up of productive technique into small units, and apportioning these skills to narrowly trained workers— gives occupational groups the opportunity to stand apart from the laity and gain a monopoly over the distribution of their skills and services. The tangible rewards of success in this project are plain. Beyond that, I believe that the conditions of work in capitalist society impel us to seek professional status. For to be a professional is to regain at least some control over the nature, the pace, and the outcome of one's work—to overcome in fair measure the alienation of labor under industrial capitalism. The professional also protects himself, or increasingly herself, from the worst rigors of competition. Tenure is our peculiar academic means to this end, but we also use other, more typical, ways of establishing our own scale of merit, defending ourselves from would-be, outside judges, and ensuring ourselves against painful recognition of failure. In their ideologies, professions also offer the comfort of identifying the worker's own welfare with that of the whole society and, at the same time, claiming to be independent of the social matrix. The bourgeois ideal of freedom finds here an almost faultless embodiment.

So do we devise our "conspiracies against the laity." Not out of venality, or no more venality than is ordinary in this society; rather, we seek to be professionals as a way of escaping the powerlessness of ordinary work and the nastier side of economic life in capitalist society. Professionalism is a claim to human dignity. Unfortunately, we succeed in the claim at a cost to others—and also at a cost to our perception of the way in which dignity for all people lies.[11]

11. A note is necessary, lest my argument be mistaken and misapplied. There is a conflict between the claims of the professions and the claims of less privileged workers. But in the midst of cries for "accountability," behavioral objectives, and vocational education; in a time of cutbacks, increased teaching loads, and lagging salaries; in a society where many leaders regard intellectuals with suspicion or exasperation, and where legislators and regents are only too willing to mount their own kind of attack on the teaching profession—I would by no means imply that our profession should now welcome annexation by the larger society. In such a context, "society" almost

Postscript

I've dwelt on the contradictions—some of them seamy—of departmental life. Do departments have to be this way? Do they have to impose their professional needs on students and the public, whatever the setting? Of course not. Institutional change is possible.

One of my batches of documents came from Forest Park Community College in St. Louis. You can read through it all without hearing about the academic honors and coups of the faculty or about a course in Sixteenth-Century Poetry offered "when enough students can be persuaded to take it." [12] The department's course booklet (1970–1971) states some aims:

The fundamental purpose of all writing courses is to teach students to express themselves clearly, effectively, and appropriately; we therefore place our emphasis on logical thinking, self-examination, and understanding of the manipulative uses of language rather than on the superficial mechanics of spelling, punctuation, usage, or dialect variation.

The fundamental purpose of all literature courses is to teach students a greater appreciation of their own experiences, and to enlarge and enrich those experiences through contact with other times and other cultures; we therefore place our emphasis on a widened understanding rather than on specialized terminology or so-called "scholarly" literary analysis.

Students should be enrolled in courses appropriate to their needs, rather than arbitrarily placed according to standardized usage tests, their declared major in college, or a unilateral decision by any member of the college staff.

Once the choice has been made, the program must contain enough flexibility that no student is frozen into any track, even for the length of a single semester, but can, instead, shift to a more appropriate section.

---

inevitably means some part of the ruling class or some reactionary body. Against these forces the institutions of our profession and of the university generally—academic freedom, independence, privacy—do somewhat protect us. Better the MLA than the FBI. Within professional walls, mavericks and communists and critics of society can survive. Partly for this reason the university is one of the institutions that occasionally turn progressive. For people who want a democratic and egalitarian and socialist society, the moral of my analysis is not to destroy professional ramparts, but to reach out over them—selectively—to poor people, minority races, workers, and in so doing build alliances that may save and humanize the intellectual life in bad times shortly to come.

12. For a fuller account of work in this department, and two other excellent junior colleges (Staten Island Community College, New York, and Hinds Junior College, Mississippi), see *College English*, vol. 35 (May, 1974).

Grading:

The English Department is also convinced that FPCC's "open door" should not become a revolving door, that students should not be admitted only to be pushed out because they do not meet arbitrary and artificial "standards." We believe strongly that grades should reflect accomplishment rather than be used punitively. That a student has not within a semester met all the aims of a course does not mean he has "failed." Backgrounds, high school experiences, self-images all indicate that some students need longer than others to meet the aims of particular courses. We see it as our responsibility to encourage them in what they have achieved rather than discourage them by further increasing their sense of inadequacy. The English Department, therefore, grades in the following way:

A]	For students who meet the aims of the course. The student
B]	and the teacher in many sections determine in conference
C]	the grade the student earns for the course.
Aud:]	for students who have attended the full semester but who have not met the aims of the course.
W or WP:]	for students who stop attending the class before the end of the semester.
Inc:]	for students who have met almost all of the course aims and who have made definite arrangements with the teacher for achieving the remainder of the aims by a specified date. Incompletes not removed by the agreed upon date will automatically become Audits. Under no circumstances will an Inc. be changed to an "F."

My informant, Greg Cowan, wrote me that his colleagues are "committed to the value of their discipline," by which he means that they "think reading and writing are so important that we aren't satisfied until we've shared that sense of importance with our students. We're trying to impart that value, rather than using it as a justification for flunking students who disagree."

Minutes of the department's meetings reflect this purpose without much piety or self-importance. They are hand-written and dittoed, and the medium helps convey the message. I close with a handful of excerpts from various meetings, in contrast with the more professional quotations scattered throughout this essay:

Meeting called to order by Garger at 2:11 after the dept. was searched out and found meeting in the wrong room.

Jerry encouraged teachers to visit each other's classes informally. The aim—to find out what's going on in other classes, exchanging ideas, techniques, methods, whatever. We probably do too little of this.

Sally warned all that, despite our understanding to the contrary, *Incs.* still change to *F's* unless you send back the proper form to the Registrar changing it to whatever you think fit—(no D or F bullshit, of course).

George Dain, a student, read a fairly strong statement about the selling of underground and aboveground publications on campus. Considerable discussion resulted in a motion, by Friedrich, amplified by Greg, that the English department write a letter (pass a resolution?) urging the administration to recognize the students' right to sell publications on campus and rescind the present policy forbidding them to do, especially since the present policy is a denial of the Constitutional guarantee of freedom of the press . . . especially since identifying and analyzing slant, propaganda, logical fallacies, and persuasive techniques is part of the content of all composition courses, and the department believes that free and easy access to all contemporary community publications is academically essential . . . . This motion was unanimous.

The meeting adjourned by the skillful, reasonable, and courageous Garger who, even though wearied of carrying heavy burdens of responsibility on his sturdy, though narrow, shoulders, remains ever ready to serve the arrogant wishes and base desires of the members of the English Department, Writing Lab and GC people, Humanities Division generally, the Junior College Board of Trustees, the vast hierarchical plethora of Administrators, Deans, sub-deans, minor administrators, the taxpayers of St. Louis and St. Louis County, the Nixon Administration, the Joint Chiefs of Staff, the Board of Directors of the recently aligned (or is it exposed) United Fund, my near and distant blood relatives, and humanity generally. Maybe even students.

V

Past and Future

I have made incidental reference throughout the book, and especially in the last five chapters, to the connection between our professional institutions and some needs of the American society that developed after the Civil War. Now I wish to discuss this history a little more systematically. In Chapter Ten, I look at the new ecology of knowing that grew up along with industrial society. Chapter Eleven traces the evolution of the modern American university as a part of this ecology. In both chapters, I argue that the growth of our field was not isolated, or a consequence of intellectual history, but rather a consequence of material history. In a way, of course, it is a truism that without the industrial revolution nothing would be as it is now, including the Department of English. Here, I try to give the truism explanatory power.

But whatever satisfaction we may get from an explanation of how we came to live and think and work as we do, I am not seeking to explain for the sake of explaining. I want to explain our present by understanding our past in order to act more wisely in the future. There is much talk about the "plight of the humanities." I have myself indulged in it. I now think most such talk cripplingly ahistorical, and far too narrow in its scope—as if the humanities were hermetically sealed, flourishing or sickening apart from the rest of the universe. Such a diagnosis makes it impossible to nurse the humanities back to health. Further, I argue, no diagnosis will point to a cure unless it is a cure for much more than just the humanities.

In Chapter Twelve, I try to draw from my account of how we got where we are implications that will indicate where to go next. But I have no specific cure, no ingenious plan for English or the humanities, no project for the National Endowment. These solutions are precisely the ones which I have meant to make a case against, in this book. The one I do endorse will not surprise readers who have come this far. And if socialist revolution sounds like a cure incommensurate with the sickness itself, one both too familiar and too difficult, I can only say: nevertheless, that's where my argument leads. I did not expect it to lead that way when I began thinking about the state of our professional health almost ten years ago. But that is where I have followed it, and, needless to say, I hope readers will also find the argument right, and urgent.

CHAPTER TEN

Culture, Knowledge, and Machines

As I have shown in earlier chapters, a common exercise for those who teach literature and the humanities is to explain why there should be people who teach literature and the humanities. In yielding to this instinct we are, I suppose, no different from stockbrokers or steelworkers. But we spend more words in justification than they, partly because we are a verbal species with lots of free access to print and lectern, but mainly, I think, because our role in society is much less *evident* than the roles of stockbrokers and steelworkers. We do not offer a tangible service like buying and selling securities or make a product like sheet metal. Customers don't pay us directly for the services we do perform, and we may nurse an uncomfortable feeling that if they had a choice they wouldn't. Is it entirely clear, after all, that universities and the whole society would find their prosperity diminished if English teachers were suddenly and totally wiped out?

The uneasiness that accompanies this question can be felt near the surface when humanists address themselves directly to their role in the economy. A survey asking faculty members if the federal government should support the humanities produced comments like these:

Scientists untrained in humanistic disciplines and values . . . can wield

power they do not understand for ends and interests contrary to the good of
a democratic society.

neglect of the humanities is one of our most crucial national problems. . . .
We will lose all our scientific gains if we fail to take early and massive action
on this aspect of our lives.

the long-range national interest is seriously endangered by the imbalance
between government funds used for the sciences and the lack of funds for the
humanities. . . . Neither scientists nor technicians will resolve the dilemma
of the arms race, the meaning of human existence, and the nature of man's
capacity for self-destruction.

That our public life is now so largely contained within a dream world is due
mainly to the neglect of the humanities.[1]

The good of a democratic society, crucial national problems, man's
capacity for self-destruction, neglect of the humanities (not to
mention the meaning of human existence)—these are the phrases
people use to equate the public weal and the ambitions of the guild
at a time when the guild seems to need defending.

But although the particular social climate of the sixties hangs over
these worried diagnoses and large promises, the justification of
humane letters is not new. It has been a lively occupation of
humanists, especially during the last hundred years or so, for reasons
not unrelated to the concern of those who think that the country will
go down the spout unless the government subsidizes English
professors. The century-long public relations effort of humanists has
come in response to the rapidly inflating role of science and
technology in the larger society. The humanities lack such demon-
strable value as science can claim; they need the support of doctrine.

So when Arnold found it necessary to *argue* the virtues of culture,
and to predict that literature would replace religion as man's "ever
surer stay," he had always in mind as an opposing force what he
called "machinery": the pragmatic and technological temperament.
Evident in his disagreement with Huxley is the perception of science
as competitor—if not adversary. And this thread has run through
most literary theory and apologetics since then. In particular, it is

1. Harold Orlans, *The Effects of Federal Programs on Higher Education* (Washington: The
Brookings Institution, 1962), pp. 106–7.

embedded in the New Criticism; somewhere behind or beneath most of the work of this school, most explicitly that of Richards, is the question, how can literature and the language of feeling and value claim attention alongside the language of science, whose power to control material reality is evident? As I indicated in Chapter 4, the New Critics answered (debatably) that literature gives us a wholeness of experience and understanding that is not available either through science or in daily living. In Trilling's mild but chauvinistic words, quoted earlier, "the study of literature has traditionally been felt to have a unique effectiveness in opening the mind and illuminating it, in purging the mind of prejudices and received ideas, in making the mind free and active."

From this awakening of the person, needless to say, it is easy to derive much social benefit, as the justifications cited earlier bear witness. From Newman's claim that liberal education "aims at raising the intellectual tone of society, at cultivating the public mind, at purifying the national taste," to Hyman's belief that the New Criticism had released "democratic possibilities" in the study of literature, our theorists have tried to confirm an alliance between humanistic education and the most progressive forces in society at large, and so stake out a safe and respected position for literature. As egalitarian ideas have gradually replaced aristocratic ones in "respectable" discourse, literary theory has moved in the direction of Hyman's remark, and beyond. Thus it is no surprise to find Michael Shugrue (then Secretary for English of the MLA) concluding his book on English in the sixties by saying that "the discipline of English, once the preserve of the Brahmin and the despair of the immigrant and the disadvantaged, will help to bring about the great social revolution now taking place in the United States" [2]—though if this event should actually come to pass, it will be surprise enough to black people, Chicanos, Puerto Ricans, Indians, and poor people generally.

But even granting the human propensity for confusing one's own

2. Michael F. Shugrue, *English in a Decade of Change* (New York: Pegasus, 1968), p. 186.

well-being with the general welfare, and even considering the century-long ascendency of science over on the other side of the campus, there is something odd about the humanist's nagging urge to defend his work, particularly in the sense one gets among humanities faculties of being in retreat, fighting for survival. What's odd is that as the justifications have become more strident over the last hundred years, and particularly over the last twenty-five, the teaching of humanities in universities has in fact burgeoned at a phenomenal rate, both absolutely and relative to the rest of the economy. There are certainly well over 150,000 people who earn a good living teaching humanities in universities now, compared to perhaps a couple of thousand in 1871. The first Ph.D. in English to be given by an American university was awarded in 1875; in the 1960's the figure crested at over 800 a year. Another fact: in 1871 there were no graduate students in English in this country; now there are 15,000. And, whereas a hundred years ago university teachers of English reached a small handful of students, now almost half the young men and women in the country pass through our classrooms. Surely there has never been so much study of the humanities and specifically of literature at a comparable level in any culture. If the humanities are without influence in the "dream world" of our public life, that is not because no one has given them the chance.

Perhaps the disquiet of humanists is due in part to the distance they feel between their goals for culture and those of the general society. And, indeed, the increase in the numbers and prosperity of humanists is not to be explained by a general cultural awakening, by a growing demand for critical education by a more literate public. On the contrary, if book publishing is any indication, the demand for literary culture has declined. It is an astonishing fact that the number of new books published in this country during 1914 was greater than for any subsequent year until 1953, and that even the paperback revolution combined with great affluence brought that number only 24% above the 1914 level by the end of the fifties.[3] This

3. Fritz Machlup, *The Production and Distribution of Knowledge in the United States* (Princeton: Princeton University Press, 1962), p. 210.

is a strong hint that the public has not been clamoring for more literary culture. Yet we custodians of literary culture have enormously improved our station in society—without explicit planning or even consent. It makes one want to ask why, and in the last five chapters I hope I have given part of an answer.

But as long as the question is posed within the conceptual boundaries implied by the quotations at the beginning of this chapter, as long as we question the role of the humanities and of literature in terms of their civilizing or spiritual value to society, we will be blocked by the image of what we wish our work to accomplish from seeing what functions it actually has, and how it comes to pass that American society pays something like 1.5 billion dollars a year to have the humanities taught and studied in universities, not to mention the much larger sum expended on teaching the same subjects in primary and secondary schools. To get a tighter grip on the question, I think we must abandon our customary approach through esthetics or literary theory and, instead, circle around through some remote precincts.

Specifically, I do not think that the growth of our field in a hundred years can be usefully pondered apart from the much deeper changes that occurred in the general culture during that period. I will argue, in this chapter and the next, that the practice of English and the humanities is what it is mainly because of some of the conditions introduced by industrial society. And to support the claim, I will offer an analysis of technological development over the last two centuries. It will be helpful, then, to scan some facts that every schoolboy once knew, and try to tease from them an understanding of the importance that this knowledge has come to have for all of us.

Start with the history of textile manufacture in England during its period of most rapid evolution. One can conveniently divide the production of cotton and wool fabrics into five stages: growing the raw materials; preparing them by sorting, cleaning, and combing, to be worked; spinning the yarn; weaving the fabric and finishing it by sizing, dying, bleaching, printing, etc. Before 1750 the most common sequence of these events was as follows: the textile merchant bought raw materials either directly from farmers or from another merchant. He then "put out" the materials to spinners and weavers who worked in cottages; a worker might own his cottage and spinning wheel or hand loom, or he might rent equipment and even the cottage itself from the merchant. Then the merchant either sold the fabric or had it finished in the shop he supervised.

In 1733, John Kay invented the flying shuttle, a simple device for beating the weft thread into the cloth, and so increasing the speed of weaving. Kay had the weaving of wool in mind, but by the 1750's his invention was used fairly widely to weave cotton. Even before this, the spinning of yarn had tended to lag behind the weaving of cloth, and the shortage of yarn became more acute after 1750, when the cotton industry in Lancashire began to grow rapidly.

This combination of circumstances put pressure on the spinning stage of production for greater output, and the need was met, not by the training and employment of more spinners, but by the development of spinning machines. John Wyatt and Lewis Paul had already achieved the fundamental mechanism: the spinning of two threads at a time. Their machines had qualified success and moderately wide use during the 1740's and, in effect, pointed the way to machines that would spin many threads at once. And these machines came, in familiar parade: Hargreaves' spinning jenny of 1764, Arkwright's water frame in 1769, Crompton's mule in 1779, and a hundred variations.

The spinning jenny had a mechanical advantage of as much as twenty-four to one over the spinning wheel. The water frame's advantage was several hundred to one. Needless to say, the increase in productivity more than met the weavers' needs; it reversed the imbalance, and created a need for mechanization of weaving. Cartwright's power loom of 1787, though crude, was the answer. By the 1820's a more sophisticated model of the original loom had increased the productivity of a worker by fifteen-fold. And the effect of Cartwright's invention is much greater than this ratio implies, since the power loom hand need not be so skilled as a weaver.

These advances at the third and fourth stages of production

naturally had their impact on the second and fifth. Cartwright patented his carding engine in 1775, and devices for cleaning and for preparation of the rove came into use about this time. The finishing processes also responded. Before machines revolutionized spinning and weaving, cloth was bleached in open meadows. The need for faster bleaching—and a lack of open land around factories—led to the use of chemical bleaching agents, first sulfuric acid and then chlorine. For printing fabrics, the cylinder press (invented earlier, but scarcely used) replaced the slower block press.

As for the first stage of production: graduates of American elementary schools well know that the demand for raw cotton grew with these improvements in the manufacture of fabric and that, in 1793, Eli Whitney, fresh from Yale, built his cotton gin during a stay on a plantation in Georgia. This invention made profitable the farming of cotton in the southern uplands, greatly lowered the price of raw cotton, and further stimulated the British cotton industry— about a seventy-fold increase in growth from 1780 to 1860.[4]

In this way all stages of cotton production were mechanized except growing the cotton itself. And Lewis Mumford would probably point out that the use of slave labor for that task foreshadowed the main idea of machine production: interchangeable parts and a central, hierarchical organization.

This dialectic of mechanization is familiar enough to have been honored with a proverb: Necessity is the mother of invention. But the absence of a complementary cliché—invention is the mother of necessity—suggests that the significance of the process has not been widely appreciated. A machine can dramatically increase the speed of an operation. It thus establishes an opportunity: the entrepreneur who can bring about a corresponding acceleration in a neighboring part of the manufacturing process can take advantage either of the greater demand for his product or of the advantage he will gain in

4. The facts mentioned in this account are, of course, commonplaces; but I have relied particularly on Albert Payson Usher, "The Textile Industry," in Melvin Kranzberg and Carroll W. Pursell, Jr., eds., *Technology in Western Civilization* (New York: Oxford University Press, 1967) and on David S. Landes, *The Unbound Prometheus* (Cambridge: Cambridge University Press, 1969).

the market because greater efficiency allows him to reduce prices. And he does not have to look far for the simplest and most profitable way to achieve this result, since the machine that provided the opportunity also stands as an example. The power loom does not resemble the spinning jenny, but it was developed in response to the same kind of challenge—to increase the productivity of a worker— and does so by the same means—the ingenious application of mechanical principles.

In other words, the technology of the Industrial Revolution gave *knowledge* a new and central place in the business of making a living. This is not to say that knowledge had no role in earlier technologies —no one who had to read Thomas Tusser's *A Hundreth Good Points of Husbandry* (later expanded to five hundred or more) for Ph.D. exams can doubt that a European farmer or craftsman of the renaissance had a rich body of lore and of tools at his disposal or that he must have known a great deal in order to perform his work. But this traditional knowledge was relatively static through any given generation, and available to workers without prior education. A farmer, craftsman, or merchant who hoped to better himself would work harder, save and invest more, and trade on more advantageous terms if he could, but not ordinarily think of gaining on his competition by using knowledge to accelerate production.

It was only with the Industrial Revolution that new applications of knowledge became, in effect, the dynamic force for an entrepreneur, for an industry, and eventually for whole economies. Success for a firm, and economic growth more generally, no longer depended upon the traditional skills of workers (e.g., spinners and weavers in their cottages) and upon sharp trading so much as on the ingenuity of inventors, of engineers, and of those who organized and combined the factors of production—with all three roles not infrequently combined in one man. It became economically critical for a firm to achieve the technology that was called for, either to catch up with competitors who had it or because a disequilibrium in the stages of manufacture offered a chance for competitive advantage.

There is an old controversy. Does the progress of technology depend on individual geniuses in the right place and right time, or does it depend mainly on the economic need that makes inventors of ordinary talented men? But whichever way this dispute is settled, there is no doubt that in the last two hundred years the application and increase of knowledge became essential to economic well-being in industrial nations. Take a broad enough view of this history, and there can be little doubt that the phenomenal increase of invention owes not to a phenomenal increase in the number of geniuses, but to the economic and technological conditions that made genius profitable, and to the way that one invention like the ball bearing might make many others possible. As the demand for innovation spread through metallurgy, energy conversion, the chemical industry, and so on, a new role for the thinker—the idea man, the engineer, the inventor—was created. With an economic premium on this kind of thinking, knowledge was for the first time systematically and innovatively applied to *work*.[5]

In drawing this inference from progress in the manufacture of cotton cloth, I am well aware of having allowed myself two heroic simplifications, which are no less inaccurate for being traditional. The sequence of inventions, the dialectic I have referred to, is, for one, a tidy pattern abstracted from a less structured reality. There were already spinning machines by the time the flying shuttle gained wide acceptance, the power loom did not come into general use for forty years after its invention, etc. In a cottage industry and a far from perfect market the response of technology to need could not have been as orderly as I have made it out to be. But if the chronology was less than sharp, the dynamic of profit, knowledge, and invention was quite clear, perhaps more clear to contemporaries than to us. Thus, in 1761, "the Royal Society of Arts offered 'rewards' for the best invention to spin six threads of wool, flax, hemp, or cotton at one time 'and that will require but one person to

5. Peter Drucker has an interesting analysis of this development in *The Age of Discontinuity* (New York: Harper & Row, 1969), pp. 269–70. He emphasizes the simplification and improvement of work, but not the competitive advantage of so using knowledge.

attend it.' " [6] If a philanthropic group like the Royal Society saw the connection between invention and economic need, we cannot be surprised that those who stood to gain from technology also saw the connection.

The other simplification lies embedded in the very concept of the Industrial Revolution. It didn't happen all that suddenly. As Mumford keeps reminding us—and as the work of Lynn White on medieval technology admirably shows—for hundreds of years before 1750 Europeans had been building a varied technology that transferred power to human use through hundreds of mechanical devices. Just to recall the windmill, the wheeled plow, the lathe, the mechanical pump, the blast furnace, the gun, and the spinning wheel itself is to realize that the garden had died long before God took the spinning jenny out of Locke's side. And Locke, along with Descartes, Ramus, Newton, and others, had helped to form a consciousness that could see and approve the opportunity for extended control of nature through technique; while the Protestant ethic (of Weber and Tawney) blessed work and individual profit. But I believe it is true that the dialectic of invention and response, the regularizing of technical innovation, and the bending of knowledge to profit all first assumed something like their modern form in the late eighteenth century in Britain and that the manufacture of cotton fabric is just a dramatic instance of a rather general process. On this hypothesis, by the way, it is not surprising that the Royal Society of the Arts, which offered monetary rewards to inventors, should have been founded in 1754.

Still other innovations in the use of knowledge help confirm the Industrial Revolution as more than an arbitrary construct. For present purposes, a critical development was the large-scale transfer of work from home to factory. The spinning frame demanded this change: it was too large to be easily moved about, and too large for the spinner's cottage. It also required more power to run it than muscle could supply. So cotton manufacturers brought workers and machines together in large buildings, and the social cataclysm brought about by the dark satanic mills received no shortage of

6. Usher, in Kranzberg and Pursell, p. 234.

attention. Beyond its spectacular effect on the lives of workers, the factory system (which had existed for many years, but never as an important mode of production) made a less evident contribution to the rebuilding of economy and society around knowledge. In the factory, it was possible to concentrate the various stages of manufacture, to link the different machines in rational combinations, all under one roof. A manager could *see* the whole sequence of processes in operation, could readily identify difficulties, and could imagine profitable simplifications. By virtue of concentration, the factory was a place where intelligence and creativity could range over a broad field. The technical skill of the mechanic and the organizational skill of the manager were essential at this point, whereas the empirical tinkering of the craftsman had sufficed before. The factory gave invention a fixed place to work, drawing attention to problems, and demanding solutions. It institutionalized "progress." [7]

If the development of high efficiency machines created an ideal place to extend technical knowledge, it also stimulated it. The use of these machines enormously raised the cost of *in*efficiency, human, mechanical, or organizational. If a single spinner is working at half speed in his cottage, that is a small matter for his employer. But if a frame with two hundred spindles is idle half the time, the employer suffers a significant loss. The high cost of slack and inefficiency, in addition to prompting new and more efficient inventions, led to a search for ways to move material smoothly through the plant and to increase the productivity of each worker.[8]

The name associated with the systematic attempt to organize work efficiently is that of Frederick W. Taylor, who analyzed production and work into their component parts, timed movements with his stopwatch, and reckoned where savings and short cuts might be

7. Though the connection is less direct, the factory and its economies of scale also contributed, through urbanization, to the ascendency of knowledge. In 1800 there were about 50 cities in the world of more than 100,000 population; now there are about 1400 such, and 140 of 1,000,000 or more. A city is a place where specialized talent congregates and where it is natural for officials and civic-minded people to see the social organism in terms of complicated problems, amenable, with luck, to collective intelligent solution.

8. See Landes, p. 302.

achieved. As a consultant for Bethlehem Steel in the 1890's, he
studied the work of shovelers in the yard of that firm, found that
workers moving different materials with the same shovel would carry
shovel-loads ranging from 38 pounds to $3\frac{1}{2}$ pounds, and determined
by a series of tests that the ideal load for a good shoveler was $21\frac{1}{2}$
pounds. It followed that workers should have shovels of different sizes
and shapes for different materials, that shovel rooms should be built
at various places in the yard to save steps, that work should be
planned at least a day in advance, that there should be an office staff
to do the planning, that there should be a telephone network to
speed communications, and, finally, that the yard itself should be
redesigned. The results must surely have earned Taylor's fee: within
three years, 140 men were doing the work that 400 to 600 had done
before, and though wages had increased 60%, the cost of moving
material was halved, at an annual saving to Bethlehem Steel of
$78,000.[9] Taylor is called the father of scientific management, but
the kind of thought process he refined was inherent in the factory
itself and must have been recognized and valued long before Taylor.

His application of measurement to work constituted a new sort of
rationality, which treated, not just the worker, but his individual
motions, as interchangeable parts of a process. Whatever the
consequences in alienation of workers, there can be no doubt that
efficiency in the use of people rewarded manufacturers, and they
were quick to put it to advantage. This meant further dependence on
old and new knowledge—on a mode of thought that was orderly,
experimental, and, after a time, sufficiently abstract to be applied to
a variety of situations. And, plainly, scientific techniques of management required that the organization of work be withdrawn from the
workers themselves and given over to specialized managers, an
ever-increasing corps whose main work was thinking.

In still another way, industrialization wedded knowledge and
economic gain. For instance, recall the improvement in techniques

9. I have taken this account from John William Ward's *Red, White, and Blue* (New
York: Oxford University Press, 1969), pp. 252–54. Ward's analysis has helped me, as
has that of Daniel Bell, *The End of Ideology*, rev. ed. (New York: The Free Press, 1962),
especially pp. 226–42, and that of Peter Drucker in *The Age of Discontinuity*, pp. 271–72.

for bleaching cotton cloth. The change from sunlight to chlorine increased profits both for cotton fabric producers and for chemical manufacturers, to whom hydrochloric acid, a source of chlorine, had been a noxious waste by-product in the production of sulfuric acid and soda. But the happy connection between waste hydrochloric acid and unbleached cotton was of course far from obvious, depending as it did on converting a by-product of one industry to a form that could be used in another. To see the chance for economic advantage in this conversion required a knowledge, not just of one manufacturing process but of remote processes. Such discoveries, of course, have since become a commonplace throughout industry, whose workings interlock in ways inconceivable before 1750. The artisan worked simple materials he produced himself or procured on the open market. He did not attempt (even if he had capital) to alter the network of connections between his craft and others or to conceive of and exploit technological improvements. But such efforts are the full-time occupation of many thousands now. Industrialization put a premium on understanding the whole system.

Though such knowledge leans on science, as does most technical innovation in industry now, science had surprisingly little to do with the early revolutions in textile and iron manufacture and in steam power, the bases of modern society. Some early inventors understood the principles behind their technical achievements, others just relied on trial-and-error and mechanical instinct. In developing the separate condenser, James Watt apparently intuited the waste of heat incurred by the warming and cooling of the cylinder, rather than relying on the ideas of the Scottish chemist Joseph Black, which partly explain the phenomenon.[10] Few inventions were projected from scientific discoveries then. In fact, the relationship was often the opposite, as in the development of thermodynamic theory partly out of attempts to understand steam engines (of which more below). And no manufacturer thought of what is now called "basic" scientific research—the discovery of hitherto unknown principles—as some-

10. A. Rupert Hall, "Cultural, Intellectual, and Social Foundations, 1600–1750," in Kranzberg and Pursell, p. 113.

thing he might sponsor or undertake as a way of increasing profits.

That came much later. It took manufacturers a while to apply science and then only in some industries. The chemical industry was one and for obvious reasons: here the inventor or mechanic, unlike his counterpart in textiles, could not *see* his problems and visualize solutions, or progress far by uninformed trial and error. So improvisation was haphazard and wasteful; the technician needed scientific theory to help him understand the unseen.

Similarly, though the steam engine had been evolving for over a hundred years before Carnot and Joule began to formulate the principle of the conservation of energy, their work grew directly out of the need to measure and increase the efficiency of steam engines. Newcomen's engine was about 2% efficient, as it turned out, and Watt's about 5%, so that there was much room for improvement—and, as I keep insisting, for profit—through application of scientific principles, once they were understood, to the steam engine. One may generalize about energy conversion: before the Industrial Revolution the sources of energy were animals, men, wind, and water, and the means of converting such energy to productive use were mechanical, visible, so that the innovator did not even have to know—though some did—the simple principles of lever, screw, inclined plane, etc. upon which conversion was founded. He could work by craft and ingenuity. The Industrial Revolution introduced sources and carriers of energy—the steam engine, the internal combustion engine, the electric motor, etc.—which could not be developed by tinkering.[11] The innovator must know more than what he can learn "by experience."

Accordingly, science and scientists have assumed a central place in technological development. By contrast with Newcomen, Watt, Hargreaves, and Arkwright, the pioneers of the radio industry were mostly well trained scientists. (Marconi is the exception.) Fessendon was trained in mathematics and physics and taught electrical engineering; DeForest wrote his Ph.D. thesis at Yale on wireless

11. For a good discussion of these matters see John B. Rae, "The Invention of Invention" and "Energy Conversion" in Kranzberg and Pursell, pp. 325–49.

telegraphy; and Armstrong studied physics under Pupin at Columbia.[12] And of course, as radio and the other new industries have grown, it has become commonplace for firms to employ hundreds of scientists in applied fields and some scientists in basic research. To dramatize the change: there were a hundred times as many research and development employees in America in 1960 as in 1920,[13] and largely because of this change in industry, the total number of scientists, engineers, and technical workers in the United States increased beyond any relationship to increase in the population: 226 times between 1880 and 1955.[14] These statistics make perfectly explicit the new economic role of scientific knowledge.

And they make clear another change that has been going on for two hundred years, the increasing concentration of economically valuable knowledge in a specialist class. Mumford speaks of the "polytechnic" culture of the earlier period, the wide diffusion of diverse traditional crafts and techniques, and contrasts it with our monotechnic industrial system, almost wholly dependent on mechanization and power. The Industrial Revolution both created *and* destroyed huge amounts of technology. The old technology spread skill and lore fairly evenly throughout society. The new demands a high concentration of special and theoretical knowledge, of the capacity to create more knowledge as needed, and of the managerial skill to bring this about.

But, of course, the modern corporation does not concentrate all its knowledge in a few supermen; it assembles a large and diverse corps of people whose main work is generating, communicating, and developing ideas. To coordinate their work is both a complex and a crucial task, about which Galbraith has useful things to say. Decisions in modern business—which I note parenthetically are the basic decisions that determine how you and I will live our material lives, and even *whether* we will live—these decisions are the

product not of individuals but of groups . . . Each contains the men possessed of the information, or with access to the information, that bears on

12. Landes, p. 430.
13. Machlup, p. 159.
14. Landes, pp. 517–18.

the particular decision together with those whose skill consists in extracting and testing this information and obtaining a conclusion. This is how men act successfully on matters where no single one, however exalted or intelligent, has more than a fraction of the necessary knowledge. It is what makes modern business possible, and in other contexts it is what makes modern government possible.[15]

To add my own emphasis again: the basic system for allocating resources in the world, and so deciding the quality of human life, is a mechanism—essentially a committee, save the mark—for sharing, organizing, and mobilizing knowledge. Within any corporation, the group of people taking part in this process is much larger than "management." It may include one-half of the workers or more in some industries. Galbraith's term for it is the "technostructure." There can be little doubt that the technostructure regularly effects decisions that serve the interest of a ruling class; it is the mechanism that makes those decisions "rational" ones.

The central place of the technostructure, according to Galbraith, depends ultimately on technology itself, whose "most important consequence, at least for purposes of economics, is in forcing the division and subdivision of any [practical] task into its component parts. Thus, and only thus, can organized knowledge be brought to bear on performance." [16] For example: metallurgy is little use in designing the whole car, but crucial in designing the engine block; chemistry is useless until it can be applied to so small a part of manufacture as, say, the enamel finish or the carburetor design. Since it takes time to coordinate all the technical solutions to problems, the period between conception and production of an item lengthens as the item becomes more complex. For the same reason, larger amounts of capital must be committed, and committed more inflexibly, to a particular task. Galbraith's telling example is the three and one-half years of preparation required before the first Ford Mustang was produced, as compared to the four *months* that elapsed between the founding of the Ford Motor Company in June, 1903

15. John Kenneth Galbraith, *The New Industrial State* (Boston: Houghton-Mifflin Company, 1967), p. 65.
16. Galbraith, p. 12.

and the time when the first Ford car reached the market. It cost sixty million dollars to produce the first Mustang, no more than $28,500 for the 1903 Ford. The difference in time and money is in no small part an investment in knowledge.

These features of industrial technology mean that a corporation must have a pretty good idea in advance how a venture will turn out. No corporation can afford many disasters of the Edsel variety. And so they plan elaborately—Galbraith uses the mild word "planning" to refer to a pervasive and central feature of our society, the management and control of economic forces. Of course it would be crude to assume that planning always tyrannizes future events. As Victor Ferkiss points out, much planning is an attempt to "take predicted behavior into account rather than to determine it. . . ." [17] Hence, the use of the computer in management decisions, to marshal data, model systems, simulate future events, and so make more "rational" decisions. Yet Galbraith insists rightly on the large element of control in industrial planning. His book presents compelling evidence that, in our present economy, markets are no longer free, since corporations have, with some success, controlled both their future supply of resources (an example is the grab for oil from the North Slope of Alaska) and the purchases of their customers (mainly through advertising). The risks of the free market must be tempered —or better, eliminated—so that corporations can make profitable use of technology. In effect, planning has replaced entrepreneurship.

Bear in mind that this sequence began with technology, the application of knowledge to practical problems, and it is evident that the very form and structure of industrial society derive from the place of knowledge within it. Knowledge (technical, scientific, managerial) is accountable, not only for the material triumphs of that system, but for the all-encompassing control it has over the way we live now and will live in the future. In the last chapter I will argue that our social control of knowledge is so primitive as to endanger the human race, but for the moment it is sufficient to

17. Victor C. Ferkiss, *Technological Man: The Myth and the Reality* (New York: Mentor, 1969), p. 152. His discussion of planning belongs to a useful chapter on technology and politics.

accept Bell's quite accurate though inelegant label, the "knowledge society."

Statistics give the label concrete meaning. In 1958, for which year Fritz Machlup measured the total product of all the knowledge industries—education, research, information machines, advice and counseling, radio and TV, telephones, advertising, and so on—it added up to 136 billion dollars, or 29% of the gross national product. And the growth rate for this sector of the economy was and is considerably faster than for the rest of the economy, so that if knowledge's share of the gross national product has increased at a steady rate since 1947 it now amounts to over 40%. Naturally it is possible to pull out from this general average specific figures that are much more spectacular—from 1947 to 1958 television enjoyed an annual growth rate of 77%, and from 1954 to 1958 the computer industry grew at a rate of 104% a year. But the major impact on our lives and for my argument is less in these explosive new industries, whatever their apologists and Cassandras may say, than on our whole pattern of work and production. Everyone knows that farm workers, the majority of the work force a hundred years ago, have declined to fewer than 10%. Less familiar but just as significant is the more recent decline in the proportion of manual and service workers from over 50% in 1940 to roughly 40% now.[18] And of course this means that white collar workers now constitute more than one-half the work force. From 1951 to 1964 their numbers increased by 10 million, while the number of blue collar workers remained constant.[19] To say it briefly, most Americans now earn their living by working with knowledge—transmitting it, transforming it, applying it, deriving it, selling it. Paradoxically, the most materially productive (and consumptive) society in the world is also the one in which mental labor has the largest part and physical labor the smallest: the less physical labor, the more physical product. The paradox resolves itself around the machine, of course: metaphorically speaking, the machine feeds on knowledge and puts out consumer goods. That is what technology means.

18. Machlup, Chapters IX and X.
19. Galbraith, p. 236.

Teachers of English in American colleges and universities are part of this social arrangement for the profitable use of knowledge. So, to the extent that apologists for the guild are self-interested, their mistrust of science as a competitor and a threat could not be more misplaced. Our increase in numbers and status is subsumed in the emergence of the industrial state and of its dependence upon science—that is the message of the statistics. But that more than a *parallel* development is involved, that the categorization of English along with other forms of knowledge is more than a statistical convenience, requires a further analytical step. If our profession derives other than numerically from the growth in importance of technology, that must be shown by an analysis of the particular institutions within which the profession exists and through which it renders to industrial society the services I have discussed in earlier chapters. That means universities. I turn next to them.

CHAPTER ELEVEN

Universities and Industrial Culture

The affluence of this society derives in part from knowledge. We could not stay effortlessly warm through northern winters, travel to the moon, own detached houses full of appliances, search for a cure for cancer, destroy revolutionary movements around the world when we think they threaten the balance of power, overeat, travel easily and swiftly upon need or whim, consume mass culture, make labor at least barely tolerable for the working class, and, in general, suffer so few impediments to our freedom and pleasure, without the particular uses of knowledge discussed in the last chapter. In so saying, I have no wish to minimize the advantages to affluent America of capitalist arrangements in the economy; on the contrary, it should be evident that capitalism was the ideal medium for such knowledge to evolve in and, certainly, that capitalism accounts for America's unequal distribution (at home and elsewhere) of the benefits of knowledge. But it is possible to have affluence without capitalism (and capitalism without affluence). It is not possible to have affluence without industrial technology and its foundation of basic knowledge.

How does the economic system obtain a continuing supply of the knowledge and the knowledgeable people that it needs to sustain the American way of life? It would be easy to answer this question by saying: from the university. Clark Kerr wrote that "the university's invisible product, knowledge, may be the most powerful single element in our culture," [1] and added that the university is constantly called upon by the larger society to generate knowledge for particular purposes. But this answer, though worth developing, is too simple, and too metaphorical. The university does not supply industry with new knowledge as Texas supplies it with oil. Of the 14 billion dollars spent for research and development in 1958, only 7% was spent in a university setting (and only 2% was provided by universities). In no direct way does industry depend upon universities for research. And if industry's demand from universities is for people, not pure knowledge, why all those history and English majors, undertrained and overeducated for the jobs many of them will get? To move closer to an adequate answer, it is necessary to pursue somewhat more deeply the nature and needs of industrial society, and their broad relationship to schooling.

It stands to reason that as a society changes in the kinds of knowledge it finds useful, its arrangements for educating the young will also change. The early stages of human technology probably did not depend on education—on teaching—at all, since a child could directly *see* the connection between means and ends in, say, the shaping of a rock into a crude axe. The first dramatic advance in stone age technology must have changed this. When people learned to shape a large piece of flint so that small tools could be struck from it, they created the extra step between securing material and finishing the product that is characteristic of all subsequent advance. Since the original stone did not resemble the tools it would eventually become, the craftsman had to have the ability to visualize a future form of his material radically different from its initial form, and to conceptualize the steps that would bring it from one form to the other. Though the young could acquire this kind of knowledge by observation and imitation, its transmission would have been greatly eased by an accompanying explanation in words, since the learner would be aided by a *concept* as well as a knack. At this point

1. Clark Kerr, *The Uses of the University* (New York: Harper & Row, 1966), pp. vi–vii.

instruction would have been valuable and may, in fact, have been given.

Saber-toothed speculation aside, there is no doubt that instruction did occur with the growth from these beginnings of what Mumford calls the "polytechnics"—a variety of skills "based primarily, as in agriculture, on the needs, aptitudes, interests of living organisms—above all on man himself." [2] The polytechnics of renaissance civilization was transmitted first by instruction within the family, which then extended out into the community and was closely linked with such other institutions as apprenticeship and the church. What about schools? Bernard Bailyn has convincingly argued that if education is "the entire process by which a culture transmits itself across the generations," then schools were, in the renaissance and seventeenth century, a very minor instrument of education. [3] And the argument is truer still if we fix our attention on that part of the culture necessary to house, feed, and clothe people and to preserve their arts. The best method for teaching the polytechnics was what we now call on-the-job training, not isolated instruction. This is not, of course, to say that pre-industrial Europeans had too little technology to require formal schooling—on the contrary, the average worker (who was, of course, rural and unspecialized) certainly learned far more techniques than the average worker in industrial society. [4] But he or she learned it best by the direct handing on of skill and knowledge, in a setting where theory was inseparable from the movement of hand and eye.

2. Lewis Mumford, "The Megamachine," *The New Yorker* (October 17, 1970), p. 134.
3. Bernard Bailyn, *Education in the Forming of American Society* (Chapel Hill: The University of North Carolina Press, 1960), p. 14. Eugene Klaaren points out to me, however, that some elements of seventeenth-century school instruction, like catechetics, were important for the value they set on the systematization of knowledge.
4. Just as even now the unspecialized—and therefore unsuccessful—farmer of Appalachia knows far more practical technology than his sophisticated, machine-dependent city counterpart—say, a factory worker or bank teller. On top of much traditional lore about soil, crops, animals, seasons, carpentry, trees, and the like, the farmer or rural worker has added knowledge of more machines than the average city person encounters—and the farmer repairs these machines himself! If technological civilization collapses, about the only Americans likely to survive are these casualties of progress, who have been forced by hardship to preserve and adapt at least some of the divers skills of their great grandfathers.

The Industrial Revolution came out of this technology and this education, by and large. The early innovators in cotton fabric manufacture and in iron were empirical tinkerers who "saw" a problem and improvised a solution, aided sometimes by book learning, but generally depending more on ingenuity and intuition.

Yet even at this stage of mechanization schools were important, and their role grew. The remarkable development of the textile industry in Lancashire during the second half of the eighteenth century drew on craftsmen's skills that went beyond know-how: an ordinary millwright was often "a fair arithmetician, knew something of geometry, levelling, and mensuration, and in some cases possessed a very competent knowledge of practical mathematics. He could calculate the velocities, strength, and power of machines: he could draw in plan and section. . . ." [5] Such a man was as much engineer as mechanic. And though there was no regular schooling to train technicians of this sort, Landes points out the presence of abundant irregular facilities for technical education, "ranging from Dissenters' academies and learned societies to local and visiting lecturers, 'mathematical and commercial' private schools with evening classes, and a wide circulation of practical manuals, periodicals, and encyclopedias." [6] This patchwork of agencies was far from a school system, but equally far from the old instruments of technical education: apprenticeship and the family. And Bailyn's *Education in the Forming of American Society* tells in a more interpretive way the story of the same shift of agency in the colonies. When both family and community proved inadequate in educating for the rapid changes that characterized life in America, evening schools and private academies of all sorts sprung up; often the terms of apprenticeship, rather than providing for the education of the boy by his master, specified that he would go out to school part of the year or during off-work hours. Over a hundred schools existed in the colonies, before

5. W. Fairbairn, *Treatise on Mills and Millwork*, 2nd ed. (London, 1864), I, vi; quoted by David S. Landes, *The Unbound Prometheus; Technological Change and Industrial Development in Western Europe from 1750 to the Present* (Cambridge: Cambridge University Press, 1969), p. 63.
6. *The Unbound Prometheus*, p. 63.

1770, for apprentices and any others who would better themselves.[7]

The necessity of schooling, however organized, was clear as the Industrial Revolution moved into what we may think of as its second phase during the nineteenth century, with work organized in factories, with sequences of production lengthened and sophisticated, and new techniques a constant competitive requirement, and with science increasingly called on to develop industrial process. For intelligent work in this setting—the work of engineers and managers —tutelage in the home was plainly an inadequate preparation, as was apprenticeship. Experience and native cunning could still carry an extraordinary man, a Carnegie or Rockefeller, to great wealth, but their entrepreneurial genius would not have sufficed without the trained intelligence of many who worked under them. For a corporation, if not always for its leader, the kind of ordered knowledge taught in schools was by then a necessity.

Nor was knowledge the only essential product of schools. Industry depended on men who also were versatile and mobile, who were not bound to a single craft or skill. In *The Idea of the English School*, Franklin stated the goal of education suited to a rapidly changing technical society: to train youths "fitted for learning any business, calling, or profession." Of course no schools of this sort existed in Franklin's time, nor would they in any number for a hundred years thereafter. Yet Franklin signaled an important turn in education and in the nature of society. When the usual experience of a technician or a manager or a man of affairs is *new* experience, when his success depends on innovation, education must prepare him to help enact change, as well as conduct a craft (or maintain traditional culture). A corollary of this change, as Bailyn says, is the ideal of social mobility.[8] Whatever the social facts, a good education has long been conceived as one that will release men (though still not many women) from acceptance of predetermined social roles, and permit them to find that place in the economic system where their abilities are required and will be rewarded.

7. *Education in the Forming of American Society*, pp. 32–33.
8. *Education in the Forming of American Society*, p. 49.

The relatively stable body of theory—laws—beneath a variable technology is science. As I indicated in the previous chapter, it was in the second phase of the Industrial Revolution that manufacturers seized on the profitable marriage between science and technology, and so made a scientific education economically important. Needless to add, science cannot conveniently be learned on the industrial job. Abstract and theoretical knowledge of this sort can best be taught in a separate, specialized agency like the school. The alternative would have been for industrial firms to teach mathematics, chemistry, etc., themselves—an inefficient proposition for large firms and an impossible one for small firms.

Furthermore, as Landes points out, science and technology do not engage one another directly. The wide gap between them is filled by applied science, which selects basic knowledge as required, and engineering, which combines applied science with other information —economic, legal, social—to solve particular problems. It was the interposition of an extra stage between raw material and product that first made a genuine technology in the stone age and, thus, created a practical use for education. As the gap widened between technique and abstract idea, engineering and applied science became necessary bodies of knowledge, distinct from the techniques they utilized. Their distinctness made school—with its array of "subjects" and its systematic presentation of disengaged knowledge —an ideal agency for developing and teaching them.

In short, by 1825, there was increasing need for the modern university, as well as for the technical institute and modern college, and the need grew. Yet it is little exaggeration to say that there were no such institutions in Britain or in America.[9] The lack in Britain is evident enough to the retrospective eye, which discerns only Oxford and Cambridge, in their non-technological splendor, and the austere Scottish universities. The true situation in America is harder to make out, since there were a large number of universities and colleges, by

9. France, by contrast, had technical institutes of some standing, and Germany's universities, though not quite what the productive system needed, were closer than anything in the English-speaking countries. More about this later.

name, in 1825. Yet in structure and method, these institutions were remarkably unsuited to the needs of industrial society. Most of them were little more than academies (there was probably not a college or university in the country whose enrollment exceeded 500, by 1850), suited to the education of clergymen, other professionals, and gentlemen, and committed to teaching the classics and the culture of Christianity within a more or less aristocratic tradition. Almost all of them were sectarian, to one degree or another, and hostile or indifferent to contemporary secular culture. Furthermore, their educational techniques were primitive: recitations stressing memory were the main pedagogical device, with a lecture thrown in from time to time. The absence of critical analysis, empirical enquiry, and Socratic dialogue indicates what the colleges were up to: transmitting a stable corpus of knowledge, embodied in a canon of classical and scriptural texts, with the purpose of confirming traditional culture and, more than incidentally, traditional class structure. The knowledge they presided over was a very long distance from the knowledge that a fluid, bourgeois, and technological society would need. Nor could they have been much practical help in educating youths who would be "fitted for learning any business, calling, or profession," in Franklin's words.

Yet few academic men saw the opportunity here for a happier marriage with society, and the universities failed to adapt themselves to the new conditions. In 1860, most of them were little different than in 1825 or 1775, and their unresponsiveness began to have a palpable result: enrollments stopped growing. It is an odd and significant fact that between 1825 and 1875, while the population of the country was rapidly growing and its industry burgeoning, the number of students attending colleges and universities in America remained almost constant. In the 1870's, at the end of this period of declining importance, enrollment at twenty of the most prestigious colleges rose only 3.5% as against a population growth in the nation of 23%.[10]

10. Laurence R. Veysey, *The Emergence of the American University* (Chicago: The University of Chicago Press, 1965), p. 4.

Public attitudes corresponded to the story these figures tell. When G. Stanley Hall—the psychologist, later president of Clark University—was admitted to study at Williams College in 1863 he tried to keep it a secret, but his friends found out, and he was "unmercifully jibed." [11] Even when universities, new and old, began answering to practical needs, these attitudes persisted. Johns Hopkins "came into existence unasked for and uncared for." Religious organizations and legislatures harassed the new universities for their secularism, Grangers demanded more teaching of agriculture, and, in general, an anti-intellectual people regarded the universities as dangerous or superfluous.[12] Men who wanted commercial success bypassed college and went to work in the school of hard knocks, where the curriculum was at least more flexible and more attuned to practical need than the rigid curriculum of the universities and colleges.

Why should a social and economic need that was clear enough in retrospect not be more clearly perceived at the time by the potential consumers, corporate and individual, of an improved education or by the academic men who stood to gain so much by supplying it? It is always hard to conceive what a new institution will be like before it exists. And the ethos of industrialism was so remote from the pious and aristocratic ethos of most existing higher education that even the possibility of adaptation must have been unthinkable. In any case, when agitation for the new university began to be heard, about 1825, it came not from manufacturers or merchants but from college officials themselves. And these latter did not, by and large, base their proposals in an appreciation of industrial progress, scientific need, and the plain chance for the academy to cash in.

There were exceptions. Jefferson had a broad and scientific concept of the university, and, in a report of 1818, the Board of Commissioners to establish a site for the University of Virginia, of which board Jefferson was a member, looked back on the "wonderful advances in the sciences and arts" of the preceding half century, and asserted the duty of each generation to advance "the knowledge and

11. *Ibid.,* p. 6.
12. *Ibid.,* pp. 15–16.

well-being of mankind" indefinitely, proposing a curriculum that
included mechanics, chemistry, mineralogy, botany, zoology, anatomy, medicine, government, law, and political economy, as well as
the more traditional subjects.[13] Jefferson's idea had its adherents, as
the demand for a "true" university increased, and occasionally a
theorist came forward who might have been speaking directly for the
nascent industrial society.

Such a one was President Wayland of Brown, who, in 1850,
blamed the colleges for not giving "scientific and literary instruction
to every class of our people," but only to brahmins. "We have in this
country," he pointed out,

one hundred and twenty colleges, forty-two theological seminaries, and
forty-seven law schools, and we have not a single institution designed to
furnish the agriculturist, the manufacturer, the mechanic, or the merchant
with the education that will prepare him for the profession to which his life
is to be devoted.

Wayland not only perceived the connection between science and
productivity—"the want of that science, which alone can lay the
foundation of eminent success in the useful arts, is extensively
felt"—but also generalized from individual to national need: "the
progress of a nation in wealth, happiness, and refinement, is
measured by the universality of its knowledge of the laws of nature,
and its skill in adapting these laws to the purposes of man. . . . It is,
therefore, of the greatest national importance to spread broadcast
over the community, that knowledge, by which alone the useful arts
can be multiplied and perfected." [14] And at this time an occasional
wealthy benefactor of universities might, like Ezra Cornell, endorse
the goal of educating "the Agricultural and Mechanical classes." [15]

But even among the strongest advocates of true universities in

13. Richard J. Storr, *The Beginnings of Graduate Education in America* (Chicago: The
University of Chicago Press, 1953), pp. 12–13.
14. Francis Wayland, *Report to the Corporation of Brown University, On Changes in the System
of Collegiate Education* (Providence, 1850), reprinted in Richard Hofstadter and Wilson
Smith, eds., *American Higher Education, A Documentary History*, vol. II (Chicago: The
University of Chicago Press, 1961), pp. 478–83.
15. Hofstadter and Smith, p. 566.

America, most rejected Wayland's rationale—an atypical repudiation of self-interest, one may add in retrospect. Henry Tappan, later president of the University of Michigan, and an indefatigable spokesman for graduate study and for genuine universities in America, nonetheless saw profit and knowledge as antagonists: "the commercial spirit of our country, and the many avenues to wealth which are opened before enterprise, create a distaste for study deeply inimical to education." And, in somewhat disdainful rebuttal of Wayland, he continues, "The manufacturer, the merchant, the gold-digger, will not pause in their career to gain intellectual accomplishments. While gaining knowledge they are losing the opportunities to gain money." So he concluded that American colleges "do not answer to the commercial and political spirit of our country," and that it would be futile to make them try.[16] Instead, Tappan saw himself helping a raw and vigorous people—the citizens of Michigan—to "refine their new homes with learning and the liberal arts," and "cause the Huron to repeat the wizard murmurs of the Ilissus." [17] The Huron in time marched to a different wizard, repeating murmurs from River Rouge and Willow Run to the material advantage of all but the fish. But the lines of debate, as drawn by Wayland and Tappan, persisted through redactions by Dewey and Hutchins, Gideonse and Flexner, to the present day. And the strength of the Tappan camp, coupled with traditional prejudices about education, no doubt helped delay the advent of the modern university, in spite of the economic need for it and the influential educators who wanted to bring it into being.

For those who might have helped create the university—legislators and wealthy men—received from educators only the cloudiest image of this desired institution, derived from diverse ideologies. Tappan was only one of many who held up the model of the German university, usually stressing the purity of its intellectual labors, its reclusion from practical reality. Within such a cloister, knowledge

16. Henry P. Tappan, *University Education* (New York, 1851), quoted by Hofstadter and Smith, p. 491.
17. Tappan, *The University: Its Constitution and its Relations, Political and Religious* (Ann Arbor, 1858); quoted by Hofstadter and Smith, p. 525.

could be pursued for its own sake; and many early images of the university placed research in the center.[18] Alongside this idea was a still cloudier one, that of the university as the carrier of virtue; Bishop Alonzo Potter, a trustee of the University of Pennsylvania, in a controversial report of 1852, opposed the elective system and vocational education, holding that a college should "inspire a generous taste for goodness truth and beauty." [19] And even those advocates who did commend the university for its practical value seldom saw, as Wayland did, the broad use of higher education—a kind of higher education that did not yet exist—in the material development of the country. Many conceived utility from the point of view of the individual student, not the economy. And it became common late in the century to hold that the university would offer service to society by training men for statesmanship and public office. Andrew White, first president of Cornell, pictured graduates of the university (according to Veysey) "pouring into the legislatures, staffing the newspapers, and penetrating the municipal and county boards of America," until pure American ideals spread throughout the world.[20] And Eliot of Harvard, in justifying the elective system, joined the ideal of utility to the individual with that of utility to the state:

For the individual, concentration, and the highest development of his own peculiar faculty, is the only prudence. But for the State, it is variety, not uniformity, of intellectual product, which is needful.[21]

And of course, among these competing ideas, the older one remained; one of an aristocratic institution modeled on the English university of the eighteenth century, with its function of cementing the cultural bonds that united a ruling class. That these strands of ideology are by no means incompatible, the universities of the 1950's

18. Veysey's well-documented discussion (pp. 121–79) of this ideal is good reading, as are his parallel accounts of the ideals of "utility" and "liberal culture."
19. Storr, p. 76.
20. Veysey, p. 85.
21. Charles William Eliot, inaugural address as President of Harvard, in Hofstadter and Smith, p. 609.

and 1960's have borne witness. But a less equivocal sense of purpose might have helped sell the university in a raw culture unaccustomed to its benefits.

For whatever reasons, there is a fifty-year history of proposals for research and graduate study in universities, of aborted attempts to found such institutions, and of disappointing reforms in existing universities. Some proposals, e.g., for the University of Albany and the University and Academy of Sciences and Arts of the City of New York, fell short of expectations; the University of the South started well, but was almost destroyed by the Civil War. And the addition of graduate programs at Columbia and Michigan in the 1850's proved unappealing to the consumers of knowledge; at Michigan only two or three graduate students a year chose to enroll outside of chemistry (which really meant agriculture); and at Columbia only the graduate program in law survived.[22] Even when the Morrill Act of 1862 provided for land grant universities, no state moved with clear purpose to create an institution with depth and spread. That did not really happen until twenty years after legislation that made it possible was passed. In short, in America around mid-century, universities languished, though there was a substantial use in the larger society for services they could have offered. To do so, they would have needed to change sharply; but even so, they were in a better position to take on this function than were family, church, or industry.

In a situation like this, it should not be surprising to find the new institution rising up quite suddenly in a number of places, as if conceived and implemented by a central authority. So it happened. Yale granted the first Ph.D. in 1861. Eliot firmly implanted the elective system, with its new tolerance for specialized learning, in 1869. And other old and prestigious colleges quickly became universities, with the characteristic pattern of modern subjects, specialized research, graduate and professional schools, departments, and complex administrations. I have shown in a bit more detail how this happened in one university (Indiana) and for one discipline (English) in Chapter Nine.

22. These and other sad stories are told in detail by Storr.

Meanwhile, and just as important, new institutes and universities sprang up. Some explicitly favored scientific and technological instruction: MIT (1861), Cornell (1865), Purdue (1869), California Institute of Technology (1891), and the ill-fated Clark (1887). Others were general universities, usually with emphasis on graduate education, specialized study, and research: Johns Hopkins (1876), Vanderbilt (1873), Stanford (1885), and Chicago (1890). Whereas at the end of the Civil War there were no universities, by the 1890's a university system existed in roughly the shape it retains today, a shape that all more recently developed universities have routinely assumed.

Yet the central authority behind this concerted transformation was mainly that of the unseen hand that guides a laissez faire economy. One of its instruments was the rationale constructed by men like Wayland of Brown and given prestige by the authority of science and of the German university. Yet Wayland was in a minority among the influential theorists and practical leaders of universities, and the preponderant ideologies of higher education were of no more use then than now in explaining what, from society's standpoint, the universities were accomplishing. Another instrument of the unseen hand was the beneficence of those wealthy men who perceived, at least dimly, a connection between the industrial system and learning, and between class and culture, and so founded universities. Yet the more felicitous of these benefactors did little to shape their creations, but gave over the executive power to academic men—John D. Rockefeller had his William Rainey Harper, Ezra Cornell his Andrew White, and Johns Hopkins his Daniel Coit Gilman. And those capitalists who did try to impose their vision directly on "their" universities generally diminished the effectiveness of the institutions: Jonas G. Clark nearly destroyed his with meddling, causing most of the faculty to leave; Leland and Jane Lathrop Stanford precipitated grave crises in academic freedom, intervening in the university they regarded as a personal memorial to their son. The unseen hand also worked through the agency of Justin Morrill and his Act in Congress that prepared the way for the land grant universities. Yet of these institutions only Cornell, itself partly a private university, was a leader in showing the way to the modern university; the rest remained small and mainly agricultural until the pattern was well established.[23]

Neither the agreement of educators nor the guidance of benefactors nor the provisions of Congress can account for the sudden emergence of the modern university. On one level of analysis these are unrelated "accidents." But on another they are concrete, if mainly unconscious and uncoordinated, responses to industry's need for concentrated and specialized learning, for theoretical understanding of natural phenomena, and for managerial ability. This need pretty well guaranteed the success of institutions patterned in the new way (short of phenomenal mismanagement as at Clark), and so attached itself to the self-interest of faculty members and administrators, whatever contempt they might allow themselves in theory for vocationalism or "mere training."[24] Similarly, though self-made businessmen liked to snort at what went on in colleges, by the turn of the century they had made it a habit to send their sons to college—nor was Carnegie the only one who indicted higher education for its vacuity while giving large sums of money to support it.[25] Finally, it is an old story that state legislatures and boards of regents, while often voicing the most blatant hostility to the life of the intellect, have with only occasional interruptions cheerfully voted the funds to support their state universities, a phenomenon duplicated in Congress in more recent years, when the reaction to Sputnik showed how natural is the identification of power with higher education. Most of the participants in the founding of the modern

23. Michigan under Tappan was a pioneer, but that was before the Morrill Act. In any case, graduate and scientific education failed to take hold there the first time, and Tappan left in the aftermath of bitter struggles with legislators who could not comprehend, much less endorse, his vision.

24. Students, of course, have known better. Among those for whom college is not an ancestral privilege, the most common motive for attendance is economic gain, and immigrant parents have rightly seen college education as a means of social advancement for their children. Nor was it to acquire fluency in Western culture or a sense of personal identity that black students beat on the doors of universities in the 1960's, but to be cut in on America's wealth and power. Such truisms would scarcely require even a footnote, were it not for the rampant mystification that has generally characterized faculty rationalization of their work.

25. See Veysey, 266–67.

university, then, acted upon a perception they misinterpreted, formulated in confusing ways, or even actively denied, but one that was likely to govern their choices as long as economic well-being, for individuals and for the nation, was closely tied to knowledge.

To recapitulate the argument: I tried to show in the last chapter that the new productive system came to rely—for profit and growth—on knowledge that was both abstract and well organized. This knowledge could best be generated and taught, not on the job, but in institutions. In America, virtually no such institutions existed until the last quarter of the nineteenth century. Meanwhile, for the fifty years before 1875, universities, which were becoming increasingly irrelevant in the American economy, declined in strength and importance. When, for many reasons, universities did begin to produce the kind of education and the kind of new knowledge that society could use, they flourished. This change took place quite rapidly. By 1900, universities were geared for the practical affairs of American society: turning out large numbers of scientifically and technically trained people; laying the groundwork for managerial competence; and accumulating new knowledge through research. They have continued since then to have an important role, and at times, like the period between 1950 and 1970, when they adapted well to further economic change, they enjoyed further spurts of growth and prosperity.

Though schematic, I think this an accurate explanation for the existence and growth of modern universities. But I want to do more: namely, account for their particular form as well. Let me note, then, how that form changed during this critical stage of development.

First, universities tended to take in all fields of knowledge that already had or had acquired economic importance, in spite of haughty proclamations about knowledge for its own sake. This is natural enough given the perspective of this chapter: universities were elite institutions, to be sure, but the new industrial system brought new elites into being, and there was much advantage and no loss to academic people and the ruling class in having those elites trained with the others.

Engineering offers a paradigm case. There were, as we have seen, a great variety of mechanics' schools in Europe and America by the first half of the nineteenth century. Furthermore, the advanced and systematic training of engineers had begun with the founding of the *École des Ponts et Chausées* in 1747, and the more famous *École Polytechnique* in 1794, and the example was soon followed in all the industrial countries of Europe (except Britain) and in America (Rensselaer Polytechnic Institute, 1824). Why did engineering "join" the university, rather than keep house separately? On one side, because it became an obviously important field, whose presence would benefit universities; and on the other, because it was clearly advantageous to engineers, newly recognizing themselves as *professionals,* to be so recognized by the institution that controlled access to all the highly valued professions.

An additional benefit, as the uses of science to industry became apparent, was the close association of engineering with basic science. The American Society for Engineering Education (originally the Society for the Promotion of Engineering Education, founded 1893) has consistently emphasized basic principles rather than practical techniques in undergraduate teaching.[26] Finally, since engineers were increasingly to share the administration of power in corporations and government, it made sense that they and those with whom they would work have a common cultural background, and common experience, common skills. So, in fact, engineering was first recognized as a university subject at London, Glasgow, Harvard, and Yale in the 1840's, and its presence in the university became almost universal in the next fifty years. And though polytechnic institutes continued to be founded, the best ones have long since followed MIT in adapting many features of full-scale universities.

The same process of amalgamation that made engineering an university subject occurred in field after field, until, by 1900, the content of university education bore little resemblance to the classical curriculum that was thought suitable in 1850. Of this

26. John B. Rae, "The Invention of Invention," in Melvin Kranzberg and Carroll W. Pursell, Jr., *Technology in Western Civilization*, vol. I (New York, Oxford University Press, 1967), p. 336.

change, at least, educational leaders were aware. John Dewey, in 1902, welcomed widespread introduction of "B.S. courses side by side with the older classical courses" and "forward movement in the direction of a specific group of commercial and social studies," as well as "the tendency of all universities of broad scope to maintain technological schools" and adapt their work "more and more to preparation for specific vocations in life." [26a] Eliot wrote with approval of the change in Harvard's function and curriculum:

All along Harvard College has produced among its Bachelors of Arts young men who went out into business, largely into businesses which required a good measure of knowledge of applied science, of sound business administration, and of the wise and considerate management of the working force; but it could hardly be said that it was a distinct object in the University to train men for business. Now it has become so.[26b]

And I have already written about Jordan's overhaul of the old "unsatisfactory" curriculum at Indiana, to make it more "useful" (Chapter Nine). In introducing the specialized curriculum and admitting professional schools to the university, educators were deliberately meeting social needs.

The peculiar *structure* of the American university also emerged during this period, but with a much less conscious design. Universities divided into undergraduate colleges and graduate schools with deans. The faculty, along with the curriculum, split into departments, with a corresponding arrangement of "majors." The "administration" emerged as a distinct part of the university and increased its power. A regular hierarchy of faculty ranks appeared, with many other arrangements that have remained virtually the same from 1900 to today. It is perhaps hard to imagine universities without these features, yet in 1875 they had none of them. Moreover, they did not assume the new structure in direct imitation of any foreign model, though German universities were doubtless influential in

26a. "The Educational Situation," in *University of Chicago Contributions to Education*, No. III (1902).
26b. C. W. Eliot, *Harvard Memories* (Cambridge, Mass., Harvard University Press, 1923), p. 70.

some respects. Nor was a clear rationale developed for this structure, any more than for the existence of the university. Veysey, who has made the most thorough survey of contemporary evidence, says that the correspondence of university leaders simply fails to explain the relevant events: "exceedingly little direct evidence may be found on decisions involving the *basic* shape of the rapidly emerging academic structure. The most fundamental assumptions were not being articulated by those who were acting upon them." [27] In such a situation, as he says, one looks for latent needs that will account for the fundamental choices.

I have already given an account (in Chapter Nine) of the latent needs served today by departments, needs of the faculty more than of any other party. Those needs surely operated to help universities settle on the departmental structure in the first place. As Veysey says, "the academic career, in a professional sense, came into being only in the late seventies and eighties," [28] and it was precisely in regularizing professional careers that departments were most effective. Departments allowed faculty members status, security, and some power; while providing for certain kinds of competition, they also set limits for the game to protect faculty members from the anxiety of too broad or too unpredictable competition. This advantage can be generalized to the whole university structure that grew up in the 1880's and 1890's.

It should be clear from the last chapter that the economic uses of knowledge that made it possible for the universities to prosper were intensely competitive. It is not surprising that competition became the principal way of organizing activity in the academic world. Veysey shows (pp. 317–32) how much of the life of the university consisted in the competition of professors with one another, of departments with other departments in the same university, and of one institution with another—*using* departments, faculty members, and students as the symbols of winning and losing. (Is it different today? How does the profession reckon it when X leaves Harvard for

27. Veysey, pp. 267–68.
28. *Ibid.*, p. 317.

Stanford or Y gets Z's chair at Chicago?) The hierarchical structure of the university both facilitated such competition and protected faculty members from its severest hurts.

University organization also derives from the larger society's use of knowledge in a second and more direct way. A system of production based on technology and managerial expertise not only requires trained personnel; it also requires criteria to classify and rank people as they finish their training and enter the market. As specialization becomes a competitive necessity, it is no longer enough for an employer to know that the young applicant spent some time at college. He will want to know what special field the candidate studied *and* how far he advanced. This requirement encouraged the division of knowledge into fields, of faculties into departments, and of students into the more and the less qualified.

To put it another way, the regular use of a college degree to certify technical, professional, and managerial workers encouraged professional behavior within the colleges: the ranking of students, the struggle for departmental prerogatives, and the growth of an administrative bureaucracy to monitor the student's progress, keep his records, and maintain relations with agencies and employers outside the university. These arrangements helped the new society make efficient use of the university's services in training personnel. Similarly, departments, learned societies, journals, and research groups facilitated discourse between professors and their industrial counterparts. Finally, the departmental system worked reasonably well to advance knowledge, at least in the sciences where discovery can be a collaborative effort and a department a congeries of research groups.

There were other causes that made the new structure of universities seem efficient and comfortable—e.g., the necessity to control student behavior *"in loco parentis"* was undoubtedly one reason for the growth of university administrations. But like the growth of universities, and the standard fields of study they came to embrace, the structure of universities came to depend, in great part, on the demands made upon them by the larger society and on the attempts of academic people to be comfortable while meeting those demands;

very little depended on conscious planning in the interests of liberal education and the advancement of learning.

It may seem improper to strain after precise causes, since we know so little about them, but, however obscure the causal connection, there can be no question that the new universities did answer society's needs far better than the old and that society distributed rewards accordingly. Thus, even the most reluctant of the old aristocratic universities—Yale, and especially Princeton—came around in time. The new model worked. Students—however obstreperous—came in larger and larger numbers, completed the course of study, and took choice jobs. Faculty members suddenly found their services in demand, their profession respected, and their promotions rapid; university presidents gloried in the growth of their institutions and the prestige of their offices. Veysey considers it a paradox that the university was a success in spite of the sometimes open warfare among its internal factions (pp. 332–33). But since the reasons for success were mainly external, the lack of common purpose and style among students, faculty, and administrators was not an impediment. All parties to the bargain gained in material and spiritual prosperity, the great reconciler of differences.

So entrenched did this bargain become—and so quickly—that the doctrinal sallies of presidents and theorists became less frequent, less polemical, more eclectic. David Starr Jordan often addressed young people on "the value of higher education," mentioning conversation with the great minds of the past, the study of nature, beneficial social influences, the virtue of hard work, the financial worth of the degree, and the idealism of the campus.[29] These benefits do not define a theory of education or even a coherent pattern of values, but they represent pretty fairly both the motives of the students in going to college and the diverse attitudes to be found within the university communities. The ideals, which in the 1860's and 1870's had contended one with the other, now were combined into a single, rather airy myth to support what existed. Success rendered philosophic self-examination unnecessary. Universities simply flourished.

29. *Ibid.*, p. 343.

It is worth noting that schools did too, though that is slightly aside from the present argument. These were the years when the American public school settled into its secure place among our institutions and when the public began to treat secondary education as an inevitable rite of passage for the young. It is easy to see why, in the context of this discussion. Industrial systems needed their trained elites, but they also needed a much larger corps of workers, both office staff and technically sophisticated laborers, who were capable of handling routine tasks, that is, to use simple tools of analysis, to pass easily between the abstract and the concrete, to translate words into acts and vice versa, and to deal with forms of organized information like catalogues, customer orders, manuals and guides, letters, and invoices. In short, the industrial system required that a large part of the work force be more than minimally literate, possess ordinary arithmetical competence, organize phenomena in rational ways, be able to apply problem solving to their work, and be cooperative. These were the skills and the sets of mind that public schooling fostered.[30]

Britain's loss of industrial leadership first to Germany and then to the United States seems in part due to her slowness in developing a system of universal education. In 1860 only one-half of the school-aged children in Britain received some kind of elementary schooling,

30. Peter Drucker argues that the lengthening out of the years of schooling is due not to the requirements of work but simply to increased human longevity and the consequent increase in the working years of an average worker. He cites jobs, such as those of salespeople, that have remained much the same for a hundred years, though the people holding them have changed from grade school to high school graduates. No doubt many people are "overeducated," and instances like this are easy to produce. But they count for nothing toward Drucker's conclusion except in the aggregate. An economic system 50% of whose labor force are people working with knowledge will require more universal schooling than one that needs only 10% white collar workers, even if some jobs change little during the transition. Nor does it seem plausible that, as Drucker says, a more educated work force has made industry produce more knowledge jobs, rather than fewer. It is not the presence of a literate and easily bored work force that has created new industries like aircraft, electronics, plastics, and tourism, which require much more brain work and less hand work than older industries. Drucker says, rightly, that it is an economic rationality for people to extend their years in school. This could hardly be so unless this choice were also economically rational from the standpoint of employers. See Peter F. Drucker, *The Age of Discontinuity* (New York: Harper & Row, 1969), pp. 178–285.

while Germany had long had excellent and nearly universal public education. The disparity makes sense when one considers also that Britain stuck longest with the old empirical methods of technological innovation (having had spectacular success with them in the first phase of the Industrial Revolution), was slow to admit scientists to a respectable station in industry, and, to this day, sends a relatively small proportion of young people to university. Attitudes toward knowledge and schooling, no less than actual practice, helped make British industry conservative and uncompetitive,[31] though now an excellent system of trade and vocational colleges exists, in the best Jeffersonian tradition.

To return to the principal subject: it should be clear that the American university, which developed belatedly in response to the second phase of the Industrial Revolution, was admirably suited to the third phase: the developments described by Galbraith in *The New Industrial State*. The emergence of the technostructure and the new reliance on planned control of markets has made organizational abilities even more critical than they were before. The use of words to bring order into complex situations, the sharing of information, the cooperative solution of problems, the mediation between concrete and abstract: such work is the daily occupation of the technostructure and of most of the 50% of our labor force who are white collar workers. Universities are (or at least were until just the other day) reasonably good at socializing young people in ways that prepare them to do committee work, to make reports, to synthesize information from diverse sources, to cooperate with others, to sublimate feelings and the impulse to action into socially acceptable —usually verbal—channels: in short, to be organization men. As Galbraith says, in the technostructure the "effective power of decision is lodged deeply in the technical, planning, and other specialized staff." [32] This means that usable knowledge, cooperative though competitive attitudes, and social and administrative graces

31. For a helpful discussion, see Landes, pp. 340–46.
32. John Kenneth Galbraith, *The New Industrial State* (Boston: Houghton Mifflin, 1967), p. 69.

must be possessed by a very large elite—certainly comprising millions of people—and not just by a few leaders. Universities are able to teach these amenities to large numbers of people and so supply Mumford's "megamachine" with its human parts.

And, as has recently become clear, the modern university is also well equipped to join the military-industrial-academic complex in more explicit ways. Though it is with startling swiftness that the marriage was effected; that two-thirds of the universities' research funds came to be provided by the Defense Department, AEC, and NASA; that universities "spun off" research corporations and institutes of all sorts to do projects for industry and government; that they came to train spies and secret police to shore up the American hegemony in divers parts of the world; that they helped develop exotic biological and chemical weapons; and that they took major responsibility for the development of whole new industries like data processing and machine teaching—though all this is new, it required no basic change in the attitudes toward knowledge, the professional ethos, or the structure that had prevailed in American universities since 1900.[33]

In fact much that was true about universities in the earlier period was a direct preparation for their present role. Woodrow Wilson was only the most influential of many academic spokesmen who called for universities to serve the nation, to train men of affairs, to assume a public duty.[34] Naturally enough, this ideal was the prevailing one in the new state universities, which Edmund J. James, President of Illinois, saw as "great civil service academ[ies], preparing the young men and women of the state for the civil service of the state, the country, the municipality, and the township." [35] And the ideal of social efficiency, which animated much talk about universities (see Veysey, pp. 113–18), was closely allied with the great success of the problem-solving approach to material production. There was long a

33. The best critical survey I know of universities' collaboration with industry and government is James Ridgeway's *The Closed Corporation; American Universities in Crisis* (New York; Random House, 1968).
34. "Princeton in the Nation's Service," Hofstadter and Smith, pp. 684–95.
35. E. J. James, "The Function of the State University," *Science*, XXII (1905), 625; quoted in Veysey, p. 73.

precedent for academic people to think of themselves as appliers of knowledge to corporate and governmental need. If flying saucers had appeared in 1900, no federal bureau would have engaged the University of Colorado to study them; but if it had, I imagine that the professors would have found that fitting enough. The ideology of value-free inquiry, which academic intellectuals have been a century in developing, lends itself well to the complacent sale of services by professors to whatever buyers appear. It is not for universities to monitor the use of their products, but only to see that professional standards of accuracy and detachment are maintained in the production.

For these reasons the American system of higher education has, since World War II, enjoyed a second spurt of prosperity, comparable to that of the 1880's and 1890's. Taken together, these two periods of growth have completely altered the university and given it an entirely new prominence in American society. The statistics are so spectacular that a few of them can carry the point. In a hundred-year period, beginning with 1870, the percentage of young Americans who attended college rose from 1.7% to over 40%. Then there were 52,000 students in post-secondary institutions; now there are 7,000,000. Most of these are undergraduates, of course, but the increase in graduate students is as spectacular and more recent. As late as 1900 there were only 5800 graduate students in the country; by 1960 there were 330,000. To translate these figures into monetary form, between 1890 and 1960 expenditures on colleges and universities went from $160 million to $18.6 *billion*, or a tenfold increase in the percentage of the GNP allocated to this purpose. Public schools shared in this social change; their share of the GNP rose from 1% to 3.7%. And the accompanying change in status is nowhere clearer than in schoolteachers' salaries, which averaged $195 annually in 1880, $936 in 1920, and $5160 in 1960,[36] far outdistancing increases in cost of living. Plainly a schoolteacher was a kind of servant in the last century (people living today in small towns still remember when

36. These figures come, as usual, from Fritz Machlup, *The Production and Distribution of Knowledge in the United States* (Princeton, N.J.: Princeton University Press, 1962), esp. pp. 71–74.

the teacher was boarded around from one home to another during the school year). Now he or she is something of a professional. And the whole institution of schooling in the United States bears little resemblance to its ancestor of 1870.

Yet, in another sense, it is not far from Woodrow Wilson and his talk of education in "the nation's service," from Charles W. Eliot's perception that universities had a role in the "unprecedented advance in civilization" of that century, or from Daniel Coit Gilman's belief that "as civilization advanced, all critical decisions and new steps must be made by experts who could command all the available knowledge in their field," [37]—not far from these noble anticipatory thoughts to their realization in James A. Perkins' statement that universities and other major institutions of our society "have now been joined together by a new kind of bloodstream, made up of the ideas, the trained intelligence, and the manpower which provide the driving energy for our society. And the university is the great pumping heart that keeps this system fresh, invigorated, and in motion," [38] or to Clark Kerr's statement that "the university has become a prime instrument of national purpose," or to Admiral Rickover's titling the first chapter of his book on education "Education is Our First Line of Defense." The earlier spokesmen had the general idea: education was to become the handmaiden to the "advance of civilization." As Galbraith says, because organized knowledge is critical for the industrial system, education now basks in "the greatest solemnity of social purpose." [39]

At the beginning of the last chapter I posed a question about the functions of literature and the humanities in American society, and the intervening discussion has been a circuitous—but I think necessary—approach to an answer. Unless you see literary and humanistic studies as part of the peculiar history I have sketched, their functions are likely to be passed over by the sanguine claims

---

37. G. Stanley Hall, *Life and Confessions of a Psychologist* (New York, 1923), in Hofstadter and Smith, p. 650.
38. James A. Perkins, *The University in Transition* (Princeton, N.J.: Princeton University Press, 1966), pp. 18–19.
39. *The New Industrial State*, p. 282.

and the good intentions we tend to improvise whenever we rationalize a position. For, if I am right, our most important function is not obvious, nor is it what the profession would choose.

English departments, for instance, have been full participants in the development of the new American university, sharing its growth, its prosperity (slightly less than the share of scientists, economists, and the like), its professional pride, and its mystifications. English departments sprang into being at the same time as other departments, and in the same unexplained way. Their antecedents, as William Riley Parker had made clear,[40] were rhetoric, oratory, and half a dozen loosely related subjects; and, though the new departments took their rationale from German philology and Matthew Arnold, their safe position within the university had more to do with rhetoric and oratory. For freshman English was the successor of these studies, and it was freshman English that university faculties, then as now, wanted from English professors—enough to make it a requirement. This meant that English departments would grow along with the university as long as they staffed freshman English, almost regardless of their success or failure in teaching the subject. For everyone agreed that college students ought to write competently, and no one knew how to achieve that result other than by delegating the job to the English department. At the same time, the professoriat took both its pleasure and its internal scale of merit from the study of *literature*. So the ideology of the field grew up around great books, not around freshman English, to the confusion of all but to the considerable benefit, psychic and financial, of professors.

Is the myth of our usefulness to the rest of the university and to society, then, totally unfounded? I think not. Recall from earlier chapters some of the things we have traditionally attempted to teach: organizing information, drawing conclusions from it, making reports, using Standard English (i.e., the language of the bourgeois elites), solving problems (assignments), keeping one's audience in mind, seeking objectivity and detachment, conducting persuasive arguments, reading either quickly or closely, as circumstances

40. "Where Do English Departments Come From?" *College English* (February, 1967).

demand, producing work on request and under pressure, valuing the
intellect and its achievements. These are all abilities that are clearly
useful to the new industrial state, and, to the extent that English
departments nourish them—even if only through the agency of
graduate assistants—they are giving value for society's money. Even
if our record of achievement is spotty in these matters—as it
certainly is—the mere fact of a student's *having to submit* to our
regimen of verbal and logical graces shows him where some of
society's values lie. We can expect that the more assiduous students
learn the lesson well. The superego needn't win every point in order
to keep the ego generally obedient.

I cannot prove, of course, that the United States would lose world
economic leadership if fewer than 40% of our young people took
freshman English or that General Dynamics needs the academic
humanities in order to keep landing those almost foolproof government contracts. Nor is it necessary to demonstrate with any such
particularity the uses of English. It is enough that both the skills
(fluency, organization, analysis) and the attitudes (caution, detachment, cooperation) that we encourage in the young are essential to
the technostructure and to the smooth functioning of liberal (not
liberated) society.[41] If they were not, I feel certain that English
literature would today draw no more teachers or students than
Greek literature, whose academic rationale is much the same, but
whose actual usefulness belongs to quite another cultural situation.

Neither do I deny the very real critical force that some teachers of
the humanities exercise. English departments house many people
who early saw the cracks in the American dream. But our main
function has been neither the making of a counter-culture nor the
laying on of the primary culture, but producing and passing on our

41. Galbraith says the humanities are "largely unaffected" by the new relation of
universities to the technostructure (*The New Industrial State*, p. 292). This is true only so
long as one restricts the issue to direct support of research, employment in industry,
and the like. The argument has made it clear, I hope, that the whole prosperity of
academic humanists—which has lagged only a bit behind that of other groups—is
indirectly due to the requirements of the new industrial state. The cry about neglect of
the humanities, which can be heard in almost every faculty, is comprehensible in
terms of local politics and internal comparisons, not by referring to any past period of
our society.

share of knowledge that has value to the technostructure. I accept the dour verdict of Galbraith: "It is the vanity of educators that they shape the educational system to their preferred image. They may not be without influence but the decisive force is the economic system." [42] As I have argued in this chapter, the "vanity of educators" can be sustained because educators do have freedom to shape their own *professions* much as they choose and because their interests coincide in important ways with those of the industrial system.

So when George Steiner cites the evidence of cultivated Nazis to prove that the humanities do not necessarily make people humane, or when the more cautious Herbert J. Muller confesses that he does not know whether they do or not,[43] I can only say that the question has been wrongly put. No one should imagine that the humanities always do the same thing simply because their content remains more or less the same. What they do, what literature does, depends on who is doing it. The humanities are not an agent but an instrument. Nazis will make different uses of Goethe and Beethoven than will liberal American professors, and "the" function of literature is almost certain to change within any given society from one century to the next: human values may be eternal, but cultural systems are not. There is just no sense in pondering the function of literature without relating it to the actual society that uses it, to the centers of power within that society, and to the institutions that mediate between literature and people. In other words, the function of literature and the role of English teachers cannot be understood except within the context of a given society and politics.

Likewise, discussion of what direction our field should take in the future must be politically grounded or it will be a coffee hour exercise. We cannot think seriously about the actions open to us without reference to what society wants of us and what knowledge is now doing for and to society.

42. Galbraith, p. 238.
43. See Muller's discussion in *The Children of Frankenstein; A Primer on Modern Technology and Human Values* (Bloomington, Ind.: Indiana University Press, 1970), p. 224.

CHAPTER TWELVE

The Politics of
Knowledge: A Polemic

A theme keeps recurring, in this account of my profession and its setting. I look at my 1966 critique and find it naive on the origins of rampant professionalism and what it would take to change our working lives: not much change can be accomplished, apart from what I call politics. I reread New Criticism and see in it a tacit politics of things-as-they-are, veiled in the claim that literature is beyond politics. Freshman English states its goals in politically neutral terms, but I find that its methods reinforce the dominance of our problem-solving liberal elites, whereas its soothing tolerance in the matter of usage covers deeper attitudes of class privilege and cultural snobbery. In English departments I see a moderately successful effort by professors to obtain some benefits of capitalism while avoiding its risks and, yet, a reluctance to acknowledge any link between how we do our work and the way the larger society is run. Always our talk about literature and teaching seems inadequately grounded in political and economic awareness. We either look too narrowly at the givens of daily work or cast our eyes upward to the transcendent realm of timeless human values and the healing force of literary culture.

I don't see how teachers and departments and university faculties can make intelligent professional choices without consciously making them political choices. Much of what's wrong in the profession reflects the needs of advanced capitalism and is remediable only through deep social change. Yet this has been an unpopular idea in the university. Most professors hold that engagement in political activity by universities, departments, and professional guilds is a threat to the academic freedom of minorities within those institutions, a lapse from professional standards of conduct, a sure way to factionalism and loss of educational focus, and (worst) a sacrifice of hard-won independence—an invitation to budget-cutters, know-nothing censors, and resentful legislators.

Though each of these arguments can be met, it will be best to stay with my general argument a little longer, before drawing my conclusions. Needless to say, since I believe that America is on the way to disintegration without radical social change, I hope that my argument will make sense to people who have not thought of themselves as radicals.

Certainly many such people, stirred to awareness by Vietnam, racial conflict, unimaginable weaponry, the excesses of capitalist technology, the "energy crisis," and the creaking of the economy, feel that this country is gravely afflicted. The poor and the political "crazies" no longer have a monopoly on the perception. When I wrote a first version of this chapter in 1970, the *New Yorker* was publishing for its affluent readers Charles Reich's *The Greening of America* and Lewis Mumford's *The Megamachine.* The latter says (between ads for a billfold size radio and a $400 watch, two minor symptoms of the disease),

During the last decade, fortunately, there has been a sudden quite unpredictable awakening to prospects of a total catastrophe. The unrestricted increase of population, the overexploitation of megatechnical inventions, the inordinate wastages of compulsory consumption, and the consequent deterioration of the environment through wholesale pollution, poisoning, bulldozing, to say nothing of the more irremediable waste products of atomic energy, have at last begun to create the reaction needed to overcome them.[1]

1. Lewis Mumford, "The Megamachine," *New Yorker* (Oct. 31, 1970), pp. 96–98.

Crisis had by then become simply a datum of intelligent experience.

As I revise now, around the turn of the new year 1975, the *New York Review of Books* announces "The World Crash" from its cover, and the *New Yorker* prints a long analysis by Richard Barnet and Ronald Müller of how international corporations are carving up the world for their own gain. The latter authors say (between ads for a full length mink coat and cruises to the Black Sea, an Oxford University Press book and a child adoption agency), "We are the first generation to have the awareness that man has the power to end history, and the first that has the destructive technology to end it ourselves." [2] Crisis remains a staple.

Mumford held that the crisis might be overcome by an "awakening." Barnet and Müller say that we can achieve the necessary new values only "if enough people are awakened" to the crisis. An awakening: better understanding, more knowledge. Beneath this hope lie the Western faith in rationality, the enlightenment idea of progress through knowledge, and two hundred years of astonishing material success in capitalistic problem solving, so that the prescription strikes us as the plainest common sense, almost a tautology. If we are in trouble, *of course* we must understand the trouble and devise a way out. And yet even a cursory glance at the experience of the twentieth century should call this conventional wisdom into question. For undeniably technical and managerial knowledge has made possible the decisions that now threaten everyone's existence, decisions to develop and use the weaponry we have, to build an industrial economy founded on consumption of goods, to use the earth's resources without restraint for these purposes, to end the reliance of most people on themselves and their immediate communities. There is good and ill in these acts, and in any case we cannot turn back from them, but if the ill is going to finish us off, that temper's one's enthusiasm for the good. We may fairly ask, is knowledge working badly for us in the long run? Is the recent history of knowledge a fatal misadventure? Might there be a contradiction in knowledge *itself* that makes it generally unhealthy for human beings?

2. "Global Reach," *New Yorker* (Dec. 9, 1974), p. 157.

If I believed so I would not be writing this book. Yet the questions are not rhetorical. A failure to answer them, or in most cases even to acknowledge their propriety, vitiates a great deal of future-talk, of both the doomsday and the millenarian sort. For it is indisputable *both* that knowledge has allowed great improvements in the human condition *and* that none of the disasters we face would be possible without enormous amounts of knowledge produced in the last 200 years. Those who look ahead to utopias of leisure, fulfillment, and decency grounded in technology fail to explain how exploitation of knowledge will result in a future so strikingly different from present tendencies. The less euphoric social scientists who project a future out of the present tendencies, e.g., most of the writers in the oddly naive *Toward the Year 2000*,[3] failed to notice that many of the tendencies knowledge has set loose point toward radical and unpleasant *dis*continuity: the perilous dynamic by which pesticides hold hunger in check, for instance, may not trace a smooth curve for long, but plunge us either into world-wide famine or world-wide poisoning. And the technicians who simply apply knowledge without thinking have no leverage at all on the future, but are prisoners of the forces they serve. On the other side, those who see modern technology as inevitably suicidal fail to explain why some countries have used it more benignly than others and why such notable improvements in the quality of life as have been achieved cannot be separated out from their unintended, ruinous concomitants.

Then does the question, "is increase of knowledge a good or an ill?" force us into a gray middle position? Many liberal academic people would accept Herbert Muller's calm verdict that "the consequences of modern technology have been profoundly, thoroughly mixed," and his "principle of essential ambiguity" in sizing up the future of what we call progress.[4] Emmanuel G. Mesthene, director of the Harvard University Program on Technology and Society, is another who carefully negotiates a course between apocalypse and euphoria, arguing that technology can be controlled

3. Ed. Daniel Bell (Boston: Houghton Mifflin, 1968).
4. Herbert J. Muller, *The Children of Frankenstein* (Bloomington, Ind.: Indiana University Press, 1970), p. xi.

by judicious use of what we know and discovery of the necessary new technology. This is close to the standard position of moderates, which comes in two variant forms: (a) Some knowledge is beneficial and some dangerous; we need more of the former to control the latter. For instance, knowledge about man and society has lagged behind technology and science; more knowledge of values and human nature would restore a balance and a future. (b) All knowledge and technology are essentially neutral; value inheres in the *use* of knowledge. We in the universities, and especially humanists, must mobilize what we know and believe to encourage the humane application and evolution of knowledge. Either version proposes that we generate and use new knowledge in the solution of problems created as by-products of previous advances in knowledge.

This is not a fantastic idea, considering that each innovation, each discovery, each technological development, each organizational improvement, *as it occurs* is a welcome aid to the welfare of the people who needed it in the first place. Thus, DDT does increase agricultural output in the short run, though it spreads death in the long run. Fossil fuels did take burdens off human backs, though they may destroy human lungs or human society in time. It is attractive to suppose that we can preserve the benefits while, through improved technology and better planning, we ameliorate the side effects, all within the present social arrangement. I feel certain, however, that we will make little headway toward maintaining civilized life into the 21st century by proceeding this way. What follows is meant to dissolve its plausibility and suggest an alternative.

The problem-solving approach to the future usually rests on two serious errors in thought, both of them natural to most of us and, therefore, hard to detect. Read any list of enticing advances tomorrow could bring:

Practical nuclear power sources for every nation on earth are well within our technical capability in this century, provided the "unforeseeable" element of political and financial support is exerted.

With "human prescriptions" we could develop nearly any type of man desired—superintelligent, highly talented, better able to survive in severe climates, in rarefied atmospheres of other planets, or underwater, etc.

Recent understanding about the nucleotides that govern life itself may eventually lead to our ability to intervene genetically and augment or introduce any protective function in the body, perhaps adding 50 years or more to expected lifespans.

Synthetic foods, textured and flavored so as to be indistinguishable from foods we now know, may be used to feed a world population that will have doubled by the end of this century.[5]

The first passage appends a salutary caution and the other three protect themselves with "may" or "could," but all these near-predictions slip into the fallacy of leaving-out-everything-in-between. When the technical solution to a problem can be conceived, or even envisioned, there is a tendency to relax and wait for the desired improvement—or, if you are a technician in the right place, to start working toward it. Aging? We can slow that down by half. Overpopulation? We can produce plenty of synthetic food. That may or may not be so—probably it is. But the social changes necessary to permit wide and humane *use* of these developments, should they be engineered, are nowhere in sight. Within our present system, and with the crises that face us, the feeding of six billion people or the provision of safe power for all might as well be written off as impossible. By skipping lightly over the hard part—"political and financial support"—the writer propels our imaginations directly into the serendipitous remote future, scarcely pausing at the battleground of the day after tomorrow. He is spellbound: if it can happen, and it sounds good, it will happen. Many writers drift in such a trance of possibility.

The second error of thought, as I have argued in Chapter Seven, is to abstract away from specific persons. This error is deeper than the first, and often responsible for it. Here, for instance, is an explicit statement of the first which commits the second inadvertently: "Anything that is theoretically possible will be achieved in practice if it is desired greatly enough." [6] What sounds like a truism vaporizes

5. Don Fabun, *The Dynamics of Change* (Englewood Cliffs, N.J.: Prentice-Hall, 1967), pp. VI 22–25.
6. Fabun quotes this from Arthur G. Clarke, but gives no reference. *The Dynamics of Change*, p. VI 21.

into nonsense as soon as you notice what the passive voice conceals: "will be achieved" by whom? "it is desired greatly enough" by whom? Dropping out the agent is critical here. Neither "science" nor any other abstraction will do as the agent of "achieve," since achievement in this important sense is a political matter. And the failure to mention whose desires will be so faithfully met shows that the writer is just not taking social reality into account. Rephrase the sentence with suitable agents, and its emptiness becomes apparent: "the governments and farmers of the rich nations will double food production if the peasants of India desire it greatly enough and can pay for it." Some people's desires count a lot; other people's desires a little or not at all.

Whenever a writer speaks of "man" and technology, there's a good chance he labors under this error: "Unlike science, technology concerns the applications of science to the needs of man and society. Therefore technology is inseparable from humanism." [7] The needs of whom? Application of science by whom? Again, I can provide a translation to bring out the delusion: "technology concerns the application of science by corporations to their own need for profit and power, and to those needs which people with money express through the market in the wealthier nations. Therefore technology is inseparable from humanism." Many "human needs" turn out on scrutiny to be of just this sort; it is apparently hard to remember that the market brings into existence many "goods" that are evils from any but the grossest perspective. "Need" implies a needer; even writers who see clearly enough what the human race needs are likely to forget how far this may be from what those in power need:

What is clearly needed is not a mindless deprecation of technology as such, but rather a reordering and redevelopment of technologies according to ecologically sound principles. We need an eco-technology that will help harmonize society with the natural world.[8]

7. Sir Eric Ashby, "Technological Humanism," *Journal of the Institute of Metals*, LXXXV (1957), p. 465; quoted in Maxwell H. Goldberg, ed. *Needles, Burrs and Bibliographies* (Pennsylvania State University, Center for Continuing Liberal Education, 1969), p. 90.
8. Murray Bookchin, "Toward an Ecological Solution," in *Eco-Catastrophe*, by the Editors of *Ramparts* (San Francisco: Canfield Press, 1970), p. 47.

Fair enough. But who are "we"? The author (an anarchist should know better!) would perhaps not write as if stating the goal were a long step toward reaching it if he tried substituting "those of us without power" for "we." For those with power, whatever their real or long range needs, now and concretely need a rapacious and profitable technology. What the one "we" needs may be the other "we's" poison.

The pronoun "we" seems to qualify as what Gilbert Ryle called a "systematically misleading expression." So does the phrase "human knowledge." Recall, for example, a passage I commented upon in Chapter Seven: "The age of cyberculture must be built by the entire corpus of human knowledge and human achievement—by an interaction of the arts, the sciences, and the philosophies." [9] Among the conceptual mastodons trotted out here, "human knowledge" requires additional comment quite aside from its portentous redundancy. In the first chapter of this book I examined the fallacy in thinking of literary studies as a cumulative body of knowledge, in the sense that science may be. Here I would add that neither science nor the humanities nor any broader accumulation of information and theory deserves the title "human knowledge," if that is to imply knowledge possessed by all people or *useful to* all people. Knowledge is power only to those who have it or can purchase it and who already have power enough to put it to use. The phrase "human knowledge" suggests a democracy of knowing, a pooling of culture's benefits, which is ill-matched by reality. For the last two hundred years the prerogatives of managing knowledge (as opposed to the exercise of specialized knowledge in one's job) have in fact become more and more concentrated, the power less democratic, the benefits for ordinary people accompanied by more and more choices in which ordinary people have had no say.

To see why—and why more knowledge won't save this civilization—re-examine a few facts about the economic and political setting within which knowledge is developed and put to use. It is well

9. Alice Mary Hilton, "The Bases of Cyberculture," in *The Evolving Society*, ed. Alice Mary Hilton (New York: The Institute for Cybercultural Research, 1966), p. 19.

known that the United States, with 6% of the world's people, controls close to 50% of the world's wealth. Even this is unduly consoling, because it implies rational control by Americans acting in concert. Actually, control lies with the huge corporations, especially the multi-national ones. And as Barnet and Müller show, these are much less responsive to any government—much less any people— than to centers of power like the Rockefeller-Morgan group of banks. The most basic decisions about how human beings will live are largely made by or through this economic system. It is this system that determines that the automobile will be king, that the United States can "afford" the Vietnam war, that there will be an oil shortage, that migrant farm workers will live in virtual slavery, that millions will starve in India and the Sahel, that industry will be moved to selected "underdeveloped" areas while unemployment and work speedups increase in the United States, and so on. To put it broadly, the economic system decides what kind of air and water we will have, how we will get from home to work, what sorts of food we will eat, how our sexual identities will be defined, who shall be rich and poor, sick and healthy. Our much-deplored use of resources, our dependence on machines, and our unequal distribution of goods all derive from the extremely advanced form of capitalism practiced in the United States and similar nations.

For my purpose the main features of this system are private ownership and the "free" market—both modified, of course, but still fundamental. They have allowed the large corporations to take over much of the power to decide how people shall live. These corporations are supported (within limits set by anti-trust laws and the like) by local and federal governments, and defended against other economic forces—e.g., revolutionaries in Chile, Vietnam, Guatemala, and the Dominican Republic who want to nationalize the corporations or close off part of the free market—by a huge military and "intelligence" establishment which is also, wondrously, the major single client of General Dynamics, United Aircraft, and the rest.

Here a natural objection to raise is that the corporations do not act independently of constraints, the two most notable being the electoral process and the dictates of consumers. But if we are speaking of how our society makes its critical decisions for the long run, these forces can be discounted. Voting is mainly a matter of choosing between two candidates with narrowly different positions on "the" issues. And the issues themselves are either meanly drawn (how fast to delegate the Vietnam war to local mercenaries) or trivial (whether unemployment is too high by a percentage point, whether we will have "double-figure" inflation through 1976). No major party candidate, so far as I know, has run recently on a plank of switching our allegiance in Vietnam to the Provisional Revolutionary Government or of nationalizing General Motors.

And though individual consumers do have an exotic array of goods before them each day, they cannot by choosing among them have a say in the basic decisions that affect their future. I do not refer here to the loss of freedom through the pressures and suasions of advertising and the media, though these are potent enough. I mean simply that you can choose to buy sardines instead of whitefish, but this choice will in no way impede the dumping of chemical wastes into Lake Erie and the accumulation of dangerous quantities of mercury in the whitefish. You can buy Granola (the same old food oligopoly will cheerfully supply it) instead of beef, but that will not get the protein you "save" to Bangladesh or alter the world agricultural system. You can waste less electricity, as Gerald Ford and the power companies sagely advise, but that won't in any way stimulate the development of fusion or solar power. Or you can choose a Jeep instead of a Chrysler, or even choose the great inconvenience of not having a car, but you cannot thereby help restore a usable railway system. Short of dropping out of the consumer society (an increasingly popular choice, but quite impossible as a general solution), you must use your power as an individual consumer (consumer groups are a different matter) within a narrow range defined for you by people and forces beyond your control. So a crucial tendency of private ownership and the "free" market is to *favor individual choices over collective ones and convenience in the short run over survival in the long run.*

To be sure, there are many in this country who suffer even in the

short run from the inhumanity of our economic and social system—
notably black and brown people and the whole one-third of the
population who are poor, but also the aged in their pathetic "homes"
and working people in their powerlessness, their tedious jobs, their
imprisonment within goals and styles of consumption set by others,
their necessarily competitive and anxiety-ridden relation to others
(e.g., poor blacks) in this society and in the Third World, their
obligation to fight remote wars while young men from the upper
social ranges are able to stay home by, for example, going to
graduate school, and so forth. The stability of the system, its
resistance to change from within in spite of the many people who
have cause to want change, is due partly to corporate use of the mass
media to sell the American way of life, and circumvent serious
criticism, and partly to the paramilitary power of the FBI, the CIA,
the police, the National Guard, and the new Law Enforcement
Assistance Agency, which ensures that poor people and the working
class will not be able to build revolutionary movements to the danger
point.

Mainly the system has until just now preserved its structure, with
all the inequities and injustices therein, because of its phenomenal
success in producing goods and in distributing them just widely
enough to enlist the support of most Americans: "You can say what
you like about the United States, but you've got to admit that we
have the best standard of living in the (whole goddam) world." The
conviction remains a focal part of ideology, in spite of recent events
that challenge it. Penetration of American capitalism into—and
dominance over—most parts of the world has helped guarantee that
privileged position, as has the remarkable development of technology and managerial skill, which allows ever-increasing "efficiency,"
in wresting materials from the earth. So most Americans above the
poverty line feel a deep investment in the very system that threatens
to destroy us.

Furthermore, those who know intellectually how many things are
amiss in America tend to have an even greater stake in the system:
university people, liberal politicians, intelligent journalists—people
who have the time and inclination to read Rachel Carson and James

Baldwin and Charles Reich and Jonathan Schell and Lewis Mumford and Richard Barnet in the pages of the *New Yorker*. Among such people the parade of perils has become a commonplace, and its composite name an adjustable cliché: Vietnam/racism/poverty/ sexism/Watergate/the _____ crisis.

But the chances of this enlightened group of people making real advances toward a better set of arrangements for living are minimal. Because liberals, however genuine their distress over the current scene, are physically and emotionally comfortable within this form of society, their critical energies are channeled into reformist politics or even, at worst, into neo-fascist forms of social engineering. Typically, liberals (and most Democratic and Republican leaders are liberals) try to cope with the disorders of the system as "problems." As I tried to show in Chapter Seven, this *modus operandi* is well embedded in liberal thought and language. We have the race problem, the Vietnam problem, the problem of crime in the streets, the problem of air pollution, the problem of campus unrest, and so on. To repeat, the trouble with reformism is this: that as soon as you identify a situation as a problem you have endorsed the perspective from which it is problematic—generally that of the economic and political status quo—and committed yourself to making it work better. New Deals and New Frontiers turn out, strangely, to leave the Rockefellers more entrenched in power, the working class in confusion, and liberals either fat and coöpted or cynical and withdrawn. Since our woes derive from the system's working all too well to serve those it serves, even an actual solution of a problem—rare as that may be—is a long-term disservice, if it helps to conceal the deeper causes of trouble to let the system continue its inhuman work less self-consciously. More of this later.

Intelligent liberals should understand this, since solving problems is what constitutes progress, and progress is what got us where we deplorably are. But to get out of this vicious circle calls for a leap into a new kind of consciousness, and this leap is risky and probably painful for anyone whose roots are in the bourgeoisie, as my own are.

For over and above the creature comforts that bourgeois life has to offer, the bourgeois frame of mind has a profound hold on all of the middle class, and especially those of us in universities. Middle-class people cherish freedom at the core of their consciousness, and merely to name it is virtually to close off critical discussion, so automatic is our wish to be free. There are many variants of bourgeois thought, but this wish is a constant. Yet nothing could be more clear than that our particular form of freedom rests on the enslavement and misery of others. We say that we want the American brand of liberty for all other nations, but this is impossible—literally impossible—when liberty means dominance.

To ward off unacceptable thoughts like this, bourgeois consciousness emphasizes isolated and individual striving, as in the interests of all. Academic freedom and freedom of inquiry are like free enterprise in this: they seek to ignore or deny our total social interdependence. Knowledge, like culture and production, has a social base, but we middle-class people like to think of knowing as an individual adventure, which mysteriously and indirectly benefits society. This set of mind has fostered, not only the growth of the industrial state and its ideology, but also, within that state's universities, the insane proliferation of disciplines, all supposedly contributing to universal knowledge, but actually making it harder and harder to understand in a unified way the human condition. The bourgeois frame of mind also helps ensure that reform, with its input of plans, techniques, committee meetings, and expertise of all sorts, will appeal to the liberal intellectual, whereas revolutionary change, with its ideal of immersion in social process, will not. The goal of the liberal is to substitute thought for action, when possible, and to live as if deep politics did not exist. For that reason, I hold, all the awareness of woe that the *New Yorker* writers can summon up will not move us toward cure unless we invest it in radical action for social change.

I want now to fit knowledge into this picture, more precisely than heretofore. In lieu of radical action, knowledge, technology, and the dynamic forces of our society remain in the service of private gain—as they have long been, but not forever. John B. Rae points out that for most of history

the process of invention had been either ignored or taken for granted. . . .
The idea that a new technological discovery is a valuable contribution to
society, for which the discoverer should be rewarded by receiving an
exclusive right to his accomplishment, is strictly a Western concept dating
from the Renaissance.[10]

The first patent was issued in Florence in 1421, and the English
Statute of Monopolies of 1623 became the model for modern patent
systems. Thus as the polytechnics gave way to the monotechnics,
knowledge and innovation were already securely assimilated to
private property and the profit motive. So firmly is this bond
established—think of copyright law and the concept of plagiarism—
that we have difficulty remembering that it is neither inevitable nor
immutable. Yet all knowledge is a social product (the greatest
innovator adds only an iota to the structure of ideas he inherits), and
it was treated as such until the Renaissance, with exceptions like
guild secrets and the knowledge bought by patrons.

That the new arrangement of ideas-for-gain took root before the
Industrial Revolution is not accidental—it was a major stimulus to
industrialization. But unfortunately those early patent laws helped
harden into unalterable assumption a concept of ownership—I shall
use "my" ideas as I choose—that has proved grotesquely inadequate
for technologies that affect literally everyone's freedom and continued life. For, as Victor Ferkiss points out,

the new technology has not at all affected any of the fundamental aspects of
the capitalist-industrial system. . . .

virtually every possible extension of man's powers over nature and himself
almost certainly will be made or not made, shaped in one direction or
another, not by considerations of what is good for man but what is good for
some men; problems that are basically scientific and ethical will be decided
in economic terms. Shall the use of a myriad of drugs become more
widespread? The drug companies will in large measure decide through

10. "The Invention of Invention," in *Technology in Western Civilization*, Vol. I., ed.
Melvin Kranzberg and Carroll W. Pursell, Jr. (New York: Oxford University Press,
1967), p. 325.

pressure on government (administrative and legislative) and through advertising.[11]

To the degree that this comes true, we can write off any hope of selecting the beneficial technology and rejecting the pernicious, of making "human knowledge" humane knowledge.

Ferkiss says that *no* fundamental aspect of capitalism has altered to accommodate the new technology. Though I accept the force of his claim, I would qualify it by agreeing with Galbraith that the profit motive itself has changed somewhat and that we must adopt a correspondingly altered definition of the "economic terms" under which basic decisions will be made. The unadorned scramble for profit belonged to the entrepreneurial phase of capitalism. Modern technology, for reasons well explained by Galbraith, subordinates profit to stability. On his analysis, some of the most important goals of corporations and their planning are (a) the survival of the firm; (b) autonomy—freedom from interference in its decisions; (c) corporate growth measured by sales; and (d) to complete the circle, improved technology.[12] Having drawn back from competition for profit only, these corporate giants will become—and take pains to seem—less narrowly rapacious than their predecessors. But that does not significantly increase the likelihood of their making basic decisions for the general welfare. Knowledge and power in the hands of the technostructure is still not knowledge and power in the hands of the people. For people generally to share knowledge and power is of course an awesome challenge. Without minimizing its difficulty, I do say that it *can* happen under socialism, and not under capitalism.

The woeful consequences of our present state of affairs can be seen in the decisions of almost any major industry, but perhaps with unusual starkness in those of the oil companies. The various oil spills, the leakage from the Santa Barbara Channel, the spoliation of the Alaskan North Slope, the oil shortage of 1973–1974 and attendant windfall profits, are only symptoms of egregious disregard for public

11. Victor C. Ferkiss, *Technological Man: The Myth and the Reality* (New York: New American Library, 1970), pp. 126–29.
12. John Kenneth Galbraith, *The New Industrial State* (Boston: Houghton-Mifflin, 1967), Chapt. XV.

welfare, except as expressed through market choices. More basic decisions in which the oil companies have had a major part include (a) to support our neurotic dependence on the private (and anti-social) automobile; (b) to endanger human and other life by using the atmosphere as a sewer; (c) to exploit fossil fuels, which took hundreds of millions of years to make, at a rate that may use them up in a century or so; (d) to push pesticides like Shell Chemical's Azodrin, even when these have been proved to become ineffective over a few years and likely to be a threat to life in the still longer run; (e) to control Middle Eastern oil through an alliance of local potentates and international corporations capable of manipulating world petroleum and money markets for their own gain; (f) generally, to support cold war ideology; and (g) to do all this with the blessing of the government and favored tax treatment, so that consumers of petroleum pay an artificially high price for oil and gas. That a group of corporations can create such policy for all of us, and make it stick against opposition and attempted reform of all sorts, shows how strongly technology and private gain are bonded together and how little hope ordinary people should attach to the oil companies' promises—reiterated daily in television, magazine, and newspaper advertising—to solve ecological problems through new knowledge.

It is extremely difficult, I repeat, for people in general to exercise socially responsible control over new (or old) knowledge. One can blame the difficulty on the ethics of the corporations—and given performances like those of the oil companies the temptation is great to do so—but I don't believe we get to the bottom of the matter by citing corporate greed and ruthlessness. For these qualities respond to opportunities created by our present technology and, furthermore, have their roots in the very social conditions and attitudes that first produced industrial technology and that nourish it still. Landes argues that advanced technology appeared first and grew fastest in those economies that assigned most freedom to the individual entrepreneur.[13] Unchecked control over economic choices by the

13. David S. Landes, *The Unbound Prometheus* (Cambridge: Cambridge University Press, 1969), p. 19.

property owner and manufacturer helped sponsor profitable new technologies and was, in the process, reinforced; so that the coincidence in the last hundred years of technological innovation and freedom for corporations is no accident: on this score, capitalist ideology is right enough. And since our culture treats knowledge as a form of property, corporate sway over knowledge follows from corporate hegemony over all our society's goods.

But the time when such arrangements could be successful in any but the blindest terms has long passed. Given the far-reaching effects of technological and economic decisions now, the reliance on economic freedom

makes it impossible to do more than tinker with the great problems facing the human species. All of these can be dealt with only by clear, conscious and sustained choices, implemented by informed and consistent social action. Space travel, use of the oceans, economic change, biological mutation—the political and administrative requirements such choices and action entail will necessarily overwhelm a political system geared to ignorance, arbitrariness and rule by special interests, and characterized by discontinuity and disjunction and general formlessness.[14]

As Ferkiss also says, it is not that our government will fail to sponsor studies, appoint commissions, and make laws touching on the effects of technology; but such action will be marginal and ineffective because it leaves basic decisions in the hands of corporations and individuals rather than the whole society (p. 160).

Of course even without adequate political power for ordinary people, it is theoretically possible that they would exercise influence on the uses of technology strictly as economic agents: as consumers and as laborers. But whatever knowledge consumers have, it is of little significance in making basic choices, partly because it operates for individual gain and without coordination or social vision and partly because the very process of planning by corporations (and governments) "consists in reducing or eliminating the independence of action of those to whom the planning unit sells. . . ."[15] That is to say, the autonomy that corporations demand is inversely proportional to any substantive autonomy of consumers.

14. Ferkiss, *Technological Man*, p. 164.
15. Galbraith, *The New Industrial State*, p. 28.

As for workers, their loss of control over the conditions of work—and hence over socially important uses of knowledge *in* work—was a logical *pre*condition of industrialized society. As an economic historian puts it, the flight from the country to the city and the resulting pool of laborers was "a necessary condition for the realization of the economist's notion of a 'market' for labor and for many kinds of agricultural, mineral, and forest products." This migration produced "a more rational (economical) allocation of productive resources." [16] That is, men not only become interchangeable units in a labor market, and alienated from their work, but they also become part of a "rationality" beyond their control. The price of this rationality is that "market forces," and not the laborer's social or individual choices, govern labor. And the process of "rationalizing" labor markets has leapt farther ahead these last ten years, as multi-national corporations have effectively put the workers of Hong Kong and Chicago into the same pool—the corporations can move, when the workers can't.

There have been attempts to reassert the worker's control over productivity. Luddism was the most dramatic and poignant. As E. P. Thompson shows,[17] far from striking out in helpless rage at machines, the Luddites wanted to have a say in the use of those machines, as well as in the conditions of labor, and they formed a sophisticated movement to advance this interest. And of course the union movement can be seen as a much broader, similar attempt. But, in the long run, such movements have done little more than gain for workers a more reasonable share of the material benefits, and even that is now dwindling. Daniel Bell's famous essay "Work and Its Discontents" traces in some analytic detail how thoroughly labor has failed to counter the assembly line "rationality" imposed by engineers and technicians in the brutalizing setting of the factory. Beyond that, labor itself has scarcely thought of demanding a say in what uses of technology will be permissible, what products will be

16. Eric E. Lampard, "The Social Impact of the Industrial Revolution," in Kranzberg and Pursell, *Technology in Western Civilization*, p. 312.
17. *The Making of the English Working Class* (London: Victor Gollancz, 1963), esp. pp. 472-602.

made, whether there will be war, etc. A condition of capitalist industrial achievement seems to be the powerlessness of labor in basic economic and human choices and the restriction of union activity to secondary goals well within the corporate design.

Because industrialism has grown up around and depends upon a deceptive notion of freedom in economic choices the people have no regular means of making these choices collectively. Because both as consumers and as laborers they have been largely coopted, they have no tradition of collective action on a large scale. So they enact what Garrett Hardin calls "the tragedy of the commons": though more automobiles, more roads, more jerrybuilt suburbs are suicidal from the standpoint of the whole community, for any one member of the community it may still make sense to buy another car and a suburban house, for his increased comfort is great, while his share in the increased public discomfort is small.[18] And the makers of cars and subdividers of land continue to encourage and to profit from this social irrationality.

So the lament of a humanist like Herbert Muller is quite beside the point, though tempting enough:

there is no question that most Americans like their cars big, powerful, and ostentatious. As certainly they want all the services that government lavishes on the automobile; as taxpayers they are more willing to pay for highway programs than for better schools. They seldom protest against all the bulldozing, the erosion of the heart of cities by parking areas. Once behind the wheel, they do not mind all the ugliness along the highways. Ultimately, in short, the American people must be blamed for the neglect of human values.[19]

The fallacy of this lies in an equivocation on "the American people." When "the American people" buy big cars they are an aggregate of individuals seeking private well-being. In order to do what Muller wants them to do to counter the effects of the automobile, however, "the American people" would have to be a collectivity. You cannot

18. Garrett Hardin, "The Tragedy of the Commons," *Science*, 162 (Dec. 13, 1968), pp. 1243–48.
19. *The Children of Frankenstein*, p. 100.

blame them for "neglect of human values" when in order to advance human values—that is, social values—they would have to live under a different economic system than the present one. To ask Americans to behave humanely with automobiles is to ask that they create a social revolution, or else it is to voice an empty piety.

Another humane writer on technology, Mesthene, speaks of "the massive task of public education that is needed if our society is to make full use of its technological potential," [20] but all the education in the world, plus uniformly high intelligence, cannot suffice to that end as long as we make decisions in the present fashion. Mesthene's example, the outcry about auto safety, might better be used to show how completely *in*effective public education is without political action. The menacing facts about car safety were "known" (to whom?) for decades, but nothing much happened until, partly through luck and scandal, Ralph Nader gathered some popular support for his political use of this knowledge. And I doubt that Nader himself would contend that his efforts have made much of a dent in corporate power or public helplessness.

Knowledge and technology as presently mobilized are not answerable to the longer range and more human needs of people in general. For reasons that emerge in analyzing the origins of advanced technology (see Chapter Ten), a society generates such knowledge mainly when there is economic demand for it. And economic demand, in our system, is expressed through the drive for profit and autonomy of those individuals and corporations who control the manufacture of goods. We get the knowledge they need, as well as that the government needs to protect the stability of the system itself. Without question, knowledge is liberating for those in power: it secures and increases their freedom. But there is no paradox in adding that this same knowledge blocks liberation and diminishes power for most human beings. For it is designed to meet only those needs they express as isolated, competing individuals under great pressure of manipulation by the corporations through the ever-pres-

20. Emmanuel G. Mesthene, *Technological Change: Its Impact on Man and Society* (Cambridge, Mass.: Harvard University Press, 1970), p. 37.

ent media: in short, as consumers. And they cannot get and mobilize enough of the knowledge they need for larger social choices because they have so few institutions—though Congress is one—through which to do so.

This analysis fits well with John McDermott's claim that technology is not neutral, but tends toward domination and exploitation.[21] It is interesting that Fritz Machlup[22] includes government as one of the "products" that make up our complement of knowledge. Social control in this form does indeed consist mainly in exchange of "information," and the converse is true enough to bear mentioning. Much exchange of information—in schools, on television, through advertising—is also a form of social control. Levi-Strauss has argued that literacy itself, at the beginning, enabled new kinds of centralized, bureaucratic control—as it does even now when Western countries bring it to unlettered cultures.[23]

Without insisting on the equation, it is still easy to see how much of the technology called into being and deployed by our government could *only* act as a form of control, by the powerful over the weak. McDermott writes of computerized bombing in Vietnam. Other obvious examples are strategic theory in the Rand Corporation mode, techniques of biological warfare, electronic surveillance, nuclear technology, and rocketry. How could the people bend such knowledge to human uses? Perhaps by using space technology to escape from an earth made uninhabitable by all the other technologies. Even those still unrealized technologies that have great promise—for example, fusion power, to solve the energy and food crises through vast increases in productivity—will call into being new kinds of centralization and control, not to mention new possibilities of dreadful miscalculation.

But the mind turns most naturally to military knowledge in this context. As Mumford points out, technology grew to maturity with

21. "Technology, Opiate of the Intellectuals," *New York Review of Books*, July 31, 1969.
22. *The Production and Distribution of Knowledge in America* (Princeton, N.J.: Princeton University Press, 1962).
23. For a discussion, see Dolores Palomo, "Homeric Epic, the Invention of Writing, and Literary Education," *College English*, vol. 36 (December, 1974), pp. 413–21.

regular assists from war. Armies required standardized products, rapidly produced, and constantly improved; factory technology was the answer on all counts. Furthermore:

Military regimentation proved to be the archetype for collective mechanization, for the megamachine it created was the earliest complex machine of specialized, interdependent parts, human and mechanical. . . . The regimentation and mass production of soldiers, to the end of turning out a cheap, standardized, and replaceable product, was the great contribution of the military mind to the machine process.[24]

The affinity between war and advanced technology represents only an extreme case of McDermott's thesis: sophisticated knowledge can best be created by powerful elites, to be used in ways that confirm their power and limit that of others.

In fact, the military example can be overdone. Oppression through knowledge is often as vicious where no violence is intended, a fact the publicity given to ecological threats has underlined. Much of the actual violence is inadvertent, an unwelcome by-product of technological "advance." Thus, Barry Commoner treats hydrocarbon pollution from cars, carbon dioxide pollution from fossil fuels, nitrate pollution from fertilizer, phosphate pollution from detergents, chlorinated hydrocarbon pollution from pesticides, and fallout pollution from bombs, all as "technological mistakes." [25] That is to say, the scientists and engineers who developed these products did not anticipate the biological consequences of innovation. Such an analysis brings out well enough the fallibility of science and industry, but fails to get at the systematic nature of the failure, and leads to conclusions like Commoner's—that we are in trouble because biology lags behind physics—which are ridiculous. Biology (read: biology at work for corporations) moves fast enough where there's profit in haste, as with development of pesticides in the first place. "Technological mistakes" are those consequences of innovation that were not *worth* anticipating to those individuals, and corporations, who effected the innovation. These mistakes, in other words, are an

24. "The Megamachine," *New Yorker* (October 17, 1970), p. 127.
25. Barry Commoner, *Science and Survival* (New York: Viking Press, 1966).

inevitable result of letting knowledge answer to economic power. Economists call pollution an "external cost," one that does not affect profit: a clearer and less technical sounding phrase would be "cost to people in general." People-in-general (*including* even the chairman of the board in his mountain retreat) pay the cost of ignorance, as only people-in-general could be expected to pay in advance the costs of making knowledge safe.

To make this point more specific, consider a notorious incident, the eruption of a Union Oil well under the Santa Barbara Channel in 1969. Harvey Molotch explains that long before this disaster, when Santa Barbara officials had tried to stop the sale of oil leases, the Interior Department assured them that "such an 'accident' could not occur, given the highly developed state of the industry." [26] The accident did occur. Furthermore, oil flowed out of control for ten days. Yet there is no reason to deny "the highly developed state of the industry." What bears mention, as Molotch says, is "the striking contrast between the sophistication of the means used to locate and extract oil and the primitiveness of the means to control and clean its spillage, e.g., hay spread on the beaches." The former are profitable knowledge, the latter not so, and no one should expect corporations to produce unprofitable knowledge for the public good.

In fact the aftermath of the Santa Barbara eruption provided an excellent example of the mechanism by which such distinctions are made. As citizens took what action they could after the fact, the Deputy Attorney General of California "complained that the oil industry 'is preventing oil drilling experts from aiding the Attorney General's office in its lawsuits over the Santa Barbara oil spill,' " and added that " 'the university experts all seem to be working on grants from the oil industry.' " A Berkeley professor of petroleum engineering, Wilbur H. Somerton, later confirmed the point rather bluntly, refusing to testify against Union Oil " 'because my work depends on good relations with the petroleum industry. My interest is serving the petroleum industry. I view my obligation to the community as

26. Harvey Molotch, "Santa Barbara: Oil in the Velvet Playground," in *Eco-Catastrophe*, p. 94.

supplying it with well-trained petroleum engineers.' " [27] To regard knowledge as neutral is to ignore this man and the millions of his less articulate counterparts in universities, industry, and government.

It is also to trust that new knowledge can be found to counter the abuse of the old, and so to embrace the liberal, problem-solving approach: Ferkiss:

Liberals . . . seem ready to accept technological change as a natural outgrowth of intellectual freedom and as benefiting society by providing a rising standard of living for all; but they seek to mitigate what they perceive as its antisocial side effects by *ad hoc,* piecemeal, palliative measures. Mrs. Johnson's highway-beautification program is typical, almost to the point of caricature, of this approach.[28]

Ferkiss must have enjoyed some more recent examples: Gerald Ford singling out for praise the family that resolved to save heat by limiting the amount of time its cat was allowed to pause at the threshold, with the door open, pondering whether to exit or not.

"Side effects" and solutions have been around for a long time. By the 1830's, large parts of the English countryside were blighted by hydrochloric acid waste and a noxious runoff of calcium sulfide from the soda industry. But the fumes, condensed, became a major source of valuable chlorine in the 1840's, and eventually the sulfide was converted to lime and sulfur and reused.[29] A vindication of Dr. Pangloss? I mention this old example to show that the technical solution of one problem in no way changes the underlying economic forces, which have produced air and water pollution of ever-increasing severity in spite of much new knowledge about feasible and even profitable use of by-products. Control of pollution is—predictably— becoming a profitable business in itself now, but this should be little cause for comfort, so long as the new firms operate within the old framework: typically enough, by 1970 "about two dozen pollution control companies [were] subsidiaries or divisions of the largest

27. *Ibid.,* pp. 95–96.
28. *Technological Man*, p. 60.
29. Robert P. Multhauf, "Industrial Chemistry in the Nineteenth Century," in Kranzberg and Pursell, p. 475.

corporations and polluters in the United States," including Monsanto, Dow, du Pont, GE, and Alcoa.[30] These crusaders are not likely to challenge private control of knowledge, but to secure it.

What about research done directly by offending corporations, in response to conscience or aroused public opinion, and in the interest of preserving profits and autonomy? The oil companies, again, have provided instructive examples during the past five years of concern about pollution. Take Chevron's additive F310, widely advertised a few years ago in dramatic commercials that showed the exhaust of a "before" car fouling up a balloon, while the same car after F310 produced clean exhaust. Oddly, the California Air Resources Board was unable to repeat these results, an independent fluid specialist concluded that "F310 is a breakthrough in advertising, not in chemistry," and Chevron admitted using an extravagantly dirty engine to foul the balloon in the commercial.[31] In brief, the oil companies' investment in knowledge of this sort is often an investment in profiting from public concern and guilt, while securing the future of the internal combustion engine, and assuring the customer that, acting as individual consumer, he can help the oil companies lick the pollution problem.

Needless to say, the more recent anxiety about running out of gas, heating oil, and energy of all kinds has produced another spate of ads about the research that corporations will do to set things right. In the summer of 1974, after a winter of shortages, the "Investor-Owned Electric Light and Power Cos." ran one titled, "What's My [!] Electric Company Doing About the Energy Problem?" Among other things,

The electric companies . . . are involved in research and development in a wide variety of new methods of power generation. Developing nuclear "breeder" reactors that would create more useable nuclear fuel than they consume. Experimenting with fusion which would create energy by combining the atoms available in ordinary water. Producing electricity directly

30. Martin Gellen, "The Making of a Pollution-Industrial Complex," in *Eco-Catastrophe*, p. 74.
31. Susan Berman, "Chevron's Pollution Solution," *Commonweal* (March 5, 1971), p. 546.

from the sun's energy. Using the earth's heat, deep underground, as an generating source. . . .

The important thing is, we in the electric companies are doing everything we can today to find ways to ease the energy problem. We are also doing everything we can for tomorrow.

Plainly this "everything" amounts to trying out technical "solutions," which will probably lead to new problems and which, in any case, will keep control of the energy field in the hands of the people who brought us *this* round of problems (including the appliance manufacturers, etc.). Advertising campaigns like this one encourage our dependency on company-paid experts, who will generate the new knowledge the company needs to stay on an even keel and draw public attention away from "solutions" of a different order, such as removing this range of social choices from the "investors" and managers and boards that now constitute "my" electric company.

The technological fix is so powerful an idea that even an activist like Ralph Nader can begin an article by saying "The modern corporation's structure, impact, and public accountability are the central issues in any program designed to curb or forestall the contamination of air, water, and soil by industrial activity" and yet end by recommending more corporate investment in research on pollution control, freedom for corporate officials to speak out in criticism of their firms, shareholder rebellions, and union agitation for cleaner air around the plant.[32] I do not at all disparage Nader's feisty attack on the giants, but I doubt that these methods will go far unless, over a period of time, they help people see how much more radical a change is actually needed in the "modern corporation's . . . public accountability." No program that sets private industry to make knowledge work well for people is likely to succeed, however much research and innovation is accomplished in this manner. What we need, for a starter, is public industry.

The fruit we pick from the tree of knowledge depends on what kind of tree it is, on the soil in which it grows, and on who does the

32. "The Profits in Pollution," *The Progressive* (April, 1970), pp. 19–22.

picking. Landes suggests that Western technology grew in, and because of, the atmosphere of individual freedom in our culture, and the value placed on rational manipulation of the environment. Lynn White, Jr. notes the contribution of "orthodox Christian arrogance toward nature," [33] and Murray Bookchin supposes that our domination of nature derives from the domination of man by man: "it was not until organic community relations, be they tribal, feudal, or peasant in form, dissolved into market relationships that the planet itself was reduced to a resource for exploitation." [34] Wherever we assign priority, it seems clear that the dynamic of individualism, private ownership, and competition is at the root of Western pragmatic knowledge and of the uses to which our economic system has put it. Theorists like Mandeville and Adam Smith offered a rationale for what was already a cultural fact—the unseen hand has always been a comfort for the exploiter, but exploitation did not wait upon the theory.

John William Ward wrote an interesting study of the reception accorded Lindberg's flight. A common theme among its celebrants was that Lindbergh resembled a lone frontiersman, a pioneer opening up a new dominion for human control. To assimilate Lindberg's trip to the myth of the questing hero, and so deny the other truly distinctive thing about it—its reliance on advanced technology—was to deny also the dependence of men on machines and the loss of human freedom in industrial society.[35] This twist of the mind is characteristic. Americans want constant reassurance as to the viability of the private life and the independence of plain men like Charles Lindbergh even in the midst of complex machinery based on complex knowledge. This is a profoundly bourgeois cast of thought, a sustaining myth whose slight value as a theory of industrial society should not blind us to its symbolic and symptomatic meaning. The innocence of a liberal society about the uses of

33. "The Historical Roots of Our Ecological Crisis," *Science* 155 (March 20, 1967), pp. 1203–7.
34. "Toward an Ecological Solution," *Eco-Catastrophe*, p. 48.
35. "The Meaning of Lindbergh's Flight," in *Red, White, and Blue: Men, Books, and Ideas in American Culture* (New York: Oxford University Press, 1969).

knowledge and the circular and repetitive quality of its attempts to remedy side effects and correct abuses owe much to the mystique of individualism and to its persistence well beyond any usefulness it once had. The kind of knowledge our society harbors in its midst is a thoroughly social product with extensive social consequences. It may well be disastrous for us to continue seeking it as if it were so much private property, a boon to independence and freedom.

Academic people have a particular weakness for this form of innocence, doubtless because their welfare is so closely bound to the privileged position of knowledge in the society and the sustaining ideology of academic freedom. Galbraith will stand for an example. It should be evident that I think Galbraith's economic analysis valuable, but when he outlines the role of universities in our "emancipation" from the power of the industrial system, his coloration is common liberal:

The proper course of action is clear. The college and university community must retain paramount authority for the education it provides and for the research it undertakes. The needs of the industrial system must always be secondary to the cultivation of general understanding and perception.[36]

Not only is this the tone ("proper course," "must retain," "must always be") of a man who thinks that to state the solution is to achieve it, not only does he suddenly believe that academics can compromise with the industrial system by serving its needs as well as their own, he also seems unaware how pliable, even vacuous, a goal "the cultivation of general understanding and perception" is. Surely the history of American academic policy over the past hundred years is one of adapting concepts like "general understanding and perception" to meet the system's needs for knowledge and skill. Relying on a principle as neutrally stated as Galbraith's, we can offer no resistance to real economic forces. When he asks that universities oppose "humane and intellectual" to "industrial" needs (p. 373), he proposes an equally attractive and equally otiose rule. If the analysis I have offered in the last three chapters has any validity,

36. *The New Industrial State*, p. 372.

it is not possible for universities to tear themselves away from the bosom of the industrial system by reaffirming pure academic values and the autonomy of the intellectual life.

Quite the opposite, in fact. To stand apart from the industrial system and its menacing uses of knowledge, universities would have to be much *more* political—less pure—than they are. They would have to relinquish the flattering ideology of the ivory tower, the dodge of academic freedom, the false security of professionalism, and all the trappings of neutrality, which conceal a subtler partisanship. They would have to shape academic policy to expressly political ends, asking not "how can we best transmit and improve the knowledge that exists?" but "what knowledge do we and our students most need for liberation?" They would have to seek out ways of making knowledge serve the powerless. They would have to dispense with the barrier between thought and action, and find ways to ensure that the *uses* of their research and teaching weighed against the present rule of corporations and the Pentagon. In short, they would have to act as allies of socialist revolution.

I have not so little regard for my own warning as to think that because I have had the pleasure of saying these things they are likely to come about. Universities will not lead a socialist revolution in the near future. But the principles outlined in the last paragraph do make a reasonable set of goals for those teachers who agree that knowledge cannot be liberating under the present system. They— we—at least should conceive and execute our work on political principles, since what teachers do is in fact political whether we say so or not, and there is much to be gained by accepting this reality.

And now it is possible to give clear answers to the reasons advanced by liberals (see p. 305) for keeping universities and departments out of politics:

1. Political engagement is a threat to academic freedom. *No.* Freedom of academic minorities is threatened as much by covert politics as by overt. What radicals threaten is the peace of mind that goes with apolitical life: the confidence that one's own

comfort and status are in the interest of society at large. We can afford to part with this belief.

2. Activism is a lapse from professional standards. *Yes,* if "professional" means "in the narrow interest of the guild." But *no,* if we take seriously our responsibility as intellectuals to understand in the broadest way our subject and its relation to the world outside the academy.

3. Political activity will cause needless conflict and distraction from our main purposes: education and scholarship. *No.* Conflict, doubtless, but needed. And distraction only from a blind and unquestioning pursuit of professional tasks defined, not by ourselves, but by segments of society with little real concern for the education that liberates.

4. To become overtly political is to ask for intervention by the most repressive forces of the right. *Yes.* This is a possibility that must be taken seriously. But to *yield* to this argument is to allow repression the victory in advance of the battle—to give the right and the corporate liberals a decisive say in our affairs through our own failure of nerve. The way to combat capitalism is to combat it, not refuse to acknowledge that a struggle exists.

It may seem inappropriate, jarring, to bring terms like "struggle" into what is after all a study of an academic field. Perhaps even if we *can* politicize our work without destroying it, we can also *refuse* to enter this struggle, and in doing so preserve the hard won disinterestedness of the intellectual life. I hope my argument has shown that what looks like a firm place to stand is actually a floating island. By withdrawing into disinterestedness we will in fact give up any chance of seriously influencing the evolution of knowledge. Our academic planning, then, will be interested in the two worst ways: it will serve our own class interests, and it will in the aggregate serve the interests of those who now hold sway over half the world. Further, it will bring those two interests closer and closer together. It is too late in the day for that. The reasons that knowledge has gone sour on us are political reasons, and they require political and collective remedies. This is a matter of survival and of reconstructing a human culture.

Perhaps some who accept the involvement of knowledge, of intellectuals, and of universities in the present crisis of politics might still wish to exempt the humanities. The academic humanities seem both well-intentioned and harmless, or, more positively, a force for decency and even liberation. Certainly this has been the message of much literary theory and esthetics in our century: the redemptive power of literature and the arts is due to their transcendence of politics and to their building a world apart from the utilitarian one where words and forms advance pragmatic interests. I sometimes wish this were true, but I don't believe it to be.

Quite aside from the use of the humanities—of high culture— within universities to harden class lines and teach the skills and habits of mind that will serve the industrial system, the humanities have a flourishing existence outside the universities. When Exxon, Mobil, Chevron, and Amoco spend millions of dollars in television advertising to cash in on their altruistic leadership in the war on pollution and the search for new forms of energy, they are using rhetoric, drama, and visual design to maintain their power over the future and proclaim the health of the free enterprise economy. Given the stakes, it seems fair to say that the oil companies' use of the humanities is the reverse of liberating. Think of other parts of our humanistic culture: music, in the romantic tradition of Engelbert Humperdinck (the younger), assuring entranced listeners that their basic needs are personal and erotic rather than social; fiction, in confession magazines, pornography, and many other profitable forms of literature, maintaining sexual and social stereotypes; history, available publicly in the form of myths about the white man's sovereign rights over darker people and their land, and of traditional American freedom threatened by the cold war enemy; architecture and design, in a thousand suburban developments, creating the illusion of independence (home, the electronic castle), denying the existence of the other half of society, and forcing complete dependence on cars, appliances, and other profit-yielding artifacts. What are the connections between these exploitative, well-financed uses of the humanities and our high culture? "Teaching literature in a discredited civilization," to repeat Grossman's title, we either teach politically with revolution as our end or we contribute to the mystification that so often in universities diverts and deadens the critical power of literature and encysts it in our safe corner of society.

I have spent a lot of time in this book debunking, uncovering "real" motives and causes, rejecting our orthodox professional beliefs as dangerous and self-serving myths. And indeed I do think that the professional field in which I have worked for twenty years has been wrapped in delusions, a great muddle at the heart of its confidence and prosperity. The argument I offer here is, among other things, a specimen of the literature of conversion. But I also believe that the contradictions I have been describing will be more and more evident. And more intolerable—we are not the helpless prisoners of guilt and class, but people to whom "only connect" can be a guide rather than a shibboleth. Furthermore, I think that we can work where we are and with what we know to oppose the tyrannies of this culture and lay the groundwork for the next. Though there is no cause for joy in this position, I do find it exhilarating in comparison to its main competitor, the idea that we must keep doing what we have been doing, only more and better. That is a dead end of history.

Index

Index